NEW CHINESE 300

NEW
CHINESE 300
A Beginning Language Course

by the Faculty of
Beijing Language Institute

1988

Cheng & Tsui Company
Boston

CHENG & TSUI COMPANY, INC.

25-31 West Street, Boston, Massachusetts 02111

Library of Congress Cataloging in Publication Data:

Beijing Language Institute
New Chinese 300: A Beginning Language Course
(C&T Asian Language Series)
I. Beijing Language Institute   II. Title   III. Series
83-73591

ISBN 0-88727-002-6   Set of book and cassette tapes

ISBN 0-88727-001-8   Paperback alone

Printed in the United States of America

PUBLISHER'S NOTE

In cooperation with the Beijing Language Institute, Beijing, People's Republic of China, the Cheng & Tsui Company is pleased to announce the introduction of its *Asian Language Series*. The Beijing Language Institute is the leading institution teaching Chinese as a foreign language in the PRC and produces many significant and valuable language texts. Unfortunately, many of these texts have not been widely known or available in the West.

The *C& T Asian Language Series* is designed to publish and widely distribute important Beijing Language Institute texts as they are completed in China, as well as other significant works in the Asian languages field.

We invite readers' comments and suggestions concerning the Series' publications. Please contact members of the Editorial Board:

Professor Shou-Hsin Teng, Chief Editor, Dept. of Asian Languages and Literature, University of Massachusetts, Amherst, MA 01003

Professor Samuel Cheung, Dept. of Oriental Languages, University of California, Berkeley, CA 94720

Professor Ying-che Li, Dept. of East Asian Languages, University of Hawaii, Honolulu, HI 96822

Professor Timothy Light, Provost, Kalamazoo College, 1200 Academy St., Kalamazoo, MI 49007

Professor Stanley R. Munro, Dept. of East Asian Languages and Literature, The University of Alberta, Edmonton, Canada.

Professor Ronald Walton, Dept. of Hebrew and East Asian Languages and Literature, University of Maryland, College Park, MD 20742

Explanatory Notes

Chinese 300 was compiled in 1980 as a crash course of Chinese for foreign students. It was reprinted the following year after some necessary revision. The thirty topical chapters with ten basic sentences in each were prepared according to the actual needs of the foreign visitors' daily life in China. There were substitution drills, dialogues, lists of new words and supplementary expressions in addition to the fundamental sentence patterns. The book with English and French translations was then adopted as a Chinese textbook for short-term trainees or as conversational course materials by some universities and colleges both at home and abroad. However we learned in the past two years that there were such problems in that book that a second revision of it would be absolutely necessary to achieve the most satisfying effect in teaching.

Our fellow teachers have generously offered their criticisms and advice which, together with the experience gained in our teaching, made the revision possible. To meet the communicative needs of foreigners living in China, we have rewritten the book by altering some of the thirty subjects first, and then reorganizing the basic sentence patterns in the manner that the essential structures, grammar and their function may be happily combined. It is hoped that students thus can learn more useful sentences and make progress through the texts arranged from very simple to fairly complicated. Now in the present book the supplementary expressions are no longer given, but the elementary grammar points and exercises are added to each lesson. A comparison is made between Chinese and English grammars so as to help students understand the prominent features of Chinese; and there is a short summary of grammar included in every ten lessons for students to take a glance at. *New Chinese 300* (so renamed, because of the great changes in its contents) contains three hundred basic sentences grouped in thirty chapters, printed seperately in English and French. The present book has been rendered into English by Comrade Xiong Wenhua.

We are pleased to record here Comrade Zhao Shuhua's enthusiastical support and assistance in reading the manuscript and her large share of contribution to revising the book; and Comrade Liu Shan's offer to do the proof reading.

Our sincere thanks are due to Comrades Zhao Shuhua, Xiong Wenhua, Liu Shan and others who kindly gave their aid as well as furtherance.

Errors and failures resulted from our limited experience may not be completely excluded in the present book. Any coments or criticisms from the users and fellow teachers are earnestly welcome.

Compilers

May 1983

说　　明

　　《汉语三百句》是一九八〇年为外国学生短期来华学习而编写的速成基础汉语教材。一九八一年重印时曾作了一些修改。全书根据外国人在中国生活的交际需要,分三十个主题,编成三十课,每课选十个日常生活中最常用的基本句型, 共三百句。除基本句型外, 每课还有替换练习、会话和生词、补充词语等四个部分。为便于外国人学习,基本句型和生词、补充词语有英、法两种文字翻译。该书曾为国内外一些学校用作短期汉语教材,或口语教材。经过两年多的教学实践,我们深深感到该书存在不少问题,亟需加以修订,以利教学。

　　我们在修订时曾征求同行专家的意见。根据他们的意见和我们的教学实践,首先按照外国人在中国生活的交际实际需要,对原书的三十个主题作了变动。其次是根据功能和句型、语法相结合的原则,对原书的基本句型作了较大的改动,力求做到既能使学生掌握有实际交际价值的句子,又能贯彻句型的循序渐进原则。此外, 还删去原书的补充词语部分,每课增加了语法和练习两个部分。语法部分的讲解,为了突出汉语的特点,同英语作了对比。同时还在每十课之后安排了一个语法小结。通过三个语法小结,使学生对汉语语法有个概括的了解。修订后仍为三十课,三百个基本句型。由于变动较大，书名改为《新汉语三百句》。为了减少篇幅，《新汉语三百句》分英、法两种文字翻译本印刷。本书是英译本。英文翻译为熊文华同志。

在《汉语三百句》修订过程中，赵淑华同志曾给予热情的支持和帮助，并参加了大量的修改和审订工作。刘山同志作了校订。

我们对赵淑华、熊文华、刘山等同志给予的支持和帮助，表示衷心的感谢。

限于水平，本书一定还存在不少缺点和错误，热切希望本书的使用者和同行专家批评指正。

编　　者
一九八三年五月

Contents

目　　录

汉 语 拼 音 字 母 表

The Chinese Phonetic Alphabet

印刷体 printed forms	书 写 体 written forms		字母名称 names	印刷体 printed forms	书 写 体 written forms		字母名称 names
A a	A	a	[a]	N n	N	n	[nɛ]
B b	B	b	[pɛ]	O o	O	o	[o]
C c	C	c	[ts'ɛ]	P p	P	p	[p'ɛ]
D d	D	d	[tɛ]	Q q	Q	q	[tɕ'iou]
E e	E	e	[ɤ]	R r	R	r	[ar]
F f	F	f	[ɛf]	S s	S	s	[ɛs]
G g	G	g	[kɛ]	T t	T	t	[t'ɛ]
H h	H	h	[xa]	U u	U	u	[u]
I i	I	i	[i]	V v	V	v	[vɛ]
J j	J	j	[tɕiɛ]	W w	W	w	[wa]
K k	K	k	[k'ɛ]	X x	X	x	[ɕi]
L l	L	l	[ɛl]	Y y	Y	y	[ja]
M m	M	m	[ɛm]	Z z	Z	z	[tsɛ]

汉 语 语 音
hàn   yǔ   yǔ   yīn

Chinese Phonetics

(一)

1. 单韵母 Simple Finals

    a [a]   o [o]   e [ɤ]

    i [i]   u [u]   ü [y]

2. 声母 Initials

  ① b [p]   p [p']   m [m]   f [f]

      d [t]   t [t']   n [n]   l [l]

      g [k]   k [k']   h [x]

      j [tɕ]   q [tɕ']   x [ɕ]

      z [ts]   ch [ts']   s [s]

      zh [tʂ]   ch [tʂ']   sh [ʂ]   r [ʐ]

  ② bo   po   mo   fo

      de   te   ne   le

      ge   ke   he

      ji   qi   xi

      zi [-ɿ]   ci [-ɿ]   si [-ɿ]

      zhi [-ʅ] chi [-ʅ] shi [-ʅ] ri [-ʅ]

3. 拼音 Combinations of Initials and Finals

    ba   bo   bi   bu

pa	po	pi	pu
ma	mo	mi	mu
fa	fo	fu	
da	de	du	
ta	te	tu	
na	ne	nu	nü
la	le	lu	lü
ga	ge	gu	
ka	ke	ku	
ha	he	hu	
ji	ju(-ü)		
qi	qu(-ü)		
xi	xu(-ü)		
za	ze	zu	zi
ca	ce	cu	ci
sa	se	su	si
zha	zhe	zhu	zhi
cha	che	chu	chi
sha	she	shu	shi
re	ru	ri	

(二)

1. 复韵母　Compound Finals

　　ai [ai]　　　ei [ei]　　　ao [au]　　　ou [ou]

　　ia [ia]　　　ie [iɛ]　　　iao [iau]　　　iu [iou]

　　ua [ua]　　　uo [uo]　　　uai [uai]　　　ui [uei]

　　üe [yɛ]

2. 拼音　Combinations of Initials and Finals

2

bai bei bao bie biao
pai pei pao pou piao
mai mei mao mou mie miao miu
fei fou
dai dei dao dou die diao diu duo dui
tai tao tou tie tiao tuo tui
nai nei nao nou nie niao niu nuo nüe
lai lei lao lou lia lie liao liu luo lüe
gai gei gao gou guo guai gui
kai kei kao kou kuo kuai kui
hai hei hao hou huo huai hui
jia jiao jiu jue
qia qie qiao qiu que
xia xie xiao xiu xue
zai zei zao zou zuo zui
cai cao cou cuo cui
sai sao sou suo sui
zhai zhei zhao zhou zhuo zhuai zhui
chai chao chou chuo chuai shui
shai shei shao shou shuo shuai shui
rao rou ruo rui

(三)

1. 鼻韵母 Nasal Finals

an [an]　　en [n]　　ang [aŋ]　　eng [ɤŋ]
ong [uŋ]　　ian [ian]　　in [in]　　iang [iaŋ]
ing [iŋ]　　iong [yŋ]　　uan [uan]　　un [uən]
uang [uaŋ]　　üan [yan]　　ün [yn]

2. 拼音 Combinations of Initials and Finals

ban ben bang beng bian bin bing

pan pen pang peng pian pin ping

man men mang meng mian min ming

fan fen fang feng

dan den dang deng dong dian ding duan dun

tan tang teng tong tian ting tuan tun

nan nen nang neng nong nian nin niang ning nuan

lan lang leng long lian lin liang ling luan lun

gan gen gang geng gong guan guang

kan ken kang keng kong kuan kuang

han hen hang heng hong huan huang

jian jin jiang jing jiong juan jun

qian qin qiang qing qiong quan qun

xian xin xiang xing xiong xuan xun

zan zen zang zeng zong zuan zun

can cen cang ceng cong cuan cun

san sen sang seng song suan sun

zhan zhen zhang zheng zhong zhuan zhun zhuang

chan chen chang cheng chong chuan chun chuang

shan shen shang sheng shuan shun shuang

ran ren rang reng rong ruan run

3. y 和 w   y and w

① y〔j〕,   w〔w〕,   yu〔y〕

② yi ya ye yao you yan yin yang ying yong

wu wa wo wai wei wan wen wang weng

yu yue yuan yun

4

（四）

1. 声调　Tones

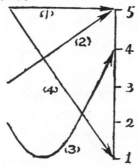

高　　High pitch

半高　Mid high pitch

中　　Middle pitch

半低　Mid low pitch

低　　Low pitch

(1) 第一声 55，调号 ˉ

The 1st tone 55, is indicated by the tone-graph ˉ

(2) 第二声 35，调号 ´

The 2nd tone 35, is indicated by the tone-graph ´

(3) 第三声 214，调号 ˇ

The 3rd tone 214, is indicated by the tone-graph ˇ

(4) 第四声 51，调号 ˋ

The 4th tone 51, is indicated by the tone-graph ˋ

2. 例　Examples

bā	bá	bǎ	bà
mā	má	mǎ	mà
fēi	féi	fěi	fèi
yāo	yáo	yǎo	yào

bài	pài	bān	pān
dāng	tāng	dòu	tòu
guǎn	kuǎn	gùn	kùn

5

nǚ	lǚ	nǜ	lǜ
jū	qū	juàn	quàn
hū	xū	hùn	xùn
zēng	zhēng	cuī	chuī
suí	shuí	ruǐ	ruǎn

3. 轻声　The Neutral Tone

轻声不标调号，如：

The neutral tone is shown without any tone-graph, e.g.

gēge	jiějie	xièxie	fūren	mùtou
zhuōzi	wǒmen	láile	zǒuzhe	xuéguo
nǐ de	hǎo ba	máng ma	tā ne	

4. 变调　Changes of Tones

① 三声连读　∨ + ∨ ⟶ ⁄ + ∨

Two 3rd tones pronounced in succession

∨ + ∨ ⟶ ⁄ + ∨

nǐ hǎo　　shǒubiǎo

zhǎnlǎn　hěn nǔlì

② 半三声　The Half 3rd Tone

měitiān　　zǔguó

qǐng jìn　wǎnshang

（五）

1. 韵母"er"　The Final "er"

ēr[ər]　ér　ěr　èr

érzi　értóng　ěrduo　èrshí　shí'èr

2. 儿化韵　The Retroflex Final

nǎr　zhèr

quānr　wánr　yǎnr　huàr

yìdiǎnr　yíxiàr　xiǎoháir　shǒujuànr

bīnggùnr　liáo tiānr

词 类 简 称 表

cí lèi jiǎn chēng biǎo

The Abbreviations of Chinese Grammatical Terms

（名）	名词	míngcí	noun
（代）	代词	dàicí	pronoun
	人称代词	rénchēng dàicí	personal pronoun
	指示代词	zhǐshì dàicí	demonstrative pronoun
	疑问代词	yíwèn dàicí	interrogative pronoun
（动）	动词	dòngcí	verb
（能动）	能愿动词	néngyuàn dòngcí	modal verb
（形）	形容词	xíngróngcí	adjective
（数）	数词	shùcí	numeral
（量）	量词	liàngcí	measure word
（副）	副词	fùcí	adverb
（介）	介词	jiècí	preposition
（连）	连词	liáncí	conjunction
（助）	助词	zhùcí	particle
	动态助词	dòngtài zhùcí	aspectual particle
	结构助词	jiégòu zhùcí	structural particle
	语气助词	yǔqì zhùcí	modal particle
（叹）	叹词	tàncí	interjection

（象声）	象声词	xiàngshēngcí	onomatopoeia
（头）	词头	cítóu	prefix
（尾）	词尾	cíwěi	suffix

问 候

wèn hòu

Greetings

1. 你好!
   Nǐ hǎo!

   Hello!

2. 身体怎么样?
   Shēntǐ zěnmeyàng?

   How are you?

3. 很好，你呢?
   Hěn hǎo, nǐ ne?

   Very well, thank you. And you?

4. 我也很好。
   Wǒ yě hěn hǎo.

   I'm O.K..

5. 张老师好吗?
   Zhāng lǎoshī hǎo ma?

   How is our teacher Mr. Zhang?

6. 好，他很好。
   Hǎo, tā hěn hǎo.

   He is all right.

7. 你工作忙吗？

   Nǐ gōngzuò máng ma?

   Very much involved in your work?

8. 不很忙。

   Bù hěn máng.

   Not very much.

9. 谢谢。

   Xièxie.

   Thank you.

10. 再见。

    Zàijiàn.

    Good bye!

替换练习　Substitution Drills

1. | 身体
工作
学习 | 怎么样？

2. | 我
他
张老师 | 也很好，

3. 你工作 | 忙
累
紧张 | 吗？

10

会 话 Dialogues

甲：你好！
Nǐ hǎo!

乙：你好！
Nǐ hǎo!

甲：你身体怎么样？
Nǐ shēntǐ zěnmeyàng?

乙：很好，谢谢。
Hěn hǎo, xièxie.

甲：你工作忙吗？
Nǐ gōngzuò máng ma?

乙：不忙，你呢？
Bù máng, nǐ ne?

甲：很忙。
Hěn máng.

乙：张老师好吗？
Zhāng lǎoshī hǎo ma?

甲：好，他很好。
Hǎo, tā hěn hǎo.

乙：再见。
Zàijiàn.

甲：再见。
Zàijiàn.

*

甲：老师好！
Lǎoshī hǎo!

11

乙：你好！
Nǐ hǎo!

甲：老师工作累吗？
Lǎoshī gōngzuò lèi ma?

乙：不累。
Bú lèi.

甲：身体好吗？
Shēntǐ hǎo ma?

乙：很好，谢谢。你呢？
Hěn hǎo, xièxie. Nǐ ne?

甲：不很好。
Bù hěn hǎo.

乙：你学习怎么样？
Nǐ xuéxí zěnmeyàng?

甲：很紧张。老师再见。
Hěn jǐnzhāng. Lǎoshī zàijiàn.

乙：再见。
Zàijiàn.

生　词　New Words

1. 你　　　　（代）nǐ　　　　　you　(singular)
2. 好　　　　（形）hǎo　　　　good, well
3. 身体　　　（名）shēntǐ　　　body, health
4. 怎么样　　（代）zěnmeyàng　how
5. 很　　　　（副）hěn　　　　very
6. 呢　　　　（助）ne　　　　　(a modal particle)
7. 我　　　　（代）wǒ　　　　　I, me
8. 也　　　　（副）yě　　　　　also

12

9. 老师	（名）	lǎoshī	teacher
10. 吗	（助）	ma	(a modal particle)
11. 他	（代）	tā	he, him
12. 工作	（动、名）	gōngzuò	to work, job
13. 忙	（形）	máng	busy
14. 不	（副）	bù	not
15. 谢谢	（动）	xièxie	to thank
16. 再见	（动）	zàijiàn	good-bye
17. 学习	（动）	xuéxí	to study
18. 累	（形）	lèi	tired
19. 紧张	（形）	jǐnzhāng	demanding

专 名 Proper Noun

张　　　　Zhāng　　　　surname of a person

语 法 Grammar

1. 形容词谓语句
Sentences with an Adjectival Predicate

汉语的形容词可以直接用作谓语，而英语的形容词作谓语时前面要加系词"be"。例如：

Unlike the English adjectives, the Chinese equivalents can be directly used as a predicate in a sentence without a linking verb "be", e.g.

(1) 你好！

(2) 工作忙吗？

这种句子叫做形容词谓语句。在肯定的陈述句中，形容词前常带副词"很"。这里的"很"表示程度的意义已不明显。例如：

13

Those are known as sentences with an adjectival predicate. In an affirmative declarative sentence the adverb 很 in a weak sense is often used before the adjective, e.g.

（3）他很累。

形容词谓语句的否定形式是在形容词前加上否定副词"不"。例如：

The negative sentence with an adjectival predicate is formed by using the adverb 不 before the adjective, e.g.

（4）我不忙。

（5）工作不很累。

常用疑问代词"怎么样"提问。例如：

To ask a question, the interrogative pronoun 怎么样 is needed, e.g.

（6）身体怎么样？

主　语 Subject	谓　语 Predicate		助　词 Modal Particle
名词或代词 Noun or Pronoun	副　词 Adverb	形容词 Adjective	
你		好。	
工作		忙	吗？
他	很	累。	
我	不	忙。	
工作	不很	累。	
身体	怎么样？		

2． 主谓谓语句

Sentences with Subject-Predicate Constructions as Their Predicates

14

汉语有的句子可以由主谓词组作谓语。例如：

A subject-predicate construction may function as a predicate in a sentence, e.g.

    (1) 他身体好。

    (2) 你身体怎么样？

    (3) 我工作很忙。

这种句子叫做主谓谓语句。

Those indicated above are known as sentences with subject-predicate constructions as their predicates.

主　　语 Subject	谓　　　　　　语 Predicate		语气助词 Modal Particle
名词或代词 Noun or Pronoun	小主语 Smaller Subject	小谓语 Smaller Predicate	
张老师 他 你	工作 身体 身体	忙。 好 怎么样？	吗？

3．疑问句(一)

Interrogative Sentences (A)

    疑问句(一)的提问方法是在陈述句尾加上表示疑问语气的助词"吗"，在词序上没有变化。例如：

The interrogative sentences (A) are formed by using a modal particle 吗 at the end of a declarative sentence without changing its word order, e.g.

    (1) 张老师好吗？

    (2) 你工作忙吗？

练　习　Exercises

1. 对话：
   Dialogues:
   (1) A：你身体怎么样？
       B：＿＿＿＿＿＿＿。
   (2) A：工作忙吗？
       B：＿＿＿＿＿＿＿。
   (3) A：我学习不很紧张，你呢？
       B：＿＿＿＿＿＿＿＿。
   (4) A：我很好，张老师也好吗？
       B：＿＿＿＿＿＿＿＿。

2. 根据答话提出用"吗"的问话：
   Ask questions with 吗：
   (1) A：＿＿＿＿＿＿＿？
       B：他身体很好。
   (2) A：＿＿＿＿＿＿＿？
       B：工作不很忙。
   (3) A：＿＿＿＿＿＿＿？
       B：我很好，张老师也很好。
   (4) A：＿＿＿＿＿＿＿？
       B：我不很累。

3. 把下列句子改成用"吗"的疑问句：
   Rewrite the following with 吗：
   (1) 你身体怎么样？
   (2) 我很忙，你怎么样？
   (3) 我工作不很紧张，你工作怎么样？
   (4) 我很好，张老师怎么样？

16

二、问姓名

wèn xìng míng

Asking about Names

11. 您贵姓？
   Nín guìxìng?

   What's your surname, please?

12. 我姓王。
   Wǒ xìng Wáng.

   My surname is Wang.

13. 您叫什么名字？
   Nín jiào shénme míngzi?

   And what's your personal name?

14. 我叫王丽。
   Wǒ jiào Wáng Lì.

   I'm called Wang Li.

15. 您是史密斯先生吗？
   Nín shi Shǐmìsī xiānsheng ma?

   You're Mr. Smith, aren't you?

16. 不，我不是，我是格林。
   Bù, wǒ bú shi, wǒ shi Gélín.

   No, I'm not. My name is Green.

17. 对不起。
    Duì bu qǐ.

    Sorry.

18. 没关系。
    Méi guānxi.

    It's O.K..

19. 那位先生是谁？
    Nà wei xiānsheng shi shuí?

    Who's that gentleman?

20. 他是布朗教授。
    Tā shi Bùlǎng jiàoshòu.

    He is Professor Brown.

替换练习　Substitution Drills

1.
您	
他	叫什么名字？
那位先生	
这位教授	

2. 您是
史密斯先生	
张老师	吗？
李同志	
布朗教授	

3. 不，
我	
他	不是，
这位	
那位	
我	
他	是格林。
这位	
那位	

18

4.
| 那 |
| 这 | 位先生是谁？

会 话 Dialogues

甲：您贵姓？
Nín guìxìng?

乙：我姓张。
Wǒ xìng Zhāng.

甲：您叫什么名字？
Nín jiào shénme míngzi?

乙：我叫张林。
Wǒ jiào Zhāng Lín.

甲：那位先生是谁？
Nà wei xiānsheng shi shuí?

乙：他叫布朗。
Tā jiào Bùlǎng.

甲：他是教授吗？
Tā shi jiàoshòu ma?

乙：不，他不是教授。
Bù, tā bú shi jiàoshòu.

丙：您是史密斯先生吗？
Nín shi Shǐmìsī xiānsheng ma?

甲：不，我不是。
Bù, wǒ bú shi.

丙：对不起。
Duì bu qǐ.

甲：没关系。
Méi guānxi.

乙：那位是。
Nà wei shì.

丙：谢谢。
Xièxie.

＊　　　＊　　　＊

甲：您好！
Nín hǎo!

乙：您好！
Nín hǎo!

甲：您是格林先生吗？
Nín shi Gélín xiānsheng ma?

乙：不，我不是，我是史密斯。您贵姓？
Bù, wǒ bú shi, wǒ shi Shǐmìsī. Nín guìxìng?

甲：我姓王。
Wǒ xìng Wáng.

乙：您叫什么名字？
Nín jiào shénme míngzi?

甲：我叫王丽。
Wǒ jiào Wáng Lì.

乙：王丽同志，这位先生是谁？
Wáng Lì tóngzhì, zhè wei xiānsheng shi shuí?

甲：他是李同志。
Tā shi Lǐ tóngzhì.

乙：他叫什么名字？
Tā jiào shénme míngzi?

甲：他叫李平。
Tā jiào Lǐ Píng.

乙：他是老师吗？
Tā shi lǎoshī ma?

甲：是。
Shì.

乙：谢谢您，再见。
Xièxie nín, zàijiàn.

甲：再见。
Zàijiàn.

生　词　New Words

1. 您　（代）nín　you (a polite form)
2. 贵姓　（名）guìxìng　What is your name
3. 姓　（动、名）xìng　surname
4. 叫　（动）jiào　to call, to be called
5. 什么　（代）shénme　what
6. 名字　（名）míngzi　personal name
7. 是　（动）shì　to be
8. 先生　（名）xiānsheng　Mr., gentleman
9. 对不起　duì bu qǐ　sorry
10. 没关系　méi guānxi　It doesn't matter
11. 那　（代）nà　that
12. 位　（量）wèi　(a measure word)
13. 谁　（代）shuí　who
14. 教授　（名）jiàoshòu　professor
15. 这　（代）zhè　this
16. 同志　（名）tóngzhì　comrade

专　名　Proper Nouns

1. 王丽　Wáng Lì　name of a person
2. 史密斯　Shǐmìsī　Smith
3. 格林　Gélín　Green

4. 布朗	Bùlǎng	Brown
5. 张林	Zhāng Lín	name of a person
6. 李平	Lǐ Píng	name of a person

语 法 Grammar

1. "是"字句

   Sentences with 是

   "是"字句是动词谓语句的一种。"是"同英语的系词 "be" 一样，作谓语时后边要带名词或代词。例如：

   A sentence with 是 belongs to those which contain a verbal predicate. Like the English linking verb "be", 是 is followed by either a noun or a pronoun in a sentence, e.g.

   (1) 我是格林。

   (2) 他是老师。

   (3) 那位先生是谁？

   "格林"、"老师"、"谁"是动词"是"的宾语（在英语语法中叫"表语"）。"是"在句中一般读轻声，前面加否定副词"不"，表示否定（注意：不能把"不"放在"是"的后边）。例如：

   As shown in the above sentences, the verb 是 takes its object (or predicative, in an English grammatical term) expressed by 格林, 老师 and 谁 respectively. 是 is generally unstressed in a sentence, and its negative form is 不是 (the two words can never be put otherwise), e.g.

   (4) 我不是格林。

   动词"姓"、"叫"作谓语时同动词"是"一样，后面也要带宾语（名词或代词）。例如：

   Both verbs 姓 and 叫 take an object signified by a noun or a pronoun, e.g.

(5) 我姓王。

(6) 他姓什么？

(7) 我叫王丽，你叫什么？

(8) 我不姓王。

(9) 我不叫王丽。

"贵姓"，用来表示客气的提问。例如：

贵姓 is a polite expression of asking someone's name, e.g.

(10) 您贵姓？

我姓张。

主　　语 Subject	谓　　　　　语 Predicate		
名词或代词 Noun or Pronoun	副　词 Adverb	动　词 Verb	名词或代词 Noun or Pronoun
我		是	格林。
他		是	老师。
那位先生		是	谁？
我	不	是	格林。
我		姓	王。
他		姓	什么？
我		叫	王丽。
你		叫	什么？
我	不	姓	王。
我	不	叫	王丽。
您			贵姓？

2．疑问句（二）

Interrogative Sentences (B)

疑问句(二)是用疑问代词("谁"、"什么"、"怎么样"等)的问句。把陈述句中需要提问的部分改成疑问代词，表示疑问所在，便构成了这种疑问句。词序同陈述句一样，不像英语要把疑问代词放在句首。例如：

Interrogative sentences (B) are made with interrogative pronouns such as "who", "what" or "how" etc.. To change a declarative sentence into an interrogative one, all one should do is to replace the part in question with an interrogative pronoun. The alteration of the word order is not necessary, e.g.

(1) 谁是格林先生？

(2) 他是谁？

(3) 你姓什么？

(4) 他叫什么名字？

(5) 身体怎么样？

练 习 Exercises

1. 对话

Dialogues:

(1) A：他是谁？

B：_____。

(2) A：你是张老师吗？

B：_____。

(3) A：谁是布朗教授？

B：_____。

(4) A：那位先生是谁？

B：_____。

2. 根据答话提出用疑问代词的问话：

Ask questions with an interrogative pronoun:

(1) A：_____？

B：我姓张。

(2) A：_____？

B：那位是布朗教授。

(3) A：_____？

B：我是布朗。

(4) A：_____？

B：我叫王丽。

3. 把下列句子改成用疑问代词"谁"、"什么"、"怎么样"的问句：

Rewrite the following with an interrogative pronoun:

(1) 他是布朗教授吗？

(2) 你叫王丽吗？

(3) 您贵姓？

(4) 他身体好吗？

4. 完成下列句子：

Complete the following sentences:

(1) 我不姓张，我_____。

(2) 我不很忙，他也_____。

(3) 你_____，我也不累。

(4) 我不是格林，我_____。

(5) 我_____，你身体怎么样？

三、介 绍
jiè   shào

Introductions

21. 这是史密斯先生。
Zhè shì Shǐmìsī xiānsheng.

This is Mr. Smith.

22. 他是我的朋友。
Tā shì wǒ de péngyou.

He is my friend.

23. 认识你很高兴。
Rènshi ni hěn gāoxìng.

I'm glad to know you.

24. 那位是格林先生，你们认识吧?
Nà wei shì Gélín xiānsheng, nǐmen rènshi ba?

That is Mr. Green. Have you ever met before?

25. 是的，我们认识。
Shì de, wǒmen rènshi.

Yes, we have.

26. 不，我们不认识。
Bù, wǒmen bú rènshi.

No, we haven't.

27. 请问，这位女士是——

Qǐng wèn, zhè wei nǚshì shì——

Could you please tell me who the lady is?

28. 她是玛丽。

Tā shì Mǎlì.

She is Mary.

29. 她是不是格林先生的秘书？

Tā shì bu shì Gélín xiānsheng de mìshū?

Is she the secretary to Mr. Green?

30. 不是，她是格林先生的夫人。

Bú shì, tā shì Gélín xiānsheng de fūren.

No, she is Mrs. Green.

替换练习 Substitution Drills

1. 他是 | 我
你
她
张先生
布朗教授 | 的朋友。

2. 请问，那位 | 女士
先生
同志
小姐 | 是——

3. 她是不是格林先生的

夫人
秘书
朋友
老师
女儿

？

会 话 Dialogues

甲：史密斯先生，这位是李平同志，他是我的朋友。
Shǐmìsī xiānsheng, zhè wei shi Lǐ Píng tóngzhì, tā shi wǒ de péngyou.

乙：你好！
Nǐ hǎo!

丙：你好！
Nǐ hǎo!

乙：认识你很高兴。
Rènshi ni hěn gāoxìng.

丙：我也很高兴。
Wǒ yě hěn gāoxìng.

乙：你身体好吗？
Nǐ shēntǐ hǎo ma?

丙：很好，谢谢。你呢？
Hěn hǎo, xièxie. Nǐ ne?

乙：我也很好。
Wǒ yě hěn hǎo.

28

丙：请问，这位女士是
Qǐng wèn, zhè wei nǚshì shì——

甲：她是史密斯先生的女儿，玛丽小姐。
Tā shi Shǐmìsī xiānsheng de nǚ'ér, Mǎlì xiǎojiě.

丙：玛丽小姐，你好！
Mǎlì xiǎojiě, nǐ hǎo!

丁：你好！
Nǐ hǎo!

*　　　*　　　*

甲：请问，那位先生是谁？
Qǐng wèn, nà wei xiānsheng shi shuí?

乙：那位是格林教授，你们认识吧？
Nà wei shi Gélín jiàoshòu, nǐmen rènshi ba?

甲：不，我们不认识。
Bù, wǒmen bú rènshi.

乙：格林教授，这是张先生。
Gélín jiàoshòu, zhè shi Zhāng xiānsheng.

丙：你好，张先生！
Nǐ hǎo, Zhāng xiānsheng!

甲：你好！
Nǐ hǎo!

丙：请问，你叫什么名字？
Qǐng wèn, nǐ jiào shénme míngzi?

甲：我叫张林。
Wǒ jiào Zhāng Lín.

丙：认识你很高兴。
Rènshi ni hěn gāoxìng.

甲：我也很高兴。
Wǒ yě hěn gāoxìng.

丙：你工作忙吗？
Nǐ gōngzuò máng ma?

甲：不很忙。
Bù hěn máng.

丙：身体怎么样？
Shēntǐ zěnmeyàng?

甲：很好，谢谢。那位女士是你的秘书吗？
Hěn hǎo, xièxie. Nà wei nǚshì shi nǐ de mìshū ma?

丙：不是，她是我的夫人。
Bú shi, tā shi wǒ de fūren.

甲：对不起。
Duì bu qǐ.

丙：没关系。
Méi guānxi.

生　词　New Words

1.	的	（助）de	of (a structural particle)
2.	朋友	（名）péngyou	friend
3.	认识	（动）rènshi	to know
4.	高兴	（形）gāoxìng	glad
5.	你们	（代）nǐmen	you (plural)
6.	吧	（助）ba	(a modal particle)
7.	是的	shì de	yes
8.	我们	（代）wǒmen	we, us

9.	请问	qǐng wèn	May I ask
10.	女士	（名）nǚshì	lady
11.	小姐	（名）xiǎojiě	miss
12.	秘书	（名）mìshū	secretary
13.	她	（代）tā	she, her
14.	夫人	（名）fūren	wife
15.	学生	（名）xuésheng	student
16.	女儿	（名）nǚ'ér	daughter

专 名 Proper Noun

玛丽	Mǎlì	Mary

语 法 Grammar

1. 表示领属关系的定语

The Possessive Adjectival Modifiers

定语，主要是修饰名词的。名词、代词、形容词等都可以充当定语。

汉语的名词同英语一样，没有"格"的变化，用作表示领属关系的定语时，后边一般要加结构助词"的"，类似英语在作定语的名词后边加"'s"。词序也和英语一样。不过，汉语只有这样一种词序（定语在所修饰的名词前面），而英语则可以通过介词"of"把定语放在所修饰的名词后面。

汉语的人称代词也没有"格"的变化（即没有"your, yours"一类的形式），作定语时，情况同名词作定语基本一样。例如：

Adjectival modifiers performed by nouns, pronouns or adjectives etc. are mainly used to qualify nouns.

There is no case ending for both Chinese and English nouns. But the possessive form of a Chinese noun can be formed

31

by adding the structural particle 的 to it (similar to "'s" for an English noun). The word order is always: a modifier + a noun. English is in common with Chinese in this aspect, though an English modifier may be put after a noun with the preposition "of" in between.

What is described above also applies to Chinese pronouns in general, e.g.

(1) 那是老师的书。

(2) 格林的夫人是我的朋友。

主　语 Subject			谓　语 Predicate			
定　语 adjec- tival Modifier	结构助词 Struc- tural Word	中心语 Central Noun	动词 Verb	宾　语 Object		
				定　语 Adjectival Modifier	结构助词 Structural Word	中心语 Central Word
格林	的	那 夫人	是 是	老师 我	的 的	书。 朋友。

2. 疑问句(三)

Interrogative Sentences (C)

把陈述句中谓语动词或形容词的肯定形式和否定形式并列起来，便构成正反疑问句。例如：

An interrogative sentence (C) may be constructed by

using the negative form of the predicate (either the verbal or adjectival one) after its affirmative form, e.g.

(1) 她是不是格林先生的朋友？

(2) 你认识不认识他？

(3) 张老师忙不忙？

(4) 王丽身体好不好？

在动词谓语句中，还可以把谓语动词的否定形式放在宾语之后。例如：

In a verbal predicate sentence, the negative form of the predicate may be placed after the object, e.g.

(5) 他是你的朋友不是？

(6) 你认识他不认识？

练 习 Exercises

1. 对话：

Dialogues:

(1) A：你认识玛丽小姐吗？

B：＿＿＿＿＿＿＿＿＿＿。

(2) A：她是谁的夫人？

B：＿＿＿＿＿＿＿＿＿＿。

(3) A：史密斯先生是不是你的朋友？

B：＿＿＿＿＿＿＿＿＿＿。

(4) A：他也是格林先生的朋友吗？

B：＿＿＿＿＿＿＿＿＿＿。

2. 根据答话提出用疑问代词"谁"的问话：

Ask questions with 谁：

(1) A：＿＿＿＿＿＿＿＿＿＿？

B：格林先生认识史密斯先生。

(2) A：＿＿＿＿＿＿＿＿？

B：玛丽是格林先生的夫人。

(3) A：＿＿＿＿＿＿＿＿？

B：张先生是我的老师。

(4) A：＿＿＿＿＿＿＿＿？

B：史密斯先生是我的朋友。

3．把下列问句改成正反疑问句：

Change the following into affirmative-negative
interrogative sentences:

(1) 你认识王丽同志吗？

(2) 王丽是张老师的朋友吗？

(3) 李平工作紧张吗？

(4) 他身体好吗？

34

四、问 时 间

wèn   shí   jiān

Asking the Time

31. 几点了？

Jǐ diǎn le?

What time is it now?

32. 现在差一刻八点。

Xiànzài chà yí kè bā diǎn.

It's a quarter to eight.

33. 八点过五分。

Bā diǎn guò wǔ fēn.

Five past eight.

34. 你们几点上课？

Nǐmen jǐ diǎn shàng kè?

When do you begin your class?

35. 我们八点上课。

Wǒmen bā diǎn shàng kè.

Our class begins at eight o'clock.

36. 下午有课吗？

Xiàwǔ yǒu kè ma?

Any classes in the afternoon?

37. 下午没有课。

Xiàwǔ méi yǒu kè.

No classes in the afternoon.

38. 明天上午我们不上课，去颐和园。

Míngtiān shàngwǔ wǒmen bú shàng kè, qù Yíhéyuán.

We're not going to have any class tomorrow
morning. We're going to the Summer Palace
instead.

39. 什么时候开车？

Shénme shíhou kāi chē?

When will the bus start?

40. 九点半开车。

Jiǔ diǎn bàn kāi chē.

It'll start at 9.30.

替换练习　Substitution Drills

1. 现在　| 差一刻八点 | 。
九点
九点过三分
九点一刻
九点半

2. 我们　| 八点 | 上课。
八点半
九点十分
上午
下午

3. 明天上午我们不上课，去 | 颐和园 |
　　　　　　　　　　　　　　长城
　　　　　　　　　　　　　　北海公园
　　　　　　　　　　　　　　故宫

4. 什么时候 | 开车 | ?
　　　　　　　上课
　　　　　　　去长城

会 话 Dialogues

甲：几点了?
Jǐ diǎn le?

乙：现在差十分八点。
Xiànzài chà shí fēn bā diǎn.

甲：你们几点上课?
Nǐmen jǐ diǎn shàng kè?

乙：我们八点上课。
Wǒmen bā diǎn shàng kè.

甲：你们下午有课吗?
Nǐmen xiàwǔ yǒu kè ma?

乙：没有。
Méi yǒu.

甲：明天上午你们上课吗?
Míngtiān shàngwǔ nǐmen shàng kè ma?

乙：明天上午我们不上课，去长城。
Míngtiān shàngwǔ wǒmen bú shàng kè, qù
Chángchéng.

37

甲：什么时候开车？
Shénme shíhou kāi chē?

乙：七点半。
Qī diǎn bàn.

*　　　　*　　　　*

甲：你好，玛丽小姐！
Nǐ hǎo, Mǎlì xiǎojiě!

乙：你好！
Nǐ hǎo!

甲：学习忙吗？
Xuéxí máng ma?

乙：很忙。
Hěn máng.

甲：你们上午几点上课？
Nǐmen shàngwǔ jǐ diǎn shàng kè?

乙：八点。
Bā diǎn.

甲：下午什么时候上课？
Xiàwǔ shénme shíhou shàng kè?

乙：下午我们没有课。
Xiàwǔ wǒmen méi yǒu kè.

甲：明天上午你们去故宫吗？
Míngtiān shàngwǔ nǐmen qù Gùgōng ma?

乙：是的，明天上午我们不上课，去故宫。
Shì de, míngtiān shàngwǔ wǒmen bú shàng kè, qù Gùgōng.

甲：什么时候开车？
Shénme shíhou kāi chē?

乙：九点一刻开车。
Jiǔ diǎn yí kè kāi chē.

生 词 New Words

1. 几 （代）jǐ which, how many
2. 点 （量）diǎn hour, o'clock
3. 了 （助）le (a modal particle)
4. 现在 （名）xiànzài now
5. 差 （动）chà less
6. 刻 （量）kè quarter
7. 过 （动）guò past, after
8. 分 （量）fēn minute
9. 上 （动）shàng to begin, to attend
10. 课 （名）kè class, lesson
11. 下午 （名）xiàwǔ afternoon
12. 有 （动）yǒu to have
13. 没 （副）méi not
14. 明天 （名）míngtiān tomorrow
15. 上午 （名）shàngwǔ morning
16. 去 （动）qù to go
17. 时候 （名）shíhou time
18. 开 （动）kāi to drive
19. 车 （名）chē car, bus etc.
20. 半 （数）bàn half

专 名 Proper Nouns

1. 颐和园 Yíhéyuán The Summer Palace

2. 长城	Chángchéng	The Great Wall
3. 北海公园	Běihǎi Gōngyuán	
		Beihai Park
4. 故宫	Gùgōng	The Palace Museum

数 词 Numerals

一	yī	one
二	èr	two
三	sān	three
四	sì	four
五	wǔ	five
六	liù	six
七	qī	seven
八	bā	eight
九	jiǔ	nine
十	shí	ten

语 法 Grammar

1. 时间表示法

The Indication of Time

汉语时间的表示法，一般是 先说 "点"，后说 "分"（再说 "秒"）。"点"字必须说出（不能像英语那样可以不说）。例如：

The word order of a Chinese time expression generally begins with "hour", proceeds with "minute" and ends up with "second". In no case can the word 点 (hour) be omitted, e.g.

3：00	三点	3：05	三点零五分
3：15	三点十五分	3：30	三点半
	三点一刻		三点三十分

40

3：20　三点二十　　　　　　3：42　三点四十二

　　3：45　三点四十五

　　　　　三点三刻

有时可以在"点"后加"过"，但词序不改变，不能像英语那样，用 "past" 或 "after" 时，把"分"放在"点"的前面。例如：

Sometimes 点 may be followed by 过, but the word order of the time expression remains unchanged. This is different from the English time expression with "past" or "after" placed before "hour" but after "minute", e.g.

　　3：15　三点过十五分　　三点过一刻

但 3：30　不能说成"三点过半"。

It is incorrect to say 三点过半.

如果分钟超过半小时而又接近下一个钟点的，可以用"差"表示，相当于英语用"to"的表示法，不过"差"的位置同"to"不同，要放在"分钟"的前面。例如：

The Chinese word 差—the equivalent of "to" in an English time expression, can be used before the "minute" to indicate a point of time between the 31st minute and the 59th minute in any specification of hours, e.g.

　　4：50　差十分五点

　　4：45　差十五分五点

　　　　　差一刻五点

2. 时间词

Time Words

时间词可以作主语和宾语。例如：

Time words may function as a subject or an object, e.g.

　　(1) 现在是十点过五分。

也可以作定语，如"下午的课"，"明天的工作"。时间词作状语时，可以放在谓语动词前面，也可以放在主语前面。例如：

Time words can also be used as adjectival modifiers as in "下午的课" and "明天的工作". When used as adverbial modifiers, they can be placed before either the verbal predicate or the subject, e.g.

(2) 我们八点上课。

(3) 你们下午去颐和园。

(4) 明天上午他们不上课。

(5) 下午两点王老师有课。

主　语	谓		语
Subject	Predicate		
状语 Adver- bial Modifier		状语 Adver- bial Modifier	动词 Verb	宾　语 Object
	现在 我们 你们 他们	八点 下午 不	是 上 去 上	十点过五分。 课。 颐和园。 课。
明天上午 下午两点	王老师		有	课。

注意：汉语同英语不同，时间词作状语时，前面不需加介词，也不能放在句尾。

N.B. When used as adverbial modifiers, the time words are neither preceded by a preposition, nor put at the end of a sentence. In this aspect, they are different from the English time words.

3. "有"字句

Sentences with 有

动词"有"作谓语,可以表示领有。一般情况下,都要带宾语。例如:

When functioning as a predicate, the verb 有 denotes possession, and often takes an object, e.g.

(1) 我们上午有课。

(2) 他有朋友。

它的否定形式是"没有"(不能用"不"否定,这同英语的"have"不同)。例如:

The negative form of 有 is 没有 (never 不有!), e.g.

(3) 我没有课。

(4) 他没有朋友吗?

(5) 王老师上午有没有课?

主 语 Subject	谓　　　语 Predicate			语 气 助 词 Modal Particle
	状 语 Adverbial Modifier	动 词 Verb	宾 语 Object	
我们	上午	有	课。	
他		有	朋友。	
我	没	有	课。	
他	没	有	朋友	吗?
王老师	上午	有没有	课?	

练 习 Exercises

1. 说出下列时间：
   Put the following into Chinese:

   6:00   3:40   9：30   7：08
   10:37   11:56   13：45   2：49

2. 用"差…"的形式说出下列时间：
   Put the following into Chinese with 差：

   5：45   3：47   2：56   4：55
   6：40   7：50   8：57   9：56

3. 用下列词语造句：
   Make sentence with the words given below:

   (1) 上午   上课   8：00
   (2) 去   颐和园   下午   2：30
   (3) 今天   没   课
   (4) 明天   不   上课

4. 根据答话提出问话：
   Ask questions corresponding to the answers given:

   (1) A：＿＿＿＿＿？
       B：现在差十分八点。
   (2) A：＿＿＿＿＿？
       B：我们十二点下课。
   (3) A：＿＿＿＿＿？
       B：我下午两点去。
   (4) A：＿＿＿＿＿？
       B：下午两点开车。

5. 把下列的问句改成用"几"的问句：

Rewrite the following with 几:

(1) 现在什么时候？

(2) 你什么时候去颐和园？

(3) 史密斯先生什么时候下课？

(4) 玛丽小姐今天什么时候去商店？

6. 把下列问句改成正反疑问句：

Change the following into affirmative-negative interrogative sentences:

(1) 你们今天上午有课吗？

(2) 你们今天下午去颐和园吗？

(3) 史密斯先生今天上课吗？

(4) 你明天去商店吗？

五、问 日 期
wèn rì qī
Asking the Day and Date

41. 今天几号？
Jīntiān jǐ hào?
What's the date today?

42. 今天十二号。
Jīntiān shí'èr hào.
Today is the twelfth.

43. 明天星期几？
Míngtiān xīngqī jǐ?
What day is tomorrow?

44. 明天是星期六吗？
Míngtiān shì xīngqīliù ma?
Will tomorrow be Saturday?

45. 昨天不是星期六，是星期日。
Zuótiān bú shì xīngqīliù, shì xīngqīrì.
Yesterday wasn't Saturday, but Sunday.

46. 明年你来中国吗？
Míngnián nǐ lái Zhōngguó ma?
Will you come to China next year?

47. 明年不来，我后年来。

Míngnián bù lái, wǒ hòunián lái.

I won't be here next year, but in the year after next.

48. 格林先生几月几号到北京?

Gélín xiānsheng jǐ yuè jǐ hào dào Běijīng?

When did Mr. Green arrive in Beijing?

49. 他七月二十六号下午到北京。

Tā qīyuè èrshí liù hào xiàwǔ dào Běijīng.

He arrived in Beijing on the 26th afternoon of July.

50. 不知道。

Bù zhīdao.

I don't know.

替换练习 Substitution Drills

1. 今天
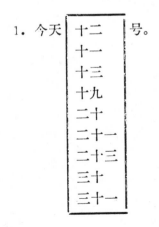
号。

2.
| 明年 | 不来，我 | 后年 | 来。 |

明年 / 一九八三年 / 一九八五年 / 一九八七年 / 一九九〇年 / 二〇〇〇年 / 二〇〇二年

后年 / 一九八四年 / 一九八六年 / 一九八八年 / 一九九一年 / 二〇〇一年 / 二〇〇三年

3. 格林先生 | 几月几号 / 什么时候 / 几点 | 到北京？

4. 他 | 七 / 一 / 二 / 三 / 四 / 五 / 六 / 八 / 九 / 十 / 十一 / 十二 | 月二十六号下午到北京。

48

会 话 Dialogues

甲：今天几号？
Jīntiān jǐ hào?

乙：今天八月十六号。
Jīntiān bāyuè shíliù hào.

甲：今天星期几？
Jīntiān xīngqī jǐ?

乙：今天星期二。
Jīntiān xīngqī'èr.

甲：昨天不是星期日吗？
Zuótiān bú shi xīngqīrì ma?

乙：不是，昨天是星期一。
Bú shi, zuótiān shi xīngqīyī.

甲：现在几点了？
Xiànzài jǐ diǎn le?

乙：现在十一点。
Xiànzài shíyī diǎn.

甲：你去颐和园吗？
Nǐ qù Yíhéyuán ma?

乙：去。
Qù.

甲：什么时候去？
Shénme shíhou qù?

乙：下午一点半。
Xiàwǔ yì diǎn bàn.

* * *

甲：请问，今天是几号？
Qǐng wèn, jīntiān shi jǐ hào?

乙：对不起，我不知道。
Duì bu qǐ, wǒ bù zhīdao.

甲：今天是星期几？
Jīntiān shi xīngqī jǐ?

乙：今天是星期四。
Jīntiān shi xīngqīsì.

甲：史密斯先生什么时候来北京？
Shǐmìsī xiānsheng shénme shíhou lái Běijīng?

乙：他九月五号来。
Tā jiǔyuè wǔ hào lái.

甲：他几点到？
Tā jǐ diǎn dào?

乙：上午十点一刻。
Shàngwǔ shí diǎn yí kè.

* * *

甲：您认识布朗先生吗？
Nín rènshi Bùlǎng xiānsheng ma?

乙：认识，他是我的朋友。
Rènshi, tā shi wǒ de péngyou.

甲：他什么时候来中国？明年来吗？
Tā shénme shíhou lái Zhōgguó? Míngnián lái ma?

乙：明年不来，后年来。
Míngnián bù lái, hòunián lái.

甲：他夫人也来吗？
Tā fūren yě lái ma?

乙：不知道
Bù zhīdao.

50

生 词 New Words

1. 今天　　（名）jīntiān　　today
2. 号　　　（名）hào　　　date
3. 星期　　（名）xīngqī　　week
4. 昨天　　（名）zuótiān　　yesterday
5. 星期六　（名）xīngqīliù　Saturday
6. 星期日　（名）xīngqīrì　　Sunday
7. 明年　　（名）míngnián　next year
8. 来　　　（动）lái　　　to come
9. 后年　　（名）hòunián　the year after next
10. 月　　　（名）yuè　　　month
11. 到　　　（动）dào　　　to arrive
12. 知道　　（动）zhīdao　to know
13. 星期二　（名）xīngqī'èr　Tuesday
14. 星期一　（名）xīngqīyī　Monday
15. 星期四　（名）xīngqīsì　Thursday
16. 年　　　（名）nián　　　year
17. 一月　　（名）yīyuè　　January
18. 二月　　（名）èryuè　　February
19. 三月　　（名）sānyuè　March
20. 四月　　（名）sìyuè　　April
21. 五月　　（名）wǔyuè　　May
22. 六月　　（名）liùyuè　　June
23. 七月　　（名）qīyuè　　July
24. 八月　　（名）bāyuè　　August
25. 九月　　（名）jiǔyuè　　September

51

26. 十月　　（名）shíyuè　　October
27. 十一月　（名）shíyīyuè　November
28. 十二月　（名）shí'èryuè　December

专　名　Proper Nouns

1. 中国　　　　Zhōngguó　　China
2. 北京　　　　Běijīng　　　Beijing (Peking)

语　法　Grammar

1. 一百以下的称数法

The Enumeration of Cardinal Numbers below One Hundred

汉语用"十进法"来称数。例如：

In Chinese the decimal system is employed for counting numbers, e.g.

一　二　三　四　五　六　七　八　九　十

十一　十二　十三　十四　十五　十六　十七　十八

十九　二十

二十一　二十二　二十三　二十四　二十五　二十六

二十七　二十八　二十九　三十

三十一　三十二　三十三　……　四十

四十一　四十二　四十三　……　五十

五十一　五十二　五十三　……　六十

六十一　六十二　六十三　……　七十

七十一　七十二　七十三　……　八十

八十一　八十二　八十三　……　九十

九十一　九十二　九十三　……　一百

2. 年、月和星期

Years, Months and Weeks

汉语说年份是直接读出每个数字。例如：

The year is given by reading each figure directly, e.g.

1979年　读作　yī-jiǔ-qī-jiǔ nián
1980年　读作　yī-jiǔ-bā-líng nián
1508年　读作　yī-wǔ-líng-bā nián
2000年　读作　èr-líng-líng-líng nián
2001年　读作　èr-líng-líng-yī nián

汉语十二个月的名称是：

The Chinese names of the twelve months are:

一月　二月　三月　四月　五月　六月　七月　八月
九月　十月　十一月　十二月

一个星期七天的名称是：

The Chinese names of the seven days of the week are:

星期一　星期二　星期三　星期四　星期五　星期六
星期日（天）

年、月、日、时连在一起时，顺序是：

The order of the year, month, date, hour used together is:

年——月——日——星期——上(下)午——时　　例如：

Year—month—date—day—morning or afternoon—hour, e.g.

一九八三年二月二十四日星期四上午十时（点）

注意：不能把年份写在月、日的后面。

N.B. The word standing for the year never appears after the month or date.

3. 名词谓语句（一）

Sentences with a Nominal Predicate (A)

汉语可以直接用时间词作谓语来表达时间。例如：

In Chinese time words can be used as predicates to indicate time, e.g.

(1) 今天四月十二号。

(2) 现在八点十分。

这一类句子叫名词谓语句（即用名词或名词词组作谓语的句子），谓语中不需要加动词"是"（这和英语不同，英语则要加动词）。这种句子没有否定形式。

Such are known as sentences with a nominal predicate. They do not need 是 as a part of the predicate, and have no negative forms.

主　语 Subject	谓　　语 Predicate
今天 现在	四月十二号。 八点十分。

练　习　Exercises

1. 读下列词组

Reading the following groups:

(1) 1905年　1917年　1900年　1983年　2001年

(2) 3月23日　4月30日　5月7日　6月1日　8月19日

(3) 星期一上午八点　　星期三下午四点十分

(4) 6月20日上午8点　　12月15日下午6点15分

2．回答下列问题：

Answer the following questions:

(1) 现在几点？

(2) 今天几号？

(3) 昨天星期几？

(4) 今天是星期五吗？

(5) 现在是九点十分吗？

(6) 明天是不是星期六？

3．把下列问句改成正反疑问句：

Change the following into affirmative-negative interrogative sentences:

(1) 今天是星期五吗？

(2) 明年你来中国吗？

(3) 史密斯先生明年来北京吗？

(4) 现在是三点一刻吗？

4．用下列词语造句：

Make sentences with the words given below:

(1) 几月几号　　到　　北京

(2) 明年　　后年　去　　中国

(3) 星期六　　来

(4) 故宫　　明天　不

六、买东西（上）
mǎi dōng xi
Go Shopping (I)

51. **您买什么?**
Nín mǎi shénme?

Can I help you?

52. **我要四个苹果。**
Wǒ yào sì ge píngguǒ.

I want four apples.

53. **多少钱一斤?**
Duōshao qián yì jīn?

How much is one *jin?*

54. **五毛六一斤。**
Wǔ máo liù yì jīn.

Fifty six fen each *jin.*

55. **再来*两盒烟，一瓶汽水。**
Zài lái liǎng hé yān, yì píng qìshuǐr.

And two packets of cigarettes and a soda water, please.

56. **您还要别的吗?**
Nín hái yào biéde ma?

Anything else?

---

* 买东西或在饭馆吃饭，都可以用"来"表示"要"什么东西。
When shopping or ordering a meal, one may use the verb 来 which means "buy" or "want".

57. 不要了，一共多少钱?

Bú yào le, yígòng duōshao qián?

That's all. How much are they?

58. 一共三块八毛四。

Yígòng sān kuài bā máo sì.

That'll make three yuan and eighty four fen.

59. 给您钱。

Gěi nin qián.

Here you are.

60. 您这是十块，找您六块一毛六。

Nín zhè shi shí kuài, zhǎo nin liù kuài yī máo liù.

Yours is a ten-yuan note, and I'll give you six yuan and sixteen fen change.

替换练习 Substitution Drills

1. 我要

| 四个苹果 |
| 半斤糖 |
| 一盒火柴 |
| 两瓶可口可乐 |
| 一本书 |

。

2. 多少钱

| 一斤 |
| 一个 |
| 一瓶 |
| 一盒 |
| 一本 |

?

3. ·共 | 三块八毛四 | 。
四块（元）
五块二毛三分
六块六毛三
七块零五分
九毛（角）三分

4. 给您 | 钱 | 。
书
火柴
汽水
烟

会 话 Dialogues

甲：您买什么？
Nín mǎi shénme?

乙：我要一斤糖，两斤苹果。
Wǒ yào yì jīn táng, liǎng jīn píngguǒ.

甲：好。
Hǎo.

乙：请问，多少钱一斤？
Qǐng wèn, duōshao qián yì jīn?

甲：糖两块四一斤，苹果五毛八一斤。
Táng liǎng kuài sì yì jīn, píngguǒ wǔ máo bā yì jīn.

乙：有可口可乐吗？
Yǒu kěkǒu-kělè ma?

甲：有。
yǒu.

乙：来一瓶。
Lái yì píng.

甲：还要别的吗？
Hái yào biéde ma?

乙：不要了，多少钱？
Bú yào le, duōshao qián?

甲：一共四块三毛一。
Yígòng sì kuài sān máo yī.

乙：给您钱。
Gěi nin qián.

甲：您这是五块，找您六毛九。
Nín zhè shi wǔ kuài, zhǎo nin liù máo jiǔ.

＊　　　＊　　　＊

甲：同志，我要买烟。
Tóngzhì, wǒ yào mǎi yān.

乙：什么烟？
Shénme yān?

甲："三五"烟，多少钱一盒？
"Sān-Wǔ" yān, duōshao qián yì hé?

乙：一块八。
Yí kuài bā.

甲：来四盒。
Lái sì hé.

乙：还要别的东西吗？
Hái yào biéde dāngxi ma?

甲：再来一盒火柴。
Zài lái yì hé huǒchái.

乙：四盒烟七块二，一盒火柴二分，一共七块两毛
二。
Sì hé yān qī kuài èr, yì hé huǒchái èr fēn, yígòng
qī kuài liǎng máo èr.

甲：给您十块。
Gěi nin shí kuài.

乙：找您两块七毛八。
Zhǎo nin liǎng kuài qī máo bā.

甲：谢谢。
Xièxle.

生 词 New Words

1. 买　　　（动）mǎi　　　　　　to buy
2. 东西　　（名）dōngxi　　　　thing
3. 要　　　（动、能动）yào　　 to want
4. 个　　　（量）gè　　　　　　(a measure word)
5. 苹果　　（名）píngguǒ　　　 apple
6. 多少　　（代）duōshao　　　 how much
7. 钱　　　（名）qián　　　　　money
8. 斤　　　（量）jīn　　　　　　(a measure word)
9. 再　　　（副）zài　　　　　　else, again, additionally
10. 两　　　（数）liǎng　　　　 two
11. 盒　　　（名、量）hé　　　　 packet
12. 烟　　　（名）yān　　　　　 cigarette
13. 瓶　　　（名、量）píng　　　bottle (a measure word)
14. 汽水　　（名）qìshuǐ　　　　soda water

60

15. 还	（副）	hái	else
16. 别的	（代）	biéde	other
17. 一共	（副）	yígòng	altogether
18. 给	（动）	gěi	to give
19. 找	（动）	zhǎo	to give change
20. 糖	（名）	táng	sweets
21. 火柴	（名）	huǒchái	match
22. 可口可乐	（名）	kěkǒu-kělè	coca-cola
23. 本	（量）	běn	(a measure word)
24. 书	（名）	shū	book
25. 块(元)	（量）	kuài(yuán)	yuan
26. 毛(角)	（量）	máo(jiǎo)	ten fen
27. 分	（量）	fēn	fen

语 法 Grammar

1. **量词**

The Measure Word

量词通常用在数词或指示代词的后面，名词的前面。例如：

A measure word is generally used after a numeral or a demonstrative pronoun, but before a noun, e.g.

数词或指示代词 Numeral or Demonstrative Pronoun	量 词 Measure Word	名 词 Noun
两 一 这 那	个 斤 位 位	苹果 糖 先生 小姐

注意：汉语的名词都有特定的量词，如只能说"这个苹果"，不能说"这位苹果"。这类量词在英语中是没有的。

N.B. Every Chinese noun can go only with its specific measure word. We can say 这个苹果, but never 这位苹果. That is not found in English.

有些名词可以用作量词，如"两盒烟"、"一瓶汽水"，英语也是这样。不过汉语把作量词用的名词直接放在所修饰的名词前边，而英语则要用介词"of"（如 a battle of sth.）。

A few nouns can be used as measure words as in 两盒烟 or 一瓶汽水. People do the same with English. However the nominal measure words can be placed right before the nouns modified. There doesn't need a word equivalent to the English "of" in it.

2. "两"的用法
The Use of 两

在量词前一般用"两"，不用"二"，如"两个苹果"、"两瓶汽水"、"两位先生"。在表示度量衡的量词前，可以用"二"，也可以用"两"，如："二斤糖"、"两斤糖"。

两 is generally put before a measure word in stead of 二, e.g. 两个苹果，两瓶汽水，两位先生. But with nouns standing for the unit of length, capacity or weight, either 两 or 二 can be employed, e.g. 二斤糖 or 两斤糖.

3. 名词谓语句（二）
Sentences with a Nominal Predicate (B)

数量词可以直接用作谓语，不需要加动词"是"，这是另一种名词谓语句。例如：

A numeral-measure word group may serve as a predicate without the linking verb "be". That belongs to another type of sentences with a nominal predicate, e.g.

    (1) 五毛六一斤。

    (2) 多少钱一瓶？

主　语 Subject	谓　语 Predicate
五毛六 多少钱	一斤。 一瓶？

这种句子可以作为一个词组当主谓谓语句的谓语。例如：

Sentences as indicated above can function as a predicate in a sentence whose predicate is a subject-predicate construction, e.g.

    (3) 苹果五毛六一斤。

    (4) 汽水多少钱一瓶？

主语 Subject	谓　　　　　语 Predicate	
名词 Noun	小主语 Smaller Subject	小谓语 Smaller Predicate
苹果 汽水	五毛六 多少钱	一斤。 一瓶？

4．双宾语动词谓语句

Verbal Predicate Sentences with a Double Object

有的动词可以带两个宾语，一个是间接宾语(一般是指人的)，在前；另一个是直接宾语(一般是指事物的)，在后。例如：

There are a few verbs taking two objects of which the first one is the indirect (in connection with persons), and the second one is the direct (in connection with things), e.g.

(1) 给你钱。

(2) 找你六块两毛六。

主语 Subject	谓　　　　　语 Predicate		
名词或代词 Noun or Pronoun	动词 Verb	名词或代词(指人) Noun or Pronoun (persons)	名词(指事物) Noun (things)
（我） （我）	给 找	你 您	钱。 六块两毛六。

这种句子是双宾语动词谓语句，词序同英语不用介词"to"的双宾语句相同。但汉语能带双宾语的动词很少。英语的"bring"、"buy"、"sell"、"read"等词可带双宾语，而汉语的"拿"、"带"、"买"、"读"等词一般不带双宾语。

The Chinese two-object sentences are the same as the English ones. However there are not many verbs taking two objects in Chinese. Verbs such as 拿，带，买，读，generally can not take two objects; but the English verbs "bring", "buy" and "read" can.

练　习　Exercises

1. 填入量词，然后再用"几"或"多少"提问：

Fill in the following blanks with a proper measure

word, and then ask questions with 几 or 多少：

例：苹果六毛九一____。

苹果六毛九一斤。

苹果多少钱一斤？

(1) 汽水四毛三一____。

(2) 我买两____苹果。

(3) 我要三____烟。

(4) 我买四____汽水。

(5) 烟一块三一____。

2．把下列数字改成汉字，并填上适当的量词：

Replace the following Arabic figures with Chinese, and add a proper measure word to each of them:

(1) 2____教授　　(2) 2____汽水

(3) 12____烟　　(4) 2____糖

(5) 22____钱　　(6) 20____苹果

3．用下列的词语造句：

Make sentences with the words given below:

(1) 给　格林　九十块钱

(2) 你　给　多少钱

(3) 找　四块　三毛

(4) 买　三斤

(5) 不要　别的　一共　钱

七、买东西（下）
mǎi dōng xi

Go Shopping (II)

61. 请问，有布鞋没有？

Qǐng wèn, yǒu bùxié méi yǒu?

Do you do cotton shoes, please?

62. 有，您穿多大号的？

Yǒu, nín chuān duō dà hàor de?

Yes, we do. What size do you take?

63. 大概是四十一号半。

Dàgài shì sìshí yī hàor bàn.

Size 41.5, I think.

64. 这双怎么样？您试试看。

Zhè shuāng zěnmeyàng? Nín shìshi kàn.

How about this pair? You may try them on.

65. 小一点儿，有大一点儿的吗？

Xiǎo yìdiǎnr, yǒu dà yìdiǎnr de ma?

They're a bit tight. Could I have a larger size?

66. 这双正合适。

Zhè shuāng zhèng héshì.

They fit me nicely.

67. 太贵了，有便宜点儿的没有？

Tài guì le, yǒu piányi diǎnr de mei yǒu?

They're too expensive. Have you got anything cheaper?

68. 这种又便宜又好。

Zhè zhǒng yòu piányi yòu hǎo.

These are cheap and nice.

69. 在哪儿交钱？

Zài nǎr jiāo qián?

Where shall I pay?

70. 请到那儿交钱。

Qǐng dào nàr jiāo qián.

Over there, please.

替换练习　Substitution Drills

1. 您穿

| 多大号 |
| 多少号 |
| 多少公分 |
| 多大 |

的？

2. 大概是

| 四十一号半 |
| 三十八号 |
| 二十六公分 |
| 二十四公分半 |

。

3.

4.

会 话 Dialogues

甲：同志，有布鞋没有？
Tóngzhǐ, yǒu bùxié mei yǒu?

乙：您穿多大号的？
Nín chuān duō dà hàor de?

甲：大概是三十九号的。
Dàgài shì sānshí jiǔ hàor de.

乙：这双怎么样？
Zhè shuāng zěnmeyàng?

甲：我试试看。小一点儿。
Wǒ shìshi kàn. Xiǎo yìdiǎnr.

乙：这双是三十九号半，您再试试。
Zhè shuāng shì sānshí jiǔ hàor bàn, nín zài shìsì

甲：这双正合适，多少钱？
Zhè shuāng zhèng héshì, duōshao qián?

乙：八块九。
Bā kuài jiǔ.

甲：太贵了，有便宜点儿的没有？
Tài guì le, yǒu piányi diǎnr de mei yǒu?

乙：这种又便宜又好。
Zhè zhǒng yòu piányi yòu hǎo.

甲：要这双。在哪儿交钱？
Yào zhè shuāng. Zài nǎr jiāo qián?

乙：请到那儿交钱。
Qǐng dào nàr jiāo qián.

*　　　*　　　*

甲：你好！
Nǐ hǎo!

乙：你好！
Nǐ hǎo!

甲：你买什么？
Nǐ mǎi shénme?

乙：我要买一双布鞋。
Wǒ yào mǎi yì shuāng bùxié.

甲：你穿多少公分的？
Nǐ chuān duōshao gōngfēn de?

乙：二十五公分。
Èrshí wǔ gōngfēn.

甲：你试试这双。
Nǐ shìshi zhè shuāng.

乙：大一点儿。
Dà yìdiǎnr.

甲：这双怎么样？
Zhè shuāng zěnmeyàng?

乙：好，正合适。多少钱？
Hǎo, zhèng héshì. Duōshao qián

甲：四块一。
Sì kuài yī.

乙：又好又便宜。
Yòu hǎo yòu piányi.

甲：买这双吗？
Mǎi zhè shuāng ma?

乙：买这双。给你钱。
Mǎi zhè shuāng. Gěi ni qián.

生　词　New Words

1.	布鞋	（名）bùxié	cotton shoes
2.	穿	（动）chuān	to wear
3.	多	（形、副）duō	how (big, much, nice etc.)
4.	大	（形）dà	big
5.	号	（名）hàor	size
6.	大概	（副）dàgài	perhaps
7.	双	（量）shuāng	pair (a measure word)
8.	试	（动）shì	to try
9.	看	（动、助）kàn	to see
10.	小	（形）xiǎo	small

70

11. （一）点儿	（量）	（yì）diǎnr	a little bit
12. 正	（副）	zhèng	just
13. 合适	（形）	héshì	suitable
14. 太	（副）	tài	too
15. 贵	（形）	guì	expensive
16. 便宜	（形）	piányi	cheap
17. 种	（量）	zhǒng	kind, type (a measure word)
18. 又…又…		yòu…yòu…	both…and…
19. 在	（介）	zài	in, at
20. 哪儿	（代）	nǎr	where
21. 交	（动）	jiāo	to pay
22. 请	（动）	qǐng	please, to invite
23. 那儿	（代）	nàr	there
24. 长	（形）	cháng	long
25. 短	（形）	duǎn	short
26. 公分	（量）	gōngfēn	centimetre

语 法 Grammar

1. 连动句（一）
Double Verbal Sentences(A)

谓语连用两个以上动词或动词词组的句子称连动句。连用的动词或动词词组不是并列关系，中间一般也不需要加连词。例如：

A double verbal sentence is one containing a predicate formed by two or more verbs or verbal groups which are not coordinative with a conjunction in between, e.g.

71

（1）他来工作。

（2）你到那儿交钱。

例（1）中的"来"、"工作"两个动词的主语都是"他"。例（2）中的"到那儿"、"交钱"两个动词词组的主语都是"你"，"交钱"表示"到那儿"去的目的。表示这种关系的动作（一个动作是另一个动作的目的）是有先后的，动词的词序不能改变（不能说"你交钱到那儿"）。说英语的人应注意这一点，因为英语中的"到那儿"常用介词词组，放在句尾。

In sentence (1) 他 is the subject of both verbs 来 and 工作. In sentence (2) 你 is the subject of 到那儿 and 交钱; and the latter indicates the purpose of the former. Sentences as such have strict verbal order only in which can the motive and purpose be expressed correctly (for example, we never say 你交钱到那儿). It is advisable for English speakers to pay close attention to that, as they do not always do the same with English.

主　语 Subject	谓　　　　语 Predicate			
名词或代词 Noun or Pronoun	动词 Verb	名词或代词 Noun or Pronoun	动词 Verb	名词或代词 Noun or Pronoun
他 你	来 到	那儿	工作。 交	钱。

这类连动句的正反疑问形式，可以有下面两种格式：

With a double verbal sentence, an affirmative-negative

question can be asked in the following two ways:

(3) 你去不去商店买鞋?

(4) 他到上海工作不工作?

2. **动词重叠(一)与助词"看"**

The Verbal Repetition (A), and the Auxiliary 看

汉语动词可以重叠,表示动作时间短。例如:"试试"、"穿穿"、"买买"等等。助词"看"用在重叠动词后边,表示尝试。例如:

Chinese verbs can be repeated to denote a brief action, e.g. 试试, 穿穿, 买买 etc.. The auxiliary 看 may go after the repeated verb to indicate "have a try", e.g.

(1) 你试试看。

(2) 这双怎么样,您穿穿看。

(3) 这里没有,你到别的商店买买看。

3. **形容词+"(一)点儿"**

An Adjective Plus (一)点儿

"点儿",量词,前面的数词限于"一",口语常省略。"(一)点儿"用在形容词后,表示程度、数量略微增加或减少。例如:

The measure word 点儿 can go after the numeral 一 which is often omitted in spoken Chinese. when preceded by an adjective(一)点儿 indicates a slight increase or decrease in number, or a minor change in degree, e.g.

大一点儿——大点儿

小一点儿——小点儿

贵一点儿——贵点儿

便宜一点儿——便宜点儿

好一点儿——好点儿

4. **介词词组作状语**

A Prepositional Group Used as an Adverbial Modifier

介词跟它的宾语构成介词词组，可以用作状语，汉语要把它放在动词前，而英语则要放在动词后。介词"在"的宾语常是处所词，"在+处所词"用作状语指动作发生的处所。例如：

A preposition-object group as an adverbial modifier comes before the verb (never after the verb as in English). The object of the preposition 在 is often a locative word. When used as an adverbial modifier, the "在 + locative word" phrase indicates where the action takes place, e.g.

（1）你在那儿交钱。

（2）格林在北京学习。

主语 Subject	谓 语 Predicate			
名词或代词 Noun or Pronoun	介词 Preposition	名词或代词 Noun or Pronoun	动词 Verb	名词或代词 Noun or Pronoun
你 我 格林	在 在 在	那儿 哪儿 北京	交 交 学习。	钱。 钱？

否定句一般是把否定副词放在介词前。例如：

In a negative sentence the negative adverb should be placed before the preposition, e.g.

（3）你不在这儿交钱。

（4）他不在北京工作。

练 习　Exercises

1. 选择适当的词语填空：
   Fill in the blanks with one of the words given below:

   学习　工作　买东西　交钱　试试

   （1）他去商店_____。
   （2）我_____这双布鞋。
   （3）你来北京_____吗？
   （4）他去上海_____。
   （5）您到那儿_____。

2. 用"形容词＋（一）点儿"填空：
   Fill in the following blanks with a proper adjective plus（一）点儿：

   （1）这双布鞋不怎么好，有____的吗？
   （2）这双大一点儿，有____的吗？
   （3）_____，有便宜点儿的吗？
   （4）太小了，有_____的吗？

3. 把下列问句改成正反疑问句：
   Change the following into affirmative-negative interrogative sentences:

   （1）这双布鞋大吗？
   （2）这双合适吗？
   （3）你明年来北京学习吗？
   （4）你明天去商店买东西吗？

八、问 住 址
wèn zhù zhǐ

Asking about Addresses

71. 请问，你家在哪儿？
Qǐng wèn, nǐ jiā zài nǎr?

Could you tell me where your home is?

72. 我家在北京。
Wǒ jiā zài Běijīng.

My home is in Beijing.

73. 你家在北京什么地方？
Nǐ jiā zài Běijīng shénme dìfang?

Where's your home in Beijing?

74. 在北京西郊学院路 8 号。
Zài Běijīng Xījiāo Xuéyuànlù bā hào.

8 Institute Road, West Suburbs, Beijing.

75. 史密斯先生，你住在哪儿？
Shǐmìsī xiānsheng, nǐ zhù zài nǎr?

Where do you live, Mr. Smith?

76. 我住在北京饭店。
Wǒ zhù zài Běijīng Fàndiàn.

I'm living in Beijing Hotel.

77. 你住在几层？

Nǐ zhù zài jǐ céng?

Which floor?

78. 我住在三层 302 号房间。

Wǒ zhù zài sān céng sān-líng-èr hào fángjiān.

I'm living in Room 302, on the third floor.

79. 格林先生是不是住在这儿？

Génlín xiānsheng shì bu shì zhù zài zhèr?

Does Mr. Green live here?

80. 他的房间是多少号？

Tā de fángjiān shì duōshao hào?

What's his room number?

替换练习　Substitution Drills

1. 你家在 | 哪儿
 什么地方 | ？

2. 我家在 | 北京
 上海
 东京
 巴黎
 纽约 | 。

3. 在 | 北京西郊学院路
 巴黎小王子街
 东京西大泉 | 8 号。

4. 史密斯先生，你住在

哪儿
什么地方
什么饭店

？

5. 我住在

北京饭店
友谊宾馆
华侨大厦

。

6. 我住在

三	层	302
五		511
八		874
一		169

号房间。

会 话 Dialogues

甲：你家在哪儿？
　　Nǐ jiā zài nǎr?

乙：我家在上海。
　　Wǒ jiā zài Shànghǎi.

甲：在上海什么地方？
　　Zài Shànghǎi shénme dìfang?

乙：我家在上海南京路81号。
　　Wǒ jiā zài Shànghǎi Nánjīnglù bāshí yī hào.

丙：你家在东京吗？
　　Nǐ jiā zài Dōngjīng ma?

甲：是的，我家在东京。
　　Shì de, wǒ jiā zài Dōngjīng.

丙：你家在东京什么地方？
Nǐ jiā zài Dōngjīng shénme dìfang?

甲：在东京西大泉。
Zài Dōngjīng Xīdàquán.

丙：山本也住在东京吗？
Shānběn yě zhù zài Dōngjīng ma?

甲：不，他住在大阪。
Bù, tā zhù zài Dàbǎn.

＊　　　　＊　　　　＊

甲：请问，布朗先生住在什么饭店？
Qǐng wèn, Bùlǎng xiānsheng zhù zài shénme fàndiàn?

乙：他住在友谊宾馆。
Tā zhù zài Yǒuyì Bīnguǎn.

甲：住在几号房间？
Zhù zài jǐ hào fángjiān?

乙：大概是 215 号房间。
Dàgài shì èr-yāo-wǔ hào fángjiān.

甲：他住在几层？是二层吗？
Tā zhù zài jǐ céng? Shì èr céng ma?

乙：啊，是二层。
À, shì èr céng.

甲：你是不是也住在友谊宾馆？
Nǐ shì bu shì yě zhù zài Yǒuyì Bīnguǎn?

乙：不，我住在学校。
Bù, wǒ zhù zài xuéxiào.

生　词　New Words

1. 家　　　（名）jiā　　　home, family
2. 在　　　（动）zài　　　to be at
3. 地方　　（名）dìfang　place
4. 西郊　　（名）xījiāo　west suburbs
5. 号　　　（名）hào　　　number
6. 住　　　（动）zhù　　　to live
7. 饭店　　（名）fàndiàn　hotel, restaurant
8. 层　　　（量）céng　　floor
9. 房间　　（名）fángjiān　room
10. 啊　　　（叹、助）à　　oh

专　名　Proper Nouns

1. 学院路　　Xuéyuànlù　　　Institute Road
2. 上海　　　Shànghǎi　　　　Shanghai
3. 东京　　　Dōngjīng　　　　Tokyo
4. 西大泉　　Xīdàquán　　　　Nisiozmi
5. 巴黎　　　Bālí　　　　　　Paris
6. 纽约　　　Niǔyuē　　　　　New York
7. 大阪　　　Dàbǎn　　　　　Osaka
8. 北京饭店　Běijīng Fàndiàn　Beijing Hotel
9. 友谊宾馆　Yǒuyì Bīnguǎn　Friendship Hotel
10. 华侨大厦　Huáqiáo Dàshà　Overseas Chinese Hotel
11. 小王子街　Xiǎo Wángzǐ Jiē　Little Prince Street
12. 南京路　　Nánjīng lù　　　Nanjing Road
13. 山本　　　Shānběn　　　　Yama Moto

80

语 法 Grammar

1. 动词"在"
The Verb 在

"在",动词,作谓语表示人或事物存在于某处所、位置,一般要带宾语(处所词)。例如:

The verb 在 indicating the locality or position of a thing or a person, often takes an object expressed by a locative word, e.g.

　　(1) 格林在家吗?
　　(2) 我家在北京。

主语 Subject	谓 语 Predicate		
名词或代词 Noun or Pronoun	否定副句 Negative Adverb	动词 Verb	处所词 Locative word
格林		在	家。
我家		在	北京。
他	不	在	上海。
史密斯先生		在	哪儿?

在一定的语言环境中,如果处所是已知的,也可以不带宾语。例如:

The object which 在 takes may be omitted if the locality is understood through the context, e.g.

　　A: 张老师在吗?
　　B: 在,请进。

注意:(1)"格林在家学习"一句中的"在",不是动词,是介词;(2)英语表示人或事物处于什么位置,可以用动词"be",相当于汉语表示处所位置的"在"，但在汉语中不能把"在"换成"是"。

N.B. (1) In 格林在家学习, the 在 is not a verb, but a preposition. (2) The English verb "to be" may be followed by a preposition-noun group or an adverb to show the locality. However in Chinese 在 can never be replaced by 是.

2．介词词组"在…"作时间处所补语（注）

The Prepositional Phrase 在… Used as a Complement of Time or Locatity

介词词组"在…"放在动词后边作补语，说明人或事物可以通过某一动作而存在于某处，"在"后面必须有宾语（处所词）。例如：

When used after a verb as a complement, the prepositional phrase 在… denotes the locality of a person or thing through an action. 在 should always be followed by an object expressed by a locative word, e.g.

（1）我住在北京。

（2）你住在几层？

主语 Subject	谓　　　　　　语 Predicate			
名词或代词 Noun or Pronoun	否定副词 Negative Adverb	动词 Verb	介词 Preposition	宾语 Object
我 他 你 格林	不	住 住 住 住	在 在 在 在	北京。 北京饭店。 几层？ 哪儿？

3. 疑问句（四）

Interrogative Sentences （D）

当提问人对某事已有一种估计，但需要进一步明确时，用"是不是"提问。"是不是"可以放在陈述句的主语和谓语的中间，也可以放在句尾。回答用"是"或"不"。例如：

是不是 can be used to ask a question by a person who has only a rough judgement of somebody or something before further certification. 是不是 can either be inserted between the subject and predicate, or put at the end of a declarative sentence. To answer the question either 是 or 不 may be used, e.g.

(1) A：格林先生是不是住在这儿？

B：是，他住在这儿。

(2) A：玛丽小姐住在北京饭店，是不是？

B：不，她住在学院路8号。

练 习 Exercises

1. 根据实际情况回答下列问题：

Give your own answers to the follwing questions:

(1) 你家在哪儿？

(2) 你住在什么地方？

(3) 现在你住在哪儿？

(4) 你住在几层？

(5) 你住在几号房间？

2. 把下列问句改成用"是不是"的疑问句：

Change the following into interrogative sentences with 是不是:

(1) 你家在不在巴黎？

(2) 你住在东京吗？

(3) 你明天去不去颐和园？

(4) 你去不去商店买东西？

(5) 你住在北京饭店，她呢？

3. 完成下列句子（要用上动词"在"或介词"在"）：

Complete the following sentences with the verbal or prepositional 在：

(1) 张老师＿＿＿吗？

(2) 我住＿＿＿，他也＿＿＿上海。

(3) 我家＿＿＿伦敦，他家也＿＿＿。

(4) 我去北京，住＿＿＿。

(5) 我到上海，住＿＿＿。

(6) 我＿＿＿朋友家。

注：时间补语例见本书第306页语法小结（三）

See *A Short Summary of Grammar* (3), page 306, for complements of time.

九、谈 家 庭
tán jiā tíng

Talking about One's Family

81. 你家有什么人？
Nǐ jiā yǒu shénme rén?

Who are there in your family?

82. 我家有父亲、母亲、一个妹妹和一个 弟弟。
Wǒ jiā yǒu fùqin, mǔqin, yí ge mèimei hé yí ge dìdi.

There's my father, mother, a younger sister and a younger brother in my family.

83. 你父亲多大岁数了？
Nǐ fùqin duō dà suìshu le?

How old is your father?

84. 他今年六十一了。
Tā jīnnián liùshí yī le.

He's 61 years old now.

85. 他在哪儿工作？
Tā zài nǎr gōngzuò?

Where does he work?

86. 他在一个公司里工作。
Tā zài yí ge gōngsī li gōngzuò.

He works in a company.

87. 他不工作了，退休了。

Tā bù gōngzuò le, tuìxiū le.

He doesn't go to work any more. He's retired.

88. 你妹妹多大了?

Nǐ mèimei duō dà le?

How old is your younger sister?

89. 她工作还是学习?

Tā gōngzuò háishi xuéxí?

Does she work or study?

90. 你弟弟几岁了?

Nǐ dìdi jǐ suì le?

How old is your younger brother?

替换练习 Substitution Drills

1.
你父亲	多大岁数了?
他母亲	
这位教授	
那位先生	

2. 他在
一个公司	里工作。
一个学校	
一家银行	
一家商店	

3. 她

工作	还是	学习	？
买烟		买火柴	
去颐和园		去长城	
在伦敦		在罗马	
在 265 号		在 365 号	

会 话　Dialogues

甲：你家在北京吗？
　　Nǐ jiā zài Běijīng ma?

乙：不，我家在上海。
　　Bù, wǒ jiā zài Shànghǎi.

甲：你家有什么人？
　　Nǐ jiā yǒu shénme rén?

乙：我家有父亲、母亲和一个妹妹。
　　Wǒ jiā yǒu fùqin, mǔqin hé yí ge mèimei.

甲：你有没有弟弟？
　　Nǐ yǒu mei yǒu dìdi?

乙：没有。
　　Méi yǒu.

甲：你父亲多大年纪了？
　　Nǐ fùqin duō dà niánjì le?

乙：他今年五十八了。
　　Tā jīnnián wǔshí bā le.

甲：他在哪儿工作？
　　Tā zài nǎr gōngzuò?

乙：他在学院工作，是教授。
Tā zài xuéyuàn gōngzuò, shì jiàoshòu.

甲：你母亲也工作吗？
Nǐ mǔqin yě gōngzuò ma?

乙：她不工作，退休了。
Tā bù gōngzuò, tuìxiū le.

甲：你妹妹工作还是学习？
Nǐ mèimei gōngzuò háishi xuéxí?

乙：她学习。
Tā xuéxí.

甲：她多大了？
Tā duō dà le?

乙：十八岁。
Shíbā suì.

*　　　　*　　　　*

甲：您认识格林吗？
Nín rènshi Gélín ma?

乙：认识，他是我的朋友。
Rènshi, tā shi wǒ de péngyou.

甲：他住在伦敦还是住在罗马？
Tā zhù zài Lúndūn háishi zhù zài Luómǎ?

乙：他住在伦敦。
Tā zhù zài Lúndūn.

甲：他家有什么人？
Tā jiā yǒu shénme rén?

乙：有母亲，一个弟弟和一个妹妹。
Yǒu mǔqin, yí ge dìdi hé yí ge mèimei.

甲：他没有父亲吗？
Tā méi yǒu fùqin ma?

乙：没有。
Méi yǒu.

甲：他母亲在哪儿工作？
Tā mǔqin zài nǎr gōngzuò?

乙：他母亲在一家银行里工作。
Tā mǔqin zài yì jiā yínháng li gōngzuò.

甲：他母亲多大岁数了？
Tā mǔqin duō dà suìshu le?

乙：四十岁。
Sìshí suì.

甲：他弟弟十几了？
Tā dìdi shíjǐ le?

乙：十四了。
Shísì le.

甲：他妹妹呢？
Tā mèimei ne?

乙：大概八岁。
Dàgài bā suì.

生 词 New Words

1. 人　　　（名）rén　　　person
2. 父亲　　（名）fùqin　　father
3. 母亲　　（名）mǔqin　　mother
4. 妹妹　　（名）mèimei　　younger sister
5. 弟弟　　（名）dìdi　　younger brother

6. 岁数	（名）	suìshu	age
7. 今年	（名）	jīnnián	this year
8. 公司	（名）	gōngsī	company
9. 里	（方）	li	in
10. 退休	（动）	tuìxiū	to be retired
11. 还是	（连）	háishi	or
12. 岁	（量）	suì	—year(s) old
13. 家	（量）	jiā	(a measure word)
14. 银行	（名）	yínháng	bank
15. 商店	（名）	shāngdiàn	shop
16. 年纪	（名）	niánjì	age
17. 学院	（名）	xuéyuàn	institute, college

专　名　Proper Nouns

1. 伦敦	Lúndūn	London
2. 罗马	Luómǎ	Rome

语　法　Grammar

1. 问年龄的几种说法
Ways of Asking One's Age

问年龄有几种说法。问老人或比自己年长的成年人，为了礼貌，常用：

There are a few ways to ask one's age. With an old person or an adult elder than the speaker , the polite expressions are:

（1）您今年多大年纪？

（2）你父亲多大岁数？

90

问一般成年人或跟自己同辈人的年龄，常用：

With an adult, or people of about one's own age, one can say:

　　　（3）你今年多大？

　　　（4）你今年多大了？

　　　（5）你二十几了？

问小孩用：

The following are good for use with a child:

　　　（6）你几岁？

　　　（7）你多大了？

　　　（8）你十几了？

这些句子都是名词谓语句，不能像英语那样加动词"是"。

What is indicated above are sentences with a nominal predicate. No 是 is needed in them.

　2. 疑问句（五）

Interrogative Sentences. (E)

　　用连词"还是"连接两种可能的答案，由回答的人选择其一，这种疑问句叫选择疑问句。例如：

An alternative question is one containing two possibilities linked by 还是. One of them may be chosen for a reply, e.g.

　　　（1）A：你妹妹工作还是学习？

　　　　　B：她工作。

　　　（2）A：你家在北京还是在上海？

　　　　　B：在上海。

　　　（3）A：你明天去颐和园还是今天去？

　　　　　B：我明天去。

"是"字句的选择疑问形式是：

The alternative question form of a sentence with 是 is:

（4）史密斯先生是你的朋友还是他的朋友？

（5）你的房间是 302 号还是 203 号？

3. 方位词"里"

The Locative Word 里

方位词"里"放在名词后面表示处所，如"家里"、"公司里"等等，可以用作宾语。例如：

A phrase made by a noun and the locative 里 as in 家里，公司里，can be used as an object，e.g.

（1）他在一个公司里工作。

（2）格林先生住在家里。

也可以用作主语。例如：

A noun-里 phrase may be treated as a subject as well，e.g.

（3）商店里有很多人。

注意：汉语方位词的意思，英语用介词来体现，说英语的人一定要注意汉语方位词的意义和用法。

N.B. The way locality is shown in Chinese can be very different from what is in English. Therefore it is advisable for English speakers to know well the meanings and usages of Chinese locative words.

4. 疑问句（六）

Interrogative Sentences (F)

在一个名词或名词词组后面，加上语气助词"呢"，可以构成疑问句。这种疑问句的疑问所在是根据上下文来决定的。例如：

An interrogative sentence can be made by using the modal particle 呢 after a noun or a nominal phrase. The part in question is always understandable through the context，e.g.

（1）我很好，你呢？

（2）他妹妹二十五岁，他弟弟呢？

如果没有上下文，这种问句是问处所的，即："…在那儿？"
例如：

A reply of a thing or a person's whereabouts is expected
if there is no context, e.g.

（3）我的火柴呢？

（4）玛丽呢？

练 习　Exercises

1．根据答话提出问话：

Ask questions to which the answers given below
are appropriate:

（1）A：＿＿＿＿＿＿＿＿？

B：我六十二了。

（2）A：＿＿＿＿＿＿＿＿？

B：我母亲今年七十。

（3）A：＿＿＿＿＿＿＿＿？

B：我弟弟十二了。

（4）A：＿＿＿＿＿＿＿＿？

B：我妹妹今年二十一岁。

（5）A：＿＿＿＿＿＿＿＿？

B：他两岁半。

（6）A：＿＿＿＿＿＿＿＿？

B：我今年二十三了。

2．把下列句子改成选择问句：

Change the following into alternative questions:

（1）我不在公司工作，在银行工作。

（2）我家在北京，不在上海。

（3）格林住在四层，不住在五层。

（4）史密斯今年不来北京，他明年来北京。

3．把下列句子改成用"是不是"的问句：

Change the following into interrogative sentences with 是不是:

（1）我妹妹在一个公司里工作。

（2）现在他在那儿买布鞋。

（3）我哥哥在这儿学习。

（4）格林先生在学院工作。

4．把下列问句改成用"呢"的问句：

Rewrite the following with 呢:

（1）今天下午我们没有课，你们有没有？

（2）他父亲退休了，他母亲工作不工作？

（3）他哥哥身体很好，他妹妹身体怎么样？

（4）格林先生在这儿，他的秘书在哪儿？

（5）张老师和我们都去颐和园，您去不去？

（6）我们买汽水，史密斯先生买不买？

十、在饭店
zài fàn diàn
In a Restaurant

91. 你们三位吃点儿什么？这是菜单。
Nǐmen sān wei chī diǎnr shénme? Zhè shi càidān.
What would you like to have, gentlemen? Here's the menu.

92. 你喜欢吃什么？
Nǐ xǐhuan chī shénme?
What would you prefer?

93. 吃什么都行。
Chī shénme dōu xíng.
Nothing particular, really.

94. 来一个香酥鸡，一个干烧鱼。
Lái yí ge Xiāngsūjī, yí ge Gānshāoyú.
One crispy chicken and one fried fish for me, please.

95. 放点儿辣椒，好吗？
Fàng diǎnr làjiāo, hǎo ma?
Put some pepper in, will you?

96. 少放点儿，别太辣了。
Shǎo fàng diǎnr, bié tài là le.
Just a little, please. I hope it's not too hot.

97. 啊，味道好极了！

A, wèidao hǎo jíle!

Mm, it's delicious!

98. 喝什么酒，葡萄酒还是啤酒？

Hē shénme jiǔ, pútaojiǔ háishi píjiǔ?

What would you like to drink? Grape wine or beer?

99. 吃米饭还是吃饺子？

Chī mǐfàn háishi chī jiǎozi?

Rice or dumplings—which do you prefer?

100. 两样都来一点儿。

Liǎng yàngr dōu lái yìdiǎnr.

Let's have some of both.

替换练习　Substitution Drills

1.

| 你
我
他
张老师 | 喜欢吃 | 什么？
苹果。
鱼。
辣椒。 |

2. 来

| 一个香酥鸡
一杯啤酒
两瓶可口可乐
半斤饺子 |

。

3. 别太

| 辣
咸
淡 |

了。

96

会 话 Dialogues

甲：你好!
Nǐ hǎo!

乙：你好!
Nǐ hǎo!

甲：你们二位吃点儿什么? 这是菜单。
Nǐmen èr wei chī diǎnr shénme? Zhè shi càidān.

乙：你喜欢吃什么?
Nǐ xǐhuan chī shénme?

丙：吃什么都行。
Chī shénme dōu xíng.

乙：有香酥鸡吗?
Yǒu Xiāngsūjī ma?

甲：有。
Yǒu.

乙：来一个香酥鸡。
Lái yí ge Xiāngsūjī.

丙：再来一个干烧鱼。
Zài lái yí ge Gānshāoyú.

甲：放点儿辣椒, 好吗?
Fàng diǎnr làjiāo, hǎo ma?

丙：少放点儿, 别太辣了。
Shǎo fàng diǎnr, bié tài là le.

甲：喝什么酒?
Hē shénme jiǔ?

乙：来两瓶啤酒。
Lái liǎng píng píjiǔ.

甲：吃米饭还是吃饺子？
Chī mǐfàn háishì chī jiǎozi?

丙：两样都来一点儿。
Liǎng yàngr dōu lái yìdiǎnr.

乙：啊，味道好极了！
À, wèidao hǎo jíle!

        *   *   *

甲：同志，我要吃饺子。
Tóngzhì, wǒ yào chī jiǎozi.

乙：您吃多少？
Nín chī duōshao?

甲：半斤。
Bàn jīn

乙：还要别的吗？
Hái yào biéde ma?

甲：来一个干烧鱼。
Lái yí ge Gānshāoyú.

乙：好。
Hǎo.

甲：我不喜欢吃辣的，别放辣椒。
Wǒ bù xǐhuan chī làde, bié fàng làjiāo.

乙：喝不喝啤酒？
Hē bu hē píjiǔ?

甲：不，我喜欢喝葡萄酒。
Bù, wǒ xǐhuan hē pútaojiǔ.

乙：来一瓶葡萄酒，好吗？
Lái yì píng pútaojiǔ, hǎo ma?

甲：好。一共多少钱？
Hǎo. Yígòng duōshao qián?

乙：一共五块四。
Yígòng wǔ kuài sì.

生　词　New Words

1. 吃　　　（动）chī　　　　to eat
2. 菜单　　（名）càidān　　menu
3. 喜欢　　（动）xǐhuan　　to like
4. 都　　　（副）dōu　　　all
5. 行　　　（形）xíng　　　O.K.
6. 放　　　（动）fàng　　　to put
7. 辣椒　　（名）làjiāo　　pepper
8. 少　　　（形）shǎo　　　a little
9. 别　　　（副）bié　　　do not
10. 辣　　　（形）là　　　hot, chilli
11. 味道　　（名）wèidao　　taste
12. 极了　　　　 jíle　　　extremely
13. 喝　　　（动）hē　　　　to drink
14. 酒　　　（名）jiǔ　　　wine
15. 葡萄酒　（名）pútaojiǔ　grape wine
16. 啤酒　　（名）píjiǔ　　beer
17. 米饭　　（名）mǐfàn　　steamed rice
18. 饺子　　（名）jiǎozi　　dumplings

19.	样	（量）yàngr	kind, type
20.	杯	（名、量）bēi	cup, glass
21.	咸	（形）xián	salty
22.	淡	（形）dàn	not salty enough

专　名　Proper Nouns

1.	香酥鸡	Xiāngsūjī	spiced crispy chicken
2.	干烧鱼	Gānshāoyú	fried fish

语　法　Grammar

1. 动宾词组作主语和宾语

A Verbal Predicate-Object Phrase Used as a Subject or an Object

动词和它的宾语构成动宾词组，可以用作主语。例如：

A phrase formed by a verb and its object can serve as a subject, e.g.

（1）吃什么都行。

（2）喝什么酒都行。

（3）穿这件也好。

也可以用作动词的宾语。例如：

The phrase may be used as an object as well, e.g.

（4）你喜欢吃什么？

（5）我喜欢喝啤酒。

　　在例（1）（2）中，代词"什么"用于"都"前，表示在所说的范围内无例外。

In sentences (1) and (2), the pronoun 什么 going before

100

都 indicates that everything related to the topic is inclusive.

2．祈使句

Imperative Sentences

祈使句是表示请求、命令、劝告等语气的句子。否定的祈使句中常用"不准"、"不许"、"别"等否定词。例如：

An imperative sentence is one expressing requests, commands or advice. Words such as 不准，不许 or 别 are often used in a negative imperative sentence, e.g.

(1) 来一个香酥鸡，一个干烧鱼。

(2) 两样都来一点儿。

(3) 请到那儿交钱！

(4) 少放点儿辣椒，别太辣了！

(5) 你别去颐和园了！

例(4)(5)是祈使句的否定形式。

Sentences (4) and (5) are the negative forms.

3．感叹句

Exclamatory Sentences

感叹句是表示强烈感情（喜爱、惊讶、赞美、感慨等等）的句子。这种句子有时前边有叹词。例如：

Exclamatory sentences express one's liking, surprise, praise or emotion, and are often begun by an interjection, e.g.

(1) 啊，味道好极了！

(2) 这双布鞋太便宜了！

练 习 Exercises

1．完成下列句子：

Complete the following sentences:

101

(1) A：你喜欢吃什么？

B：我喜欢＿＿＿＿。

(2) A：你喜欢去什么地方？

B：我喜欢＿＿＿＿。

(3) A：你穿什么去？

B：＿＿＿＿去都行。

(4) A：你喜欢住在什么地方？

B：我住在什么地方＿＿＿＿。

2．按照下面的句型完成句子：

Complete the following sentences after the model:

例：喝什么酒，葡萄酒还是啤酒？

(1) 吃什么，＿＿＿＿？

(2) 买什么，＿＿＿＿？

(3) 你明天去哪儿，＿＿＿＿？

(4) ＿＿＿＿，啤酒还是汽水？

(5) 你在＿＿＿＿学习，北京还是上海？

(6) 你家＿＿＿＿地方，巴黎还是伦敦？

3．回答下列问题：

Answer the following questions:

(1) 您来点什么？

(2) 来个干烧鱼，好吗？

(3) 这个菜味道怎么样？

(4) 味道不大好，是不是？

(5) 来瓶可口可乐，好吗？

(6) 你喜欢吃香酥鸡吗？

语 法 小 结 (一)
yǔ fǎ xiǎo jié

A Short Summary of Grammar (1)

1. 汉语的句子按照谓语的结构可以分为：

According to their predicates, Chinese sentences can be classified as:

A. 名词谓语句（5课　6课）

Sentences with a Nominal Predicate

(1) 今天星期三。

(2) 现在十二点一刻。

(3) 他今年十九岁。

(4) 三毛五一斤。

B. 形容词谓语句（1课）

Sentences with an Adjectival Predicate

(1) 他很好。

(2) 这种布鞋很便宜。

(3) 我不累。

C. 主谓谓语句（1课）

Sentences with a Subject-Predicate Construction as Their Predicate

(1) 他工作很忙。

(2) 苹果四毛七一斤。

(3) 我今天身体不太好。

D. 动词谓语句（2课　4课　6课　7课）
Sentences with a Verbal Predicate
(1) 这位是格林先生。
(2) 我不是王丽，我姓张，叫张丽。
(3) 我今天下午没课，明天上午有课。
(4) 我有一个妹妹和一个弟弟。
(5) 格林先生明天不来。
(6) 今天下午我们去颐和园。
(7) 他父亲不在北京工作，在上海工作。
(8) 他给我一双布鞋。
(9) 他不去商店买东西。

2. 汉语的句子按照句子的用途和语气可以分为：

According to their use and modes, Chinese sentences can be divided into:

A. 陈述句　Declarative Sentences
(1) 他去友谊宾馆看朋友。
(2) 吃什么都行。

B. 祈使句（10课）Imperative Sentences
(1) 请到那儿交钱！
(2) 来一瓶啤酒！
(3) 我不喜欢吃辣的，别放辣椒！

C. 感叹句（10课）Exclamatory Sentences
(1) 啊，味道好极了！
(2) 这种布鞋便宜极了！

D. 疑问句　Interrogative Sentences
(a) 用"吗"的疑问句（1课）

104

Questions with 吗
(1) 张老师好吗？
(2) 你工作忙吗？
(3) 你明天上午有课吗？
(4) 今天星期二吗？

(b) 正反疑问句（3课）
Affirmative-Negative Questions
(1) 你是不是格林先生？
(2) 你认识不认识她？
(3) 你有没有妹妹？
(4) 你明年来不来北京学习？
(5) 你忙不忙？
(6) 他身体好不好？

(c) 用疑问代词的疑问句（2课）
Questions with an Interrogative Pronoun
(1) 谁是格林先生？
(2) 她是谁的秘书？
(3) 今天星期几？
(4) 你今年十几了？
(5) 苹果多少钱一斤？
(6) 你家在哪儿？
(7) 你住在什么地方？
(8) 你要什么？
(9) 他明天什么时候来？
(10) 你身体怎么样？

(d) 用"还是"的选择疑问句（9课）

Alternative Questions with 还是

(1) 你今天有课还是没课？

(2) 你喜欢吃米饭还是吃饺子？

(3) 喝什么酒，葡萄酒还是啤酒？

(e) 用"是不是"的疑问句（8课）

Questions with 是不是

(1) 你是不是有个弟弟？

(2) 你明天去上海，是不是？

(3) 你们学习很紧张，是不是？

(f) 用"呢"的疑问句（9课）

Questions with 呢

(1) 我明天上课，你呢？

(2) 四十一号的布鞋太小，四十二号的布鞋呢？

(3) 张老师呢？

3. 句子的主要成分有六个：

There are six important elements in a sentence:

A. 主语（10课）The Subject

(1) 格林夫人在一个公司里工作。

(2) 他是史密斯先生的好朋友。

(3) 他身体很好。

(4) 今天星期五。

(5) 吃什么都行。

B. 谓语（1课 2课 5课）The Predicate

(1) 现在两点半。

(2) 这种布鞋贵，那种布鞋便宜。

(3) 弟弟工作，妹妹学习。

(4) 中国的啤酒味道很好。

(5) 多少钱一斤。

C. 宾语（10课）The Object

(1) 这位是王老师。

(2) 我有工作，父亲不给我钱。

(3) 我去商店买苹果。

(4) 我的朋友在上海学习。

(5) 我喜欢吃米饭。

D. 定语（3课）The Adjectival Modifier

(1) 这是谁的东西？

(2) 那是张先生的房间。

(3) 我们是好朋友。

E. 状语（4课 7课）The Adverbial Modifier

(1) 我们不去北京饭店。

(2) 我们都喜欢穿布鞋。

(3) 这种酒太辣。

(4) 明天我们去朋友家吃饺子。

(5) 星期二下午我在家里学习。

F. 补语（7课 8课）The Complement

(1) 这双布鞋小一点儿，有大一点儿的吗？

(2) 我们的老师都住在学校里。

练 习 Exercises

阅读下面的短文并复述：

Read and retell the following passages:

(1) 我是英国人，名字叫格林。你呢？你是哪国人？你是学生吧？我是学生，现在在北京学习。我有两个老师，他们都是中国人。他们有十五个学生，学生都不是中国人。我们的老师工作很忙，我们学习也很紧张。你学习怎么样？是不是也很紧张？

星期一到星期五，我们上午都有课。明天是星期六，我们不上课。上午老师和我们去故宫，九点一刻开车。下午去颐和园，大概差十分两点开车。

你喜欢去北京的公园吗？星期日我们去北海公园看看，怎么样？什么时候去？上午八点半好不好？

好，再见。

(2) 昨天我去商店买东西，我的朋友也去买东西。我买苹果、糖和别的东西。苹果又便宜又好，糖也不贵。我买二斤苹果、一斤糖、两瓶汽水、两盒烟和一盒火柴，一共九块七毛二。

我的朋友很喜欢中国布鞋，他买了一双布鞋。商店的同志给他一双四十二号的，不大也不小，正合适，他很高兴。

这个商店不太大，东西很多，很好，也很便宜。我和我的朋友都喜欢在这个商店买东西。

(3) 今天是八月二十三号，星期六。下午我去朋友家吃饺子。他住在西郊学院路十号。他家在二层，有三个房间，都很大。

我朋友家有五个人。父亲在一个公司里工作，母亲退休了。今天他父亲不在家。我朋友有一个弟弟和一个妹妹。弟弟二十

108

五岁，他是老师。妹妹是学生，她今年十八岁。今天他们都在家。

　　中国的啤酒味道很好，我们都很喜欢喝。我朋友的母亲喜欢喝葡萄酒。他妹妹不喝酒，她喝汽水。我们吃饺子，还有香酥鸡、干烧鱼，味道好极了。我们都很高兴。

十一、谈 语 言
tán　yǔ　yán
Talking about Languages

101. **你是哪国人?**
　　　Nǐ shì nǎ guó rén?
　　　What country do you come from?

102. **我是日本人。**
　　　Wǒ shì Rìběn rén.
　　　I'm a Japanese.

103. **你会说英语吗?**
　　　Nǐ huì shuō Yīngyǔ ma?
　　　Can you speak English?

104. **我不会。**
　　　Wǒ bú huì.
　　　No, I can't.

105. **我说得不好。**
　　　Wǒ shuō de bù hǎo.
　　　I can't speak it well.

106. **你汉语说得怎么样?**
　　　Nǐ Hànyǔ shuō de zěnmeyàng?
　　　Do you speak Chinese very well?

110

107. 我只会说一点儿。

Wǒ zhǐ huì shuō yìdiǎnr.

I can say only a few words.

108. 你能看中文书不能？

Nǐ néng kàn Zhōngwén shū bu néng?

Can you read Chinese books?

109. 我能看。

Wǒ néng kàn.

Yes, I can.

110. 你说的话，我不懂，请你说得慢一点儿。

Nǐ shuō de huà, wǒ bù dǒng, qǐng nǐ shuō de màn yìdiǎnr.

I don't understand what you said. Will you say it slowly?

替换练习　Substitution Drills

1. 我是 | 日本人 |。
　　　　| 美国人 |
　　　　| 法国人 |
　　　　| 中国人 |
　　　　| 英国人 |
　　　　| 德国人 |

2. 你会说 | 英语 | 吗？
　　　　　| 汉语 |
　　　　　| 法语 |
　　　　　| 日语 |
　　　　　| 德语 |

111

3. 你汉语说得 | 怎么样？
| 很好。
| 不太好。
| 好极了。

4. 你能看 | 中文书 | 不能？
| 中文报 |
| 法文杂志 |

会 话 Dialogues

甲：你是哪国人？
　　Nǐ shi nǎ guó rén?

乙：我是法国人。
　　Wǒ shi Fǎguó rén.

甲：你会说英语吗？
　　Nǐ huì shuō Yīngyǔ ma?

乙：不会。
　　Bú huì.

甲：你会说德语吗？
　　Nǐ huì shuō Déyǔ ma?

乙：我只会说一点儿。
　　Wǒ zhǐ huì shuō yìdiǎnr.

甲：你汉语说得怎么样？
　　Nǐ Hànyǔ shuō de zěnmeyàng?

乙：我说得不好。
　　Wǒ shuō de bù hǎo.

甲：你能看中文报吗？
Nǐ néng kàn Zhōngwén bào ma?

乙：不能。
Bù néng.

甲：你能不能看中文书？
Nǐ néng bu néng kàn Zhōngwén shū?

乙：你说的话，我不懂，请你说得慢一点儿。
Nǐ shuō de huà, wǒ bù dǒng, qǐng nǐ shuō de màn
yìdiǎnr.

甲：你能看中文书吗？
Nǐ néng kàn Zhōngwén shū ma?

乙：我只能看一点儿。
Wǒ zhǐ néng kàn yìdiǎnr.

＊　　　　＊　　　　＊

甲：你好！
Nǐ hǎo!

乙：你好！
Nǐ hǎo!

甲：你叫什么名字？
Nǐ jiào shénme míngzi?

乙：我叫安东尼。
Wǒ jiào Āndōngní.

甲：你是美国人吗？
Nǐ shi Měiguó rén ma?

乙：我不是美国人。
Wǒ bú shi Měiguó rén.

甲：对不起。
Duì bu qǐ.

乙：没关系。
Méi guānxi.

甲：你是哪国人？
Nǐ shì nǎ guó rén?

乙：我是法国人。
Wǒ shì Fǎguó rén.

甲：那位先生是——
Nà wei xiānsheng shì——

乙：他是威尔逊先生。
Tā shì Wēi'ěrxùn xiānsheng.

甲：他是哪国人？
Tā shì nǎ guó rén?

乙：他是英国人。
Tā shì Yīngguó rén.

甲：他汉语说得怎么样？
Tā Hànyǔ shuō de zěnmeyàng?

乙：他汉语说得很好。
Tā Hànyǔ shuō de hěn hǎo.

甲：他能看中文书不能？
Tā néng kàn Zhōngwén shū bu néng?

乙：他能看。
Tā néng kàn.

甲：你呢？
Nǐ ne?

乙：我也能看。
Wǒ yě néng kàn.

114

生 词 New Words

1. 哪　　（代）nǎ　　　　which
2. 国　　（名）guó　　　country
3. 会　　（能动）huì　　　can
4. 说　　（动）shuō　　　to speak
5. 得　　（助）de　　　　(a structural particle)
6. 只　　（副）zhǐ　　　only
7. 能　　（能动）néng　　can
8. 话　　（名）huà　　　spoken language
9. 懂　　（动）dǒng　　to understand
10. 慢　　（形）màn　　　slow
11. 报　　（名）bào　　　newspaper
12. 杂志　（名）zázhì　　magazine

专 名 Proper Nouns

1. 日本　　Rìběn　　　　Japan
2. 英语　　Yīngyǔ　　　English
3. 汉语　　Hànyǔ　　　　Chinese
4. 中文　　Zhōngwén　　Chinese
5. 美国　　Měiguó　　　U.S.A
6. 法国　　Fǎguó　　　　France
7. 英国　　Yīngguó　　　Britain
8. 德国　　Déguó　　　　Germany
9. 法语　　Fǎyǔ　　　　French
10. 日语　　Rìyǔ　　　　Japanese
11. 德语　　Déyǔ　　　　German

115

12. 法文	Fǎwén	French
13. 安东尼	Āndōngní	Anthony
14. 威尔逊	Wēi'ěrxùn	Wilson

语 法 Grammar

1. 能愿动词
Modal Verbs

能愿动词"会"、"能"， 相当于英语的 can (could)，否定用"不"放在能愿动词前面(不同于英语的词序)。能愿动词的肯定和否定形式并列起来构成正反疑问句。例如：

The modal verbs 会 and 能 are equivalent to the English "can (could)", and preceded by 不 if the negative form is required. The affirmative and negative forms of a modal verb together can be used to make an interrogative sentence, e.g.

主语 Subject	谓		语		
	Predicate				
	状语 Adverbial Modifier	能愿动词 Modal Verb	动词 Verb	宾语 Object	语气助词 Modal Particle
你 我 格林 他 你	 不 不	会 会 会 能 会不会	说 说。 说 看 说	英语 中文。 中文书。 英语？	吗？

在对话中，能愿动词可以单独用作谓语。例如：

In spoken Chinese a modal verb can function as a predicate by itself, e.g.

    (1) A：你会说英语吗？

          B：（我）会。

    (2) A：你能不能看中文书？

          B：不能。

注意：虽然"会"和"能"都可译作"can （could)"，但这两个词的意义并不完全相同。如果是表示通过学习掌握了某种技术，则用"会"；如果只是表示有能力作某事，则用"能"。

N.B. Although both 会 and 能 may be translated into English as "can （could)", they do not always have the equal meanings. Sometimes 会 expresses know-how through learning, while 能 indicates one's ability to do sth..

2. 程度补语

Complements of Degree

动词后边的补充说明成分叫补语。说明动作所达到的程度或结果的补语，叫程度补语。程度补语和动词之间要用结构助词"得"来连接。简单的程度补语一般由形容词充任，形容词前可带程度副词。否定用"不"，放在程度补语前。

A complement is a word or a phrase used after a verb for further qualification. A complement of degree shows the extent or result of an action. Between the complement and the verb the structural particle 得 should be inserted. An adjective (sometimes preceded by an adverb of degree) may serve as a simple complement of degree. If required, the negative adverb 不 may be followed by a complement of degree.

主语 Subject	谓　语　Predicate		
	动词 Verb	结构助词 Structural Particle	程度补语 Complement of Degree
他	说	得	慢。
我	说	得	不快。
他	吃	得	很好。

这种句子常用"怎么样"来提问。例如：

The interrogative form of such a sentence requires 怎么样, e.g.

　　(1) 他说得怎么样？

　　(2) 他吃得怎么样？

正反疑问句是把作补语的形容词的肯定和否定形式并列起来。例如：

A yes-or-no question is formed by the affirmative and negative complements expressed by an adjective, e.g.

　　(3) 他说得好不好？

如果动词带宾语，则要在宾语后重复一下动词，再接由"得"引出的补语。例如：

If the verb takes an object, the word order of the sentence is:

Subject—verbal predicate—object—verbal predicate—得——complement, e.g.

　　(4) 你说中文说得很好。

为了突出宾语，可以让宾语出现在动词前边。例如：

The object can be prefixed to the verb to obtain a prominent effect, e.g.

（5）我英语说得不太好。

（6）你汉语说得怎么样？

主语 Subject	谓 语 Predicate					
	宾语 Object	动词 Verb	宾语 Object	重复的动词 Repeated Verb	结构助词 Structrual Particle	程度补语 Complement of Degree
他		说			得	怎么样？
他		说			得	好不好？
你		说	中文	说	得	很好。
我	英语	说			得	不太好。

　　注意：·英语动词后面的补充部分，如"well"直接放在动词或宾语后面。这是与汉语不同之处。

　　N.B. The English complement such as "well" used right after the verb or the object is different from its Chinese equivalent.

3. **主谓词组作定语**

Subject–Object Phrase Used as an Adjectival Modifier

主谓词组作定语，后面一定要用结构助词"的"。例如：

A subject-object phrase requires the structural particle 的 when used as an adjectival modifier, e.g.

　　（1）这是格林先生买的东西。

　　（2）那是他住的房间。

　　（3）你说的话，我不懂，请你说得慢一点儿。

定 语 Adjectival Modifier		结构助词 Structural Particle	中 心 语 Central Word
小主语 Smaller Subject	小谓语 Smaller Predicate		名词 Noun
格林先生 他 你	买 住 说	的 的 的	东西 房间 话

练 习 Exercises

1. 把下列各句改成正反疑问句：
   Change the following into affirmative-negative interrogative sentences:
   (1) 我会说英语。
   (2) 他能看中文书。
   (3) 格林先生汉语说得很好。
   (4) 我汉语说得不好。

2. 用选择问句完成下列句子：
   Complete the following by using alternative sentence
   forms and adding necessary words to them:
   (1) 你能说汉语_____？
   (2) 你会说_____，还是会说汉语？
   (3) 格林先生是英国人_____？
   (4) 他英语说得好_____？

120

3. 用下列主谓词组作定语造句：

Make sentences with the following subject-predicate phrases as an adjectival modifier:

例：我买——→这是我买的书。

(1) 他看

(2) 你买

(3) 他住

(4) 你穿

(5) 玛丽要

(6) 母亲喜欢

(7) 格林先生喝

(8) 我认识

十二、上　课
shàng　kè
Going to a Class

111. 打铃了，上课了。

Dǎ líng le, shàng kè le.

The bell has gone. It's time for class.

112. 都来了吗？

Dōu lái le ma?

Is everybody here?

113. 玛丽和格林没(有)来。

Mǎlì hé Gélín méi(yǒu) lái.

Mary and Green are absent.

114. 他们怎么了？

Tāmen zěnme le?

What's the matter with them?

115. 玛丽有事，去大使馆了。

Mǎlì yǒu shì, qù dàshǐguǎn le.

Mary has got something to do. She has gone to the embassy.

116. 格林请假，他病了。

Gélín qǐng jià, tā bìng le.

Green has asked for leave. He's ill.

117. 保罗迟到了。
Bǎoluó chídào le.

Paul was late.

118. 同学们都进教室去了。
Tóngxuémen dōu jìn jiàoshì qu le.

All the students went into the classroom.

119. 拿出本子来。
Náchu běnzi lai.

Take out your note-books, please.

120. 听懂了吗?
Tīngdǒng le ma?

Understand?

替换练习 Substitution Drills

1.

玛丽和格林	没(有)	来
王老师		去
他		买
我		看

。

2. 玛丽有事,去

大使馆
北京饭店
上海

了。

3.

同学们	都进	教室	去了。
他们		商店	
学生们		学校	

4. 拿出

本子	来。
书	
杂志	
报	

会 话 Dialogues

甲：打铃了。
Dǎ líng le.

乙：上课了。
Shàng kè le.

甲：我们进教室去吧!
Wǒmen jìn jiàoshì qu ba!

......

丙：同学们好!
Tóngxuémen hǎo!

同学们：老师好!
Lǎoshī hǎo!

丙：都来了吗?
Dōu lái le ma?

甲：玛丽和格林没有来。
Mǎlì hé Gélín méiyǒu lái.

丙：他们怎么了？
Tāmen zěnme le?

乙：玛丽有事，去大使馆了。
Mǎlì yǒu shì, qù dàshǐguǎn le.

丙：格林也去大使馆了吗？
Gélín yě qù dàshǐguǎn le ma?

甲：格林请假了，他病了。
Gélín qǐng jià le, tā bìng le.

丙：保罗，你迟到了。
Bǎoluó, nǐ chídào le.

丁：老师，对不起！
Lǎoshī, duì bu qǐ!

丙：你们拿出本子和书来。听懂了吗？
Nǐmen náchu běnzi hé shū lai. Tīngdǒng le ma?

同学们：听懂了。
Tīngdǒng le.

*　　　　*　　　　*

甲：开车了，都来了吗？
Kāi chē le, dōu lái le ma?

乙：王丽和张林没有来。
Wáng Lì hé Zhāng lín méiyǒu lái.

甲：他们怎么了？病了吗？
Tāmen zěnme le? Bìng le ma?

乙：没有，王丽不去颐和园，她去故宫。
Méiyǒu, Wáng Lì bú qù Yíhéyuán, tā qù Gùgōng.

甲：张林呢？
Zháng Lín ne?

125

乙：张林去北京饭店了。
Zhāng Lín qù Běijīng Fàndiàn le.

甲：李平来没来？
Lǐ Píng lái mei lái?

乙：他没来，他病了。
Tā méi lái, tā bìng le.

甲：今天下午我们去颐和园，三点到那儿。我说的话，听懂了吗？
Jīntiān xiàwǔ wǒmen qù Yíhéyuán, sān diǎn dào nàr.
Wǒ shuō de huà, tīngdǒng le ma?

乙：你说的两句话，我只听懂了一句。
Nǐ shuō de liǎng jù huà, wǒ zhǐ tīngdǒng le yī jù.

生　词　New Words

1. 打	（动）	dǎ	to strike
2. 铃	（名）	líng	bell
3. 没有	（副）	méiyou	not
4. 他们	（代）	tāmen	they
5. 怎么	（代）	zěnme	why, how
6. 事	（名）	shì	business, thing
7. 大使馆	（名）	dàshǐguǎn	embassy
8. 请假		qǐng jià	ask for leave
9. 病	（动、名）	bìng	to be ill, illness
10. 迟到	（动）	chídào	late
11. 同学们	（名）	tóngxuémen	students
12. 进	（动）	jìn	to enter
13. 教室	（名）	jiàoshì	classroom

126

14. 拿	（动）ná	to take, to bring
15. 出	（动）chū	out
16. 本子	（名）běnzi	note-book, exercise-book
17. 听	（动）tīng	to listen
18. 句	（量）jù	sentence

专 名 Proper Noun

保罗　　　　　　Bǎoluó　　　　Paul

语 法 Grammar

1. 动词的完成态

The Perfect Aspect of Verbs

同英语不同，汉语动词本身没有"时"和"态"的分别。完成态
是"动词＋了"（"了"是动态助词，表示动作的实现或完成）。否
定式是"没（有）＋动词"（去掉"了"）。例如：

Unlike English verbs, the Chinese ones have neither
tense forms nor voice forms. The perfect aspect of a Chinese
verb is expressed by the aspectual particle 了 (indicating a
complete or perfect action) preceded by a verb. Its negative
form is 没(有) plus a verb (without 了), e.g.

(1) 玛丽来了吗？
(2) 他买了一双布鞋。
(3) 玛丽没去大使馆。
(4) 李平没有去颐和园。

"动词＋了"后面如果有宾语，宾语需要带数量词或其他定

语。例如：

The object after the group "verb + 了" is always preceded by a numeral-measure word phrase or an adjectival modifier. E.g.

（3）他买了一双布鞋。

（4）玛丽看了很多中文书。

否定句或疑问句中，宾语一般不需带数量词。例如：

In a negative or an interrogative sentence, the object is seldom qualified by a numeral-measure word phrase, e.g.

（5）他没（有）买布鞋。

（6）他买布鞋了吗？

如果宾语很简单，则常用"动词＋宾语＋了"来表示完成。例如：

The word group "verb + object + 了" is often used to indicate the perfection of something if the object is very simple, e.g.

（7）玛丽去大使馆了。

正反疑问句是：

Its affirmative-negative question form is:

（8）玛丽来没来？

（9）李平去颐和园了没有？

注意：汉语不表示动作的动词如"是"没有完成态，不能说"我是了一个教师。"

N.B. In Chinese the actionless verbs such as 是 do not have their perfect aspect form. Therefore it is incorrect to say 我是了一个教师.

2. 趋向补语

Directional Complements

A. 简单趋向补语 Simple Directional Complements

动词"来"和"去"可以放在其他动词后边作补语，表示趋向，即"动词＋来/去"。如果动词带表示处所的宾语，趋向补语放在宾语后面，即"动词＋处所词＋来/去"。如果宾语不是表示处所的，可以放在"来"或"去"之前，也可以放在"来"或"去"之后，即"动词＋宾语＋来/去"或"动词＋来/去＋宾语"。例如：

Verbs like 来 or 去 can be preceded by another verb to show the direction of an action. If a verb takes an object of locality, the directional complement should be placed after the object, i.e. "verb + locative word + 来/去". Otherwise 来 or 去 may be either preceded or followed by the object, i.e. "verb + object + 来/去"; or "verb + 来/去 + object". E.g.

    (1) 格林进来了。

    (2) 他进教室去了。

    (3) 我没买汽水，只买来了一瓶啤酒。

    (4) 请他拿一个本子来。

B. 复合趋向补语　Compound Directional Complements

动词"进"、"出"等后面加上"来"或"去"，可以作其他动词的补语，表示趋向，即："动词＋进/出＋来/去"。如果动词带表示处所的宾语，宾语只能放在"来"或"去"的前面；如果宾语不是表示处所的，则放在"来"或"去"的前后均可。即："动词＋进/出＋宾语＋来/去"或"动词＋进/出＋来/去＋宾语"。例如：

If followed by 来 or 去, verbs such as 进 and 出 can be used as a directional complement, i.e. "verb + 进/出 + 来/去". The locatve object of the verb can be placed only before 来 or 去; and the non-locative object may go either before or after 来 or 去, i.e. "verb + 进/出 + object + 来/去"; or "verb + 进/出 + 来/去 + object". E.g.

(1) 都拿出来了吗？

(2) 同学们都走进教室去了。

(3) 请拿出书来！

(4) 他拿出来一个本子。

练 习 Exercises

1. 请把下列否定句改成肯定句：

Change the following into affirmative sentences:

    (1) 格林昨天没来。

    (2) 他没有去大使馆。

    (3) 他在商店没有买布鞋。

    (4) 玛丽今天没迟到。

    (5) 我没懂。

2. 请把下列句子改成用"是不是"的疑问句：

Change the following into interrogative sentences with 是不是：

    (1) 格林昨天请假了。

    (2) 我说的你都听懂了。

    (3) 同学们都进教室去了。

    (4) 玛丽没来上课，她病了。

    (5) 她昨天去颐和园了。

3. 请把下列句子改成正反疑问句：

Change the following into affirmative-negative interrogative sentences:

    (1) 昨天他没来。

130

（2）他去大使馆了。
（3）他没买东西。
（4）他工作了。

十三、谈 学 习

tán xué xí

Talking about Chinese Study

121. 你们以前学过中文吗？

Nǐmen yǐqián xuéguo Zhōngwén ma?

Have you ever studied Chinese before?

122. 我学过，他没学过。

Wǒ xuéguo, tā méi xuéguo.

Yes, I have, but he hasn't.

123. 你学过多长时间？

Nǐ xuéguo duō cháng shíjiān?

How long did you study it?

124. 我学过两年。

Wǒ xuéguo liǎng nián.

I studied it for two years.

125. 你觉得中文难不难？

Nǐ juéde Zhōngwén nán bu nán?

Do you think Chinese is difficult?

126. 发音和汉字比较难。

Fāyīn hé Hànzì bǐjiào nán.

Chinese pronunciation and characters are fairly difficult.

127. 教你们的老师是中国人吗？

Jiāo nǐmen de lǎoshī shi Zhōngguó rén ma?

Are your teachers Chinese?

128. 有一位是中国人，他教我们口语。

Yǒu yí wei shi Zhōngguó rén, tā jiāo wǒmen kǒuyǔ.

One of them is a Chinese. He teaches us the oral.

129. 这本书你学完了吗？

Zhè běn shū nǐ xuéwán le ma?

Have you finished learning this book?

130. 没学完。

Méi xuéwán.

Not yet.

替换练习 Substitution Drills

1.

你们	以前学过	中文	吗？
你		英文	
他		法文	
老师		日文	

2. 你觉得

中文	难不难？
发音	
汉字	
日语	
这本书	

3. 教你们的老师是 | 中国人吗 | ？

| 哪国人 |
| 不是英国人 |
| 美国人不是 |

4. | 这本书 | 你 | 学 | 完了吗？
这本杂志		看
饭		吃
汽水		喝

会　话　Dialogues

甲：你以前学过中文吗？
Nǐ yǐqián xuéguo Zhōngwén ma?

乙：我学过。
Wǒ xuéguo.

甲：你学过多长时间？
Nǐ xuéguo duō cháng shíjiān?

乙：我只学过一年。
Wǒ zhǐ xuéguo yì nián.

甲：这本书你学完了吗？
Zhè běn shū nǐ xuéwán le ma?

乙：学完了。
Xuéwán le.

甲：你觉得汉字怎么样？难吗？
Nǐ juéde Hànzì zěnmeyàng? Nán ma?

乙：难极了。
Nán jíle.

甲：中文发音难不难？
Zhōngwén fāyīn nán bu nán?

乙：我觉得比较难。
Wǒ juéde bǐjiào nán.

甲：教你们的老师是中国人吗？
Jiāo nǐmen de lǎoshī shi Zhōngguó rén ma?

乙：不，是英国人。
Bù, shì Yīngguó rén.

甲：你汉语说得很好。
Nǐ Hànyǔ shuō de hěn hǎo.

乙：不太好。
Bú tài hǎo.

＊　　　　＊　　　　＊

甲：你是中国人吗？
Nǐ shi Zhōngguó rén ma?

乙：我不是中国人。
Wǒ bú shi Zhōngguó rén.

甲：你是哪国人？
Nǐ shi nǎ guó rén?

乙：我是日本人。
Wǒ shi Rìběn rén.

甲：你汉语说得好极了。
Nǐ Hànyǔ shuō de hǎo jíle.

乙：说得不太好。
Shuō de bú tài hǎo.

135

甲：你以前学过多长时间？
Nǐ yǐqián xuéguo duō cháng shíjiān?

乙：我学过五年。
Wǒ xuéguo wǔ nián.

甲：你觉得汉语难不难？
Nǐ juéde Hànyǔ nán bu nán?

乙：发音比较难。
Fāyīn bǐjiào nán.

甲：你现在能看中文杂志不能？
Nǐ xiànzài néng kàn Zhōngwén zázhì bu néng?

乙：能看。
Néng kàn.

甲：教你们的老师是哪国人？
Jiāo nǐmen de lǎoshī shi nǎ guó rén?

乙：有两位是日本人，一位是中国人。
Yǒu liǎng wei shi Rìběn rén, yí wei shi Zhōngguó rén.

甲：中国老师教你们什么？
Zhōnguó lǎoshī jiāo nǐmen shénme?

乙：教我们口语。
Jiāo wǒmen kǒuyǔ.

生 词 New Words

1. 以前　　（名）yǐqián　　before, in the past
2. 学　　　（动）xué　　　to study
3. 过　　　（助）guo　　　(a particle)
4. 多长　　duō cháng　　how long

136

5. 时间	（名）	shíjiān	time
6. 觉得	（动）	juéde	to feel
7. 难	（形）	nán	difficult
8. 发音	（名）	fāyīn	pronunciation
9. 和	（连）	hé	and
10. 汉字	（名）	Hànzì	Chinese character
11. 比较	（动、副）	bǐjiào	to compare, comparatively
12. 教	（动）	jiāo	to teach
13. 口语	（名）	kǒuyǔ	oral, spoken language
14. 完	（动）	wán	to finish

语　　法 Grammar

1. 动词的经验态
The Aspect of Experience

动词的经验态是"动词＋过"，"过"是动态助词，表示某种动作曾在过去发生过，重点在说明有过这种经历。否定式是"没（有）＋动词＋过"。宾语放在"过"后，即"动词＋过＋宾语"。例如：

The "verb + 过" group serves as an expression of the aspect of experience. As a aspectual particle, 过 denotes an action that took place in the past, or refers to one's past exprience. Its negative form is "没（有）＋verb＋过". The object, if there is any, is put after 过, i.e. "verb＋过＋object", e.g.

（1）你们以前学过中文吗？
（2）我学过两年。
（3）我没（有）来过北京。

正反疑问句是：

Its affirmative-negative question form is:

  (4) 你去过颐和园没有?

  (5) 你以前学过没学过中文?

  注意：英语现在完成时用法之一是表示经验，如："I have been to Shanghai once"，译成汉语是"我曾经去过上海"。但并不是所有的英语"完成时"，汉语都要用动词的经验态来表示。

  N.B. The Aspect of experience may be used for the translation of English present perfect tense, for example, "I have been to Shanghai once（我曾经去过上海）". However that does not apply to all cases.

2. 结果补语

Resultative Complements

  动词或形容词放在其他动词的后边作补语，说明动作的结果。这种补语叫结果补语。如果有宾语，要把它放在结果补语的后面，即："动词＋结果补语＋宾语"。否定式一般用"没（有）"，即"没（有）＋动词＋结果补语"。例如：

  A verb (or an adjective) used after another verb as a resultative complement indicates the result of an action. The object, if there is one, should be placed after the complement, i.e. "verb + resultative complement + object". Its negative form is generally "没（有）+ verb + resultative complement", e.g.

  (1) 我说的话你听懂了吗?

  (2) 我能学好中文吗?

  (3) 这本书我没学完。

正反疑问句是：

Its affirmative-negative question form is:

  (4) 这本书你看完没看完?

138

（5）你听懂了没有？

3．动词词组作定语

A Verbal Phrase used as an Adjectival Modifier

动词词组包括动宾词组、动补词组和状动词组。动词词组可以作定语，但后面要加结构助词"的"，即"动词词组＋的＋名词"。例如：

Verbal phrases include verb-object phrases, verb-complement phrases and adverbial modifier-verb phrases. They can be used as an adjectival modifier, but the structural particle 的 is always attached to the end of it, i.e. "verbal phrase + 的 + noun", e.g.

（1）他是学过中文的学生。

（2）教我们口语的老师是北京人。

（3）昨天来的同学都去故宫了。

练　习　Exercises

1．请把"了"、"过"分别填入以下各句中：

Fill in the following blanks with 了 or 过：

（1）布鞋好，我以前穿＿＿。

（2）我昨天到商店买＿＿点东西。

（3）以前，他到北京来＿＿。

（4）昨天他在我这儿拿＿＿本书。

（5）我以前在日本学＿＿两年英文，你没有学＿＿吗？

（6）我在北京饭店住＿＿，你呢？

2．根据下列句子造出带主谓词组作定语的问句和答句：

Ask questions and give their corresponding answers with a subject-predicate group as its adjectival modifier in each based on the informative sentences below:

例：**有一位老师是中国人，他教我们口语。**

教你们口语的老师是哪国人？

教我们口语的老师是中国人。

（1）有一位老师是巴黎人，他教我们法语。

（2）有一位老师是北京人，他教我们汉语。

（3）有一位老师中国人，他教格林口语。

（4）有一位老师是美国人，他教王丽英文。

（5）有一位老师是日本人，他教我们日语。

3. 回答：

Answer the following questions:

（1）你在日本学过中文吗？

（2）你学过多长时间？

（3）你以前来过北京吗？

（4）你去过长城没有？

（5）你到过上海没有？

（6）你在上海住过没有？

（7）你在上海住过多长时间？

（8）你吃过中国饭吗？

4. 把下列句子改成正反疑问句：

Change the following into affimative-negative inter-rogative sentences:

（1）这本书你看完了吗？

（2）我说的话，你听懂了，是吗？

（3）你以前到中国来过，是不是？

（4）你以前是不是学过中文？

（5）你以前是不是在北京饭店住过？

140

十四、在 朋 友 家
zài péng you jiā
At a Friend's House

131. **请进!**
Qǐng jìn!

Come in, please!

132. **请坐! 请喝茶!**
Qǐng zuò! Qǐng hē chá!

Sit down, and have a cup of tea, please.

133. **我可以吸烟吗?**
Wǒ kěyǐ xī yān ma?

May I smoke here?

134. **别客气,就跟在家里一样,好吗?**
Bié kèqi, jiù gēn zài jiāli yíyàng, hǎo ma?

Be at home, will you?

135. **我自己来!**
Wǒ zìjǐ lái!

I'll help myself.

136. **够了,谢谢。我吃不下了。**
Gòu le, xièxie. Wǒ chī bu xià le.

Enough, thanks. I can't eat any more.

137. 太麻烦你了。
Tài máfan nǐ le.

Sorry to have given you so much trouble.

138. 不早了，我该走了。
Bù zǎo le, Wǒ gāi zǒu le;

It's getting late. I must be off now.

139. 我说汉语，你现在都能听得懂吧？
Wǒ shuō Hànyǔ, nǐ xiànzài dōu néng tīng de dǒng ba?

Did you understand every Chinese word I said just now?

140. 不，有些话还听不懂。
Bù, yǒuxiē huà hái tīng bu dǒng.

Not all of them.

替换练习 Substitution Drills

1. 我可以

吸烟
坐
走
请假
试试

吗？

2. 太

麻烦
谢谢
对不起

你了！

142

3. 不早了，

我	该	走	了。
我们		告辞	
你		休息	

会 话 Dialogues

甲：请进!
Qǐng jìn!

乙：你好!
Nǐ hǎo!

甲：你好! 请坐!
Nǐ hǎo! Qǐng zuò!

乙：谢谢。
Xièxie.

甲：请喝茶!
Qǐng hē chá!

乙：我可以吸烟吗?
Wǒ kěyǐ xī yān ma?

甲：可以，请吸吧!
Kěyǐ, qǐng xī ba!

......

乙：啊! 这么多菜，太麻烦你了。
Ā! Zhème duō cài, tài máfan ni le.

甲：你喜欢吃什么? 这是香酥鸡。
Nǐ xǐhuan chī shénme? Zhè shi Xiāngsūjī.

143

乙：谢谢。
Xièxie.

甲：别客气，就跟在家里一样，好吗？
Bié kèqi, jiù gēn zài jiālǐ yíyàng, hǎo ma?

乙：好，我自己来！
Hǎo, wǒ zìjǐ lái!

甲：你汉语说得很好了。
Nǐ Hànyǔ shuō de hěn hǎo le.

乙：不，不太好。
Bù, bú tài hǎo.

甲：我说汉语，你现在都能听得懂吧？
Wǒ shuō Hànyǔ, nǐ xiànzài dōu néng tīng de dǒng ba?

乙：不，有些话还听不懂。
Bù, yǒuxiē huà hái tīng bu dǒng.

甲：再吃一点儿饭。
Zài chī yìdiǎnr fàn.

乙：够了，谢谢。我吃不下了。
Gòu le, xièxie. Wǒ chī bu xià le.

甲：喝点茶吧。
Hē diǎnr chá ba.

乙：不早了，我该走了。
Bù zǎo le, wǒ gāi zǒu le.

甲：再见。
Zàijiàn.

乙：再见。
Zàijiàn.

生 词 New Words

1. 坐 （动）zuò to sit
2. 茶 （名）chá tea
3. 可以 （能动）kěyǐ can, may
4. 吸 （动）xī to smoke
5. 客气 （形）kèqi polite
6. 就 （副）jiù just (like)
7. 跟…一样 gēn…yíyàng same as…
8. 自己 （代）zìjǐ oneself
9. 够 （形）gòu enough
10. 下 （动）xià to go down
11. 麻烦 （动、名、形）máfan to trouble
12. 早 （形）zǎo early
13. 该 （能动）gāi should, must
14. 走 （动）zǒu to leave, to go
15. 有些 （代）yǒuxiē some
16. 告辞 （动）gàocí take leave (of one's host)
17. 这么 （代）zhème so, such
18. 菜 （名）cài dish
19. 饭 （名）fàn steamed rice, meal

语 法 Grammar

1. 可能补语
Potential Complements

在结果补语或趋向补语前加结构助词"得"就构成可能补语，

145

即:"动词 + 得 + 结果补语/趋向补语"。否定形式是把"得"换成
"不",即:"动词 + 不 + 结果补语/趋向补语"。可能补语表示可
能。有时为了加重语气可以在动词前加能愿动词。例如:

A potential complement can be formed by using the
structural particle 得 before either a resultative complement
or a directional complement, i.e. "verb + 得 + resultative com-
plement/directional complement". Its negative can be formed
by replacing 得 with 不, i.e. "verb + 不 + resultative com-
plement/directional complement". As its name implies, a
potential complement indicates the possibility of doing something. A modal verb may be used before the verb in this type
of sentences for emphasis, e.g.

(1)《汉语三百句》,我们学得完吗?

(2)你说汉语我听不懂。

(3)汉语你能学得好吗?

(4)够了,我吃不下了。

正反疑问句是:

Its affirmative-negative question form is:

(5)我说的话你听得懂听不懂?

(6)这双布鞋小不小?你穿得下去穿不下去?

2. 语气助词"了"

The Modal Particle 了

A. 语气助词"了",可以表示一种新情况的出现,即:表示
情况有所变化。形容词谓语句、"是"字句、"有"字句、否定句以
及带能愿动词的句子等,句尾的"了",往往就是表示这种意思的
语气助词。

The modal particle 了 implies the changing of a situation.
It is particularly so when used at the end of a sentence with

146

an adjectival predicate, a sentence with 是 or 有, a negative
sentence, or a sentence with a modal verb, e.g.

    (1) 够了，我吃不下了。

    (2) 不早了，我该走了。

    (3) 现在学的东西难了，以前学的不难。

    (4) 他以前是学生，现在是老师了。

    (5) 谢谢你，我有本子了，不要了。

    (6) 现在我可以吸烟了吧！

  B 、语气助词"了"也可以表示确定的语气，有时还能使句子
带有一些感叹的意味。例如：

The modal particle 了 also indicates a certainty, sometimes
with a touch of deep emotion, e.g.

    (1) 太麻烦你了！

    (2) 味道好极了！

    (3) 我们今天太高兴了！

练 习 Exercises

1. 请把下列问句改成带可能补语的问句,并用否定句回答:
   Change the following into interrogative sentences
   with a potential complement and then give negative
   answers to them:

    (1) 你能听懂中国人说话吗?

    (2) 中文报你能看懂吗?

    (3) 这本书你今天能看完吗?

    (4) 你能不能学好汉语?

    (5) 你能拿来那本书吗?

 2. 完成下列对话:

Complete the following dialogues:

(1) A：昨天你到哪儿去了？

    B：_____。

    A：你买东西了没有？

    B：_____。

(2) A：_____？

    B：我有事，没有上课。

    A：_____？

    B：我去朋友家了。

(3) A：你朋友说话你都听得懂吗？

    B：_____。

    A：中文你学过多长时间？

    B：_____。

(4) A：昨天没上课，你病了吗？

    B：_____。

    A：_____？

    B：我到颐和园去了。

3．请把"可以"、"能"、"该"填入以下各句：

Complete the following sentences with 可以、能 or 该：

(1) 十二点了，____吃饭了。

(2) 七点五十了，____去上课了。

(3) 今天星期六，____去朋友家了。

(4) 我____在这儿吸烟吗？

(5) 中文书他____看得懂。

(6) 他学过五年，____听懂汉语。

148

十五、问　　路
wèn　　lù

Asking the Way

141. 劳驾，到百货大楼怎么走？
Láojià, dào Bǎihuò Dàlóu zěnme zǒu?

Excuse me, but can you tell me how to get to the Department Store?

142. 往前走，到十字路口往右拐。
Wàng qián zǒu, dào shízì-lùkǒur wàng yòu guǎi.

Go straight forward, and then turn right at the junction.

143. 离这儿远不远？
Lí zhèr yuǎn bu yuǎn?

Is it far from here?

144. 不远，走五分钟就到了。
Bù yuǎn, zǒu wǔ fēnzhōng jiù dào le.

Not very far. It's only about five minutes' walk.

145. 请问，去天安门坐几路车？
Qǐng wèn, qù Tiān'ānmén zuò jǐ lù chē?

Excuse me, what bus should I take for Tian An Men?

146. 坐103路无路轨电车。
Zuò yāo-líng-sān lù wúguǐ diànchē.

You want a No. 103 trolley bus.

147. 在哪儿换车？
Zài nǎr huàn chē?

Where to change?

148. 在北海公园换5路汽车。
Zài Běihǎi Gōngyuán huàn wǔ lù qìchē.

Change to a No. 5 bus at Beihai Park.

149. 劳驾，到北京饭店还有多远？
Láojià, dào Běijīng Fàndiàn hái yǒu duō yuǎn?

Excuse me, how much further is it from Beijing Hotel?

150. 不远了，前边一拐弯就是。
Bù yuǎn le, qiánbiān yì guǎi wānr jiù shì.

It's not very far. Take the first turning ahead, and you can't miss it.

替换练习　Substitution Drills

1. 劳驾，到 | 百货大楼 | 怎么走？
颐和园
动物园
东风市场
友谊商店
法国大使馆

150

2. 往 | 前 / 右 / 左 / 东 / 西 / 南 | 走，到十字路口，往 | 右 / 左 / 右 / 西 / 南 / 北 | 拐。

3. 离这儿 | 远不远 / 近不近 / 远吗 | ？

4. 在哪儿 | 换车 / 下车 / 上车 | ？

会　话　Dialogues

甲：劳驾，到北京饭店怎么走？
Láojià, dào Běijīng Fàndiàn zěnme zǒu?

乙：往前走。
Wàng qián zǒu.

甲：离这儿远不远？
Lí zhèr yuǎn bu yuǎn?

乙：不太远，走三分钟就到了。
Bú tài yuǎn, zǒu sān fēnzhōng jiù dào le.

* * *

甲：请问，去颐和园坐几路车？
Qǐng wèn, qù Yíhéyuán zuò jǐ lù chē?

乙：坐 111 路无轨电车。
Zuò yāo-yāo-yāo lù wúguǐ diànchē.

甲：在哪儿换车？
Zài nǎr huàn chē?

乙：在动物园换332路汽车。
Zài Dòngwùyuán huàn sān-sān-èr lù qìchē.

甲：谢谢您。
Xièxie nín.

* * *

甲：对不起，请问，到美国大使馆怎么走？
Duì bu qǐ, qǐng wèn, dào Měiguó Dàshǐguǎn zěnme zǒu?

乙：往东走，到十字路口往右拐。
Wàng dōng zǒu, dào shízì-lùkǒur wàng yòu guǎi.

甲：离这儿远不远？
Lí zhèr yuǎn bu yuǎn?

乙：不远。
Bù yuǎn.

甲：走多少分钟？
Zǒu duōshao fēnzhōng?

乙：十几分钟。
Shíjǐ fēnzhōng.

甲：能坐车去吗？
Néng zuò chē qù ma?

152

乙：能，坐113路无轨电车。
Néng, zuò yāo-yāo-sān lù wúguǐ diànchē.

甲：在哪儿下车？
Zài nǎr xià chē?

乙：在三里屯下。
Zài Sānlǐtún xià.

·······

甲：请问，美国大使馆在哪儿？
Qǐng wèn, Měiguó Dàshǐguǎn zài nǎr?

乙：前边一拐弯就是。
Qiánbiān yī guǎi wānr jiù shì.

甲：谢谢。
Xièxie.

乙：不谢。
Bú xiè.

生 词 New Words

1.	劳驾	(动) láojià	excuse (me), would you ---
2.	往	(介) wàng	toward
3.	前	(名) qián	front
4.	十字路口	shízì-lùkǒur	junction
5.	右	(名) yòu	right
6.	拐	(动) guǎi	to turn
7.	离	(介) lí	from
8.	远	(形) yuǎn	far
9.	分钟	(量) fēnzhōng	minute
10.	路	(名) lù	road, number (of buses etc.)

153

11.	无轨电车		wúguǐ diànchē	trolley bus
12.	换	(动)	huàn	to change
13.	汽车	(名)	qìchē	bus, car
14.	前边	(名)	qiánbiān	ahead
15.	拐弯		guǎi wānr	to turn
16.	动物园	(名)	dòngwùyuán	zoo
17.	左	(名)	zuǒ	left
18.	东	(名)	dōng	east
19.	西	(名)	xī	west
20.	南	(名)	nán	south
21.	北	(名)	běi	north
22.	下	(动)	xià	to get off

专 名 Proper Nouns

1.	百货大楼	Bǎihuò Dàlóu	Department Store
2.	天安门	Tiān'ānmén	Tian An men
3.	东风市场	Dōnhfēng Shìchǎng	Dongfeng Market
4.	友谊商店	Yǒnyì Shāngdiàn	Friendship Store
5.	三里屯	Sānlǐtún	name of a place

语 法 Grammar

1. 时量补语

Time-Measure Complements

表示时间数量的词语（如"两年"、"五分钟"）可以放在动词后面作补语，说明一个动作或一种状态持续的时间。动词如果有宾语，可以放在主语前面；如果宾语在原来的位置，要重复动词。有时也可以把表示时间的词语放在宾语前面。即：

A、宾语 + 动词 + 时量补语

B、动词 + 宾语 + 重复的动词 + 时量补语

C、动词 + 时间词语（ + 的） + 宾语

例如：

A time-measure word group such as 两年，五分钟 may be used after a verb as a complement, indicating the duration of an action or a state. The object can go before the subject, or between the verb and its repeated form. Sometimes the time words may appear before the object, i.e.

A. object + verb + time-measure complement;

B. verb + object + repeated verb + time-measure complement;

C. verb + time words (+ 的) + object. E.g.

（1）我在北京饭店住了一个星期。

（2）不远，走五分钟就到了。

（3）汉语他学过两年。

（4）他学汉语学了两年半。

（5）他学了两年（的）汉语。

时量补语也可以表示从动作发生到某时的一段时间，这类动作大都是不能持续的，如"来"、"去"、"下（课）"等。如果有宾语，时量补语要放在宾语之后。例如：

The time-measure complement may express the time period of an action which is unlikely, in most cases, to last long. 来，去，下（课）are such actions. If there is an object, the complement should be put after it, e.g.

（6）我来北京一个多月了。

（7）下课二十分钟了，他早走了。

要注意时量补语的位置。汉语时量补语有的放在动词后面，

有的放在宾语后面，不能像英语词序那样，把时量补语一律放在句尾。

Note that close attention should be paid to the position of the time-measure complement which is differently expressed in English.

2. 用"多"提问

Ask Questions with 多

"多"，用来询问数量、程度，后接形容词，前面常用"有"，即："有＋多＋形容词"。例如：

When preceded by 有 and followed by an adjective, 多 is good for asking a question about the number or extent of people or something. The order is "有＋多＋adjective", e.g.

  （1）到北京饭店还有多远？

  （2）您（有）多大岁数了？

  （3）你汉语学过多长时间？

  （4）那双布鞋是多大号的？

练 习 Exercises

1. 用下列词语造出带有时量补语的句子：

Make sentences with a time-measure complement, using words given below:

  （1）在朋友家 坐

  （2）看 中文报

  （3）走 就 到 家

  （4）来 中国

  （5）上课

2. 根据答话写出用"多"的问话：

156

Ask questions with 多 corresponding to the answers given below:

(1) A: _____ ?
    B: 我来中国一个多星期了。

(2) A: _____ ?
    B: 我坐了两个多小时的飞机。

(3) A: _____ ?
    B: 我学过三年汉语。

(4) A: _____ ?
    B: 我在上海住过两个月。

(5) A: _____ ?
    B: 我父亲今年五十岁了。

(6) A: _____ ?
    B: 我妹妹今年十六了。

(7) A: _____ ?
    B: 离这儿不远，走几分钟就到了。

十六、坐 公 共 汽 车

zuò gōng gòng qì chē

Taking a Bus

151. 请问，331路汽车站在哪儿？

Qǐng wèn, sān-sān-yāo lù qìchēzhàn zài nǎr?

Excuse me, but could you please tell me where the 331 bus stop is?

152. 在马路对面。

Zài mǎlù duìmiàn.

It's just on the other side of the road.

153. 请问，这路车到天安门吗？

Qǐng wèn, zhè lù chē dào Tiān'ānmén ma?

Does this bus go to Tian An Men, please?

154. 不到，请到前边坐22路汽车。

Bú dào, qǐng dào qiánbiānr zuò èrshí èr lù qìchē.

No, it doesn't. You can go straight on and take a No. 22 bus there.

155. 有买票的没有？

Yǒu mǎi piào de mei yǒu?

Fares, please!

156. 劳驾，到北京饭店在哪儿下车？

Láojià, dào Běijīng Fàndiàn zài nǎr xià chē?

Would you please tell me where to get off for Beijing Hotel?

157. 买一张到北京饭店的票。

Mǎi yì zhāng dào Běijīng Fàndiàn de piào.

One ticket for Beijing Hotel, please.

158. 从哪儿上的?

Cóng nǎr shàng de?

Where did you get on this bus?

159. 刚上的。

Gāng shàng de.

At the last stop.

160. 下一站就是。

Xià yì zhàn jiù shì.

It's the next stop.

替换练习 Substitution Drills

1. 请到

前边	坐	22 路	汽车。
左边		13 路	
右边		302 路	
马路对面		331 路	

2. 请问，这路车

到	天安门吗?
去	
开往	

3. 有 | 买票 / 下车 / 上车 | 的没有？

4. | 刚 / 颐和园 / 语言学院 / 前一站 | 上的。

会 话 Dialogues

甲：劳驾，这路车到人民剧场吗？
Láojià, zhè lù chē dào Rénmín Jùchǎng ma?

乙：不到，请到那边坐22路汽车。
Bú dào, qǐng dào nàbiān zuò èrshí èr lù qìchē.

甲：请问，22路汽车站在哪儿？
Qǐng wèn, èrshí èr lù qìchēzhàn zài nǎr?

乙：在马路对面。
Zài mǎlù duìmiàn.

甲：谢谢。
Xièxie.

乙：不客气。
Bú kèqi.

*   *   *

甲：有买票的没有？
Yǒu mǎi piào de mei yǒu?

乙：劳驾，到人民剧场在哪儿下车？
Láojià, dào Rénmín Jùchǎng zài nǎr xià chē?

甲：在平安里下。
Zài Píng'ānlǐ xià.

乙：我买一张到平安里的票。
Wǒ mǎi yì zhāng dào Píng'ānlǐ de piào.

甲：从哪儿上的？
Cóng nǎr shàng de?

乙：刚上的。
Gāng shàng de.

甲：一毛。
Yì máo.

乙：给您钱。
Gěi nǐ qián.

＊　　　＊　　　＊

甲：劳驾，这路车到哪儿？
Láojià, zhè lù chē dào nǎr?

乙：这路车开往天桥。
Zhè lù chē kāiwǎng Tiānqiáo.

甲：去北京语言学院坐几路车？
Qù Běijīng Yǔyán Xuéyuàn zuò jǐr lù chē?

乙：您坐332路汽车。
Nín zuò sān-sān-èr lù qìchē.

甲：在哪儿换车？
Zài nǎr huàn chē?

乙：在中关村换331路汽车。
Zài Zhōngguāncūn huàn sān-sān-yāo lù qìchē.

甲：坐 332 路汽车，在哪儿上车？
Zuò sān-sān-èr lù qìchē, zài nǎr shàng chē?

乙：在马路左边。
Zài mǎlù zuǒbiān.

甲：谢谢！
Xièxie!

*　　　　　*　　　　　*

甲：有买票的吗？
Yǒu mǎi piào de ma?

乙：这路车到中关村吗？
Zhè lù chē dào Zhōngguāncūn ma?

甲：到。
Dào.

乙：我买一张到中关村的票。
Wǒ mǎi yì zhāng dào Zhōngguāncūn de piào.

甲：哪儿上的？
Nǎr shàng de?

乙：动物园。
Dòngwùyuán.

甲：下一站就是中关村。
Xià yí zhàn jiù shì Zhōngguāncūn.

生　词　New Words

1. 站　　　（名）zhàn　　　bus stop, station
2. 马路　　（名）mǎlù　　　street, road
3. 对面　　（名）duìmiàn　　the opposite

162

4. 票	（名）	piào	ticket
5. 张	（量）	zhāng	(a measure word)
6. 从	（介）	cóng	from
7. 刚	（副）	gāng	just
8. 左边	（名）	zuǒbiān	left
9. 右边	（名）	yòubiān	right
10. 开	（动）	kāi	to drive, to go
11. 往	（动）	wǎng	to go to

专 名　Proper Nouns

1. 人民剧场	Rénmín Jùchǎng	Peope's Theatre
2. 平安里	Píng'ānlǐ	name of a place
3. 天桥	Tiānqiáo	name of a place
4. 北京语言学院	Běijīng Yǔyán Xuéyuàn	
		Beijing Languages Institute
5. 中关村	Zhōngguāncūn	name of a place

语　法　Grammar

1. "的"字词组

Phrases with 的

动词、形容词、名词或词组加上"的"字，即可构成"的"字词组，后面不带中心语，在句中代替名词。例如：

A phrase with 的 can be constructed by attaching 的 to a verb, an adjective, a noun or a word group. With no word modified, the phrase stands for a noun in a sentence, e.g.

(1) 吃的、穿的、住的都很好。

(2) 我不能吃辣的。

(3) 有买票的没有？

(4) 我说的你都听懂了吗？

2. 语气助词"的"

The Modal Particle 的

动作已在过去发生，而要强调发生的时间、地点或方式等时，就可以在句尾用上语气助词"的"来表示强调的语气。例如：

The time, place or way in which an action took place can be shown in an emphatic manner by ending the sentence with 的, e.g.

(1) 从哪儿上的？

(2) 刚上的。

(3) 你什么时候来的？

(4) 我八点到的。

3. 介词词组"从…"

The Prepositional Phrase 从 …

介词"从"同表示处所（或时间）的词语构成介词词组，用在动词前面作状语。如果宾语是一个指人的名词或代词，必须在它后面加上"这儿"或"那儿"，以表示处所。这点，说英语的人要特别注意。例如：

The prepositional phrase formed by 从 and a locative or time word can be used bofore a verb as an adverbial modifier. If it is expressed by a personal noun or pronoun, the object should be followed by either 这儿 or 那儿 to denote the locality. This might be new to English speakers, e.g.

(1) 你从哪儿上的？

(2) 我从巴黎来。

(3) 我从王丽那儿来。

(4) 格林从我这儿拿走了一本中文书。

164

4. 名词词组作定语

A Nominal Phrase Used as an Adjectival Modifier

名词词组作定语，后面要加结构助词"的"。例如：

When used as an adjectival modifier, the nominal phrase is always followed by the structural particle 的, e.g.

(1) 在马路对面的车站上车。

(2) 我在学校前边的商店买了点儿东西。

(3) 王丽左边的那个人，你认识吗？

练 习 Exercises

1. 请把下列句子改成有"的"字词组的句子：

Rewrite the following sentences with a nominal phrase with 的：

(1) 买东西的人很多。

(2) 从日本来的人都学过汉语吗？

(3) 我认识那个上车的人。

(4) 那个买票的同志，我认识，她是我的老师。

(5) 我说的话，你听得懂听不懂？

2. 回答：

Answer the following questions:

(1) 你从哪儿去格林那儿？

(2) 你从哪儿去颐和园？

(3) 你什么时候上车的？

(4) 你什么时候到中国来的？

(5) 你什么时候从北京来的？

3. 把下列句子改成由名词词组作定语的句子：

Rewrite the following sentences with a nominal

phrase as an adjectival modifier:

例： **马路对面有一个商店，我在那儿买了点儿东西。**

我在马路对面的那个商店买了点儿东西。

(1) 商店左边有个车站，我在那儿上的。

(2) 331 路汽车站右边有一家商店，我在那儿买了双布鞋。

(3) 商店对面有一个饭店，我们到那儿去吃饭。

(4) 北京饭店对面有汽车站，我们到那儿去坐车。

4．把下列句子改成由动词结构作定语的句子：

Rewrite the following sentences with a verbal structure as an adjectival modifier:

例： **我去上海，请给我一张票。**

请给我一张到上海的票。

(1) 我到北京饭店，请给我一张票。

(2) 我去西安，买一张票。

(3) 我们到北京去，买两张票。

(4) 去颐和园，买一张票。

十七、看 电 影
kàn diàn yǐng

Seeing a Film

161. 今天晚上礼堂里有电影。
Jīntiān wǎnshang lǐtáng li yǒu diànyǐng.

There'll be a film shown in the auditorium tonight.

162. 什么电影? 几点开演?
Shénme diànyǐng? Jǐ diǎn kāiyǎn?

What film will it be? When will it begin?

163. 这是一部很好的电影。
Zhè shi yí bù hěn hǎo de diànyǐng.

This is a very good film.

164. 现在离开演还有几分钟?
Xiànzài lí kāiyǎn hái yǒu jǐ fēnzhōng?

How many minutes are there left before the film begins.

165. 你的票是双号还是单号?
Nǐ de piào shi shuānghào háishi dānhào?

Is yours an even number or an odd number?

166. 我的票是楼下15排2号。
Wǒ de piào shi lóuxia shíwǔ pái èr hào.

My seat is 2 in the 15th row in the stalls.

167. 座位不错。
Zuòwèi búcuò.

A very good seat!

168. 以前你看过中国电影吗?
Yǐqián nǐ kànguo Zhōngguó diànyǐng ma?

Have you seen any Chinese film before?

169. 来中国以后，你看过几次电影?
Lái Zhōngguó yǐhòu, nǐ kàngguo jǐ cì diànyǐng?

How many films did you see after you came to China?

170. 我看过两次。
Wǒ kànguo liǎng cì.

I saw two films.

替换练习 Substitution Drills

1. 这是一部 | 很好 | 的电影。
   很新
   很有意思
   很不错
   很不好

2. 现在离 | 开演 | 还有几分钟?
   开车
   上课
   下课

3. 以前你 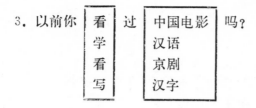 吗？

看	过	中国电影
学看		汉语
看		京剧
写		汉字

4. 我 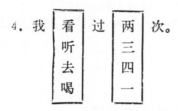 次。

看	过	两
听		三
去		四
喝		一

会 话 Dialogues

甲：今天晚上礼堂里有电影，你看不看？
Jīntiān wǎnshang lǐtáng li yǒu diànyǐng, nǐ kàn bu kàn?

乙：是中国电影吗？
Shì Zhōngguó diànyǐng ma?

甲：是，是中国电影《少林寺》。
shì, shì Zhōngguó diànyǐng 《Shàolín Sì》.

乙：这部电影怎么样？
Zhè bù diànyǐng zěnmeyàng?

甲：这是一部很好的电影。
Zhè shi yí bù hěn hǎo de diànyǐng.

乙：你买票了吗？
Nǐ mǎi piào le ma?

169

甲：买了。
Mǎi le.

乙：你的票是双号还是单号？
Nǐ de piào shi shuānghào háishi dānhào?

甲：单号，楼下 20 排 7 号。
Dānhào, lóuxia èrshí pái qī hào.

乙：座位不错。以前你看过中国电影吗？
Zuòwèi búcuò. Yǐqián nǐ kànguo Zhōngguó diànyǐng ma?

甲：没有。
Méiyǒu.

乙：来中国以后，你看过几次电影？
Lái Zhōngguó yǐhòu, nǐ kànguo jǐ cì diànyǐng?

甲：我看过两次。
Wǒ kànguo liǎng cì.

＊　　　＊　　　＊

甲：格林，你好！
Gélín, nǐ hǎo!

乙：你好！
Nǐ hǎo!

甲：今天下午人民剧场有京剧，你去看吗？
Jīntiān xiàwǔ Rénmín Jùchǎng yǒu jīngjù, nǐ qù kàn ma?

乙：去看。
Qù kàn.

甲：你以前看过京剧吗？
Nǐ yǐqián kànguo jīngjù ma?

甲：我看过两次。
Wǒ kànguo liǎng cì.

乙：你有票没有？
Nǐ yǒu piào mei yǒu?

甲：我有两张票，上午买的。
Wǒ yǒu liǎng zhāng piào, shàngwǔ mǎi de.

乙：座位怎么样？
Zuòwèi zěnmeyàng?

甲：不错，楼下 14 排 4 号和 6 号。
Búcuò, lóuxia shísì pái sì hào hé liù hào.

乙：几点开演？
Jǐ diǎn kāiyǎn?

甲：七点半。
Qī diǎn bàn.

乙：现在离开演还有几分钟？
Xiànzài lí kāiyǎn hái yǒu jǐ fēnzhōng?

甲：还有二十分钟。
Hái yǒu èrshí fēnzhōng.

乙：该走了！
Gāi zǒu le!

生 词 New Words

1. 晚上　（名）wǎnshang　evening
2. 礼堂　（名）lǐtáng　auditorium
3. 电影　（名）diànyǐng　film
4. 开演　（动）kāiyǎn　to begin (a performance)
5. 部　（量）bù　(a measure word)

6. 双	(形)	shuāng	even
7. 单	(形)	dān	odd
8. 楼	(名)	lóu	floor
9. 排	(名)	pái	row
10. 座位	(名)	zuòwèi	seat
11. 不错	(形)	búcuò	not bad
12. 以后	(名)	yǐhòu	after
13. 次	(量)	cì	time (a measure word)
14. 新	(形)	xīn	new
15. 有意思		yǒu yìsi	interesting
16. 京剧	(名)	jīngjù	Beijing Opera
17. 写	(动)	xiě	to write

专 名 Proper Noun

少林寺　　　Shàolín Sì　　Shaolin Temple

语 法 Grammar

1. 形容词词组作定语
An Adjectival Phrase Used as an Adjectival Modifier

形容词词组作定语，后面要加结构助词"的"。例如：

When used as an adjectival modifier, the adjectival phrase should be followed by the structural particle 的, e.g.

(1) 这是一部很好的电影。
(2) 那是一本很不错的书。
(3) 我看了个比较好的电影。
(4) 他买了本很有意思的书。

2. 动量补语

172

Action-Measure Complements

动量词"次"、"遍"等同数词结合放在动词后面作补语，说明动作发生的次数。如果动词带名词宾语，动量补语一般放在宾语前面；如果是代词宾语，动量补语一般放在宾语后面。即：

（A）动词＋动量补语＋名词宾语

（B）动词＋代词宾语＋动量补语

例如：

The phrase formed by a numeral and a verbal measure word such as 次 or 遍, may be used after a verb as a complement to indicate the frequency of an action. If the verb takes a nominal object, the complement is placed before the object; but in a sentence where the verb takes a pronominal object, the complement is put after the object, i.e.

（A）verb＋action-measure complement＋nominal object;

（B）verb ＋ pronominal object ＋ action-measure complement.

E.g.

(1) 来中国以后，你看过几次电影？

(2) 我看过两次。

(3) 那个电影很好，我看过两遍。

(4) 我去过那儿两次。

(5) 来北京以后，我找了他三次。

如果宾语是指人的名词，动量词也可以放在宾语后边。例如：

If the object is expressed by a personal noun, the action-measure word may be preceded by it, e.g.

(6) 我到北京来以后，看了王先生两次。

3. "以前"和"以后"

以前 and 以后

"以前"和"以后"，可以表示时间，也可以表示方位。表示时间时，可以单独作状语。例如：

Both 以前 and 以后 refer to either "time" or "direction". When referring to "time", they can be employed as adverbial modifiers, e.g.

(1) 以前你看过中国电影吗？

(2) 你以前在哪儿学习汉语？

(3) 以后我们再去长城吧！

(4) 他1980年来过中国，以后再也没来。

也可以在前面加上时间名词、动词或动词词组、主谓词组等。例如：

They may be preceded by a time word, a verb, a verbal group or a subject-predicate group, etc.. E.g.

(5) 出发以前，老师还要讲几句话。

(6) 去上海以前，你能到我这儿住几天吗？

(7) 一年以前，你学过汉语吗？

(8) 下课以后，你到哪儿去？

(9) 他走以前，我们去看看他，好不好？

练 习 Exercises

1. 请给下列句子加上动量补语：

Add an action-measure complement to each of the following sentences:

(1) 我看过这个电影。

(2) 我以前来过北京。

(3) 来北京以后我到张老师家去过。

174

(4) 这本书很有意思，我看过。

(5) 这个汉字我写了。

2．回答下列问题：

Answer the following questions:

(1) 来中国以前，你学过几年汉语？

(2) 到北京以后，你到北京饭店去过几次？

(3) 以前你在上海住过多长时间？

(4) 以前你来过中国几次？

(5) 你以后还到中国来学习吗？

(6) 昨天下课以后，你到哪儿去了？

3．完成下列对话：

Complete the following dialogues:

(1) A：北京饭店在哪儿？离这儿远不远？

B：_____，_____。

(2) A：长城离这儿远吗？

B：_____。

A：你坐火车去吗？

B：_____。

(3) A：车几点开？

B：_____。

A：离开车还有五分钟。

B：_____。

(4) A：不早了，该上车了。

B：_____？

A：八点开，离开车还有三分钟。

B：_____。

4．把下列句子改成带有形容词词组作定语的句子：

Change the following into sentences with an adjectival

175

phrase as an adjectival modifier:

例：这本书很好。

这是一本很好的书。

(1) 这部电影很有意思。

(2) 那本书很新。

(3) 楼下 15 排 2 号，这个座位很不错。

(4) 楼下30排28号，那个座位很不好。

十八、周末度假

zhōu mò dù jià

Weekend Holidaying

171. 周末你打算到哪儿去度假?

Zhōumò nǐ dǎsuan dào nǎr qù dù jià?

Where are you going this weekend?

172. 我还没拿定主意, 你呢?

Wǒ hái méi nádìng zhǔyi, nǐ ne?

I haven't made up my mind yet. What about you?

173. 我决定去承德。

Wǒ juédìng qù Chéngdé.

I've decided to visit Chengde.

174. 什么时候动身? 怎么去?

Shénme shíhou dòng shēn? Zěnme qù?

When are you leaving? And how?

175. 星期六早上走, 坐火车去。

Xīngqīliù zǎoshang zǒu, zuò huǒchē qù.

On Saturday morning, by train.

176. 从北京到承德有多远? 火车走几个小时?

Cóng Běijīng dào Chéngdé yǒu duō yuǎn? Huǒchē zǒu jǐ

ge xiǎoshí?

How far is it from Beijing to Chengde? How long will
it take to go there by train?

177. 从北京到承德有256公里，火车走4个多小时。

Cóng Běijīng dào Chéngdé yǒu èrbǎi wǔshí liù gōnglǐ,
huǒchē zǒu sì ge duō xiǎoshí.

The distance between Beijing and Chengde is 256
kilometres. It'll take more than 4 hours to go there by
train.

178. 你为什么不去大同?

Nǐ wèi shénme bú qù Dàtóng?

Why aren't you going to Datong?

179. 承德是避暑的地方，夏天去那儿度假最合适。

Chéngdé shi bì shǔ de hǎo dìfang, xiàtiān qù nàr dù jià
zuì héshì.

Chengde is a good place for summer holiday makers,
and summer is the best season for one to visit there.

180. 既然这样，我就跟你一起去承德吧！

Jìrán zhèyàng, wǒ jiù gēn ni yìqǐ qù Chéngdé ba!

In that case, I'll go to Chengde with you.

替换练习 Substitution Drills

1. | 周末
 今年夏天
 明年 | 你打算到哪儿去 | 度假
 旅行
 学汉语 | ？

2. 星期六早上走，坐 | 火车
 汽车
 飞机
 轮船 | 去。

3. 从 | 北京
 伦敦
 上海
 东京 | 到 | 承德
 巴黎
 纽约
 大阪 | 有多远？

4. 既然 | 这样
 这部电影好
 汉语不难学 | ，我就跟你一起去 | 承德
 看
 北京学 | 吧！

会 话 Dialogues

甲：周末你去度假吗？
　　Zhōumò nǐ qù dù jià ma?

179

乙: 是的。
Shì de.

甲: 你打算去哪儿？
Nǐ dǎsuan qù nǎr?

乙: 我还没有拿定主意。
Wǒ hái méi nádìng zhǔyi.

甲: 我们一起去承德吧！
Wǒmen yìqǐ qù Chéngdé ba!

乙: 为什么去承德？
Wèi shénme qù Chéngdé?

甲: 承德是避暑的好地方，夏天去那儿度假最合适。
Chéngdé shi bì shǔ de hǎo dìfang, xiàtiān qù nàr dù jià zuì héshì.

乙: 从北京到承德有多远？火车走几个小时？
Cóng Běijīng dào Chéngdé yǒu duō yuǎn? Huǒchē zǒu jǐ ge xiǎoshí?

甲: 从北京到承德有256公里，火车走4个多小时。
Cóng Běijīng dào Chéngdé yǒu èrbǎi wǔshí liù gōng-lǐ, huǒchē zǒu sì ge duō xiǎoshí.

乙: 好，我决定去承德。
Hǎo, wǒ juédìng qù Chéngdé.

甲: 我们什么时候动身？
Wǒmen shénme shíhou dòng shēn?

乙: 星期六早上走，坐火车去。
Xīngqīliù zǎoshang zǒu, zuò huǒchē qù.

*　　　　*　　　　*

甲: 今年夏天你打算到哪儿去旅行？
Jīnnián xiàtiān nǐ dǎsuan dào nǎr qù lǚxíng?

乙：我还没有拿定主意，你呢？
Wǒ hái méi nádìng zhǔyi, nǐ ne?

甲：我打算去青岛。
Wǒ dǎsuan qù Qīngdǎo.

乙：为什么去青岛？
Wèi shénme qù Qīngdǎo?

甲：夏天去青岛最合适，那儿是避暑的好地方。
Xiàtiān qù Qīngdǎo zuì héshì, nàr shì bì shǔ de hǎo dìfang.

乙：我觉得庐山也是很好的避暑地方。
Wǒ juéde Lúshān yě shì hěn hǎo de bì shǔ dìfang.

甲：既然这样，那你去庐山，我去青岛。
Jìrán zhèyàng, nà nǐ qù Lúshān, wǒ qù Qīngdǎo.

乙：好。你什么时候动身？怎么去？
Hǎo. Nǐ shénme shíhou dòng shēn? Zěnme qù?

甲：我打算十五号动身，坐火车去。你呢？
Wǒ dǎsuan shíwǔ hào dòng shēn, zuò huǒchē qù. Nǐ ne?

乙：我十二号动身，坐飞机去。
Wǒ shí'èr hào dòng shēn, zuò fēijī qù.

生　词　New Words

1. 周末　（名）zhōumò　weekend
2. 打算　（动、名）dǎsuan　to plan
3. 度假　dù jià　to spend a holiday
4. 拿定　nádìng　to make up (one's mind)
5. 主意　（名）zhǔyi　plan, decision
6. 决定　（动、名）juédìng　to decide, decision

181

7. 动身		dòng shēn	to set off
8. 早上	(名)	zǎoshang	morning
9. 火车	(名)	huǒchē	train
10. 从…到…		cóng…dào…	from… to…
11. 小时	(名)	xiǎoshí	hour
12. 公里	(量)	gōnglǐ	kilometre
13. 为什么		wèi shénme	why
14. 避暑		bì shǔ	away on holiday at a summer resort
15. 夏天	(名)	xiàtiān	summer
16. 最	(副)	zuì	the most
17. 既然	(连)	jìrán	since, in that case
18. 这样	(代)	zhèyàng	like this
19. 跟…一起		gēn…yìqǐ	together with
20. 旅行	(动)	lǚxíng	to travel
21. 飞机	(名)	fēijī	aeroplane
22. 轮船	(名)	lúnchuán	steamship

专 名 Proper Nouns

1. 承德	Chéngdé	name of a place
2. 大同	Dàtóng	name of a place
3. 青岛	Qīngdǎo	name of a place
4. 庐山	Lúshān	Lushan Mountain

语 法 Grammar

1. 动词词组作主语和宾语

   A Verbal Phrase Used as a Subject or an Object

182

汉语动词词组可以在句中作主语和宾语。例如：

A Chinese verbal phrase may function as a subject or an object in a sentence, e.g.

(A) 作主语　As a Subject

(1) 夏天去那儿度假最合适。

(1) 星期日早上走比较好。

(3) 从北京到承德有多少公里？

(4) 看完电影去也可以。

(B) 作宾语　As an Object

(5) 周末你打算到哪儿去度假？

(6) 我决定去承德。

(7) 我觉得应该去上海。

(8) 格林打算明年去中国学习。

2. "既然…就…"

The Structure 既然…就…

"既然"，连词，用来构成复句。"既然"用于前一分句，提出已肯定的前提，后一分句根据这一前提推出结论，常用"就"、"也"、"还"呼应。"既然"后边可以接指示代词"这样"。例如：

The conjunction 既然 often appears in a complex sentence. It is used in the first clause to introduce the premise. In the second clause where the conclusion is reached, 就, 也 or 还 can be used. 既然 may be followed by the demonstrative pronoun 这样, e.g.

(1) 既然这样，我就跟你一起去承德吧！

(2) 既然你决定去承德，我也决定去承德。

如果前后两个分句的主语相同，"既然"一般放在主语后边。例如：

If both clauses share the same subject, 既然 is often

placed after the subject, e.g.

(3) 你既然来了，就别走了。

(4) 他既然有病，就不要去上课了。

练习 Exercises

1. 完成下列对话：

Complete the following dialogues:

(1) A：夏天你打算去哪儿？

B：_____。

A：你打算在那儿住多长时间？

B：_____。

(2) A：到哪儿度假，你还没有拿定主意吗？

B：_____。

A：你决定去哪儿？

B：_____。

(3) A：你打算明年去北京学习吗？

B：_____。

A：你打算学多长时间？

B：_____。

(4) A：你决定什么时候去上海？

B：_____。

A：坐火车去还是坐飞机去？

B：_____。

A：从这儿到上海，火车要走多长时间？

B：_____。

2. 完成下列句子：

Complete the following sentences:

(1) 既然＿＿＿＿＿＿＿＿＿，我也去上海。

(2) 你既然有事，＿＿＿＿＿＿＿＿＿。

(3) 既然你决定明天走，＿＿＿＿＿＿＿＿＿。

(4) 你既然决定在这儿学习，＿＿＿＿＿＿＿＿＿。

(5) 既然＿＿＿＿＿＿＿＿＿，我就跟你一起去长城吧！

3．用疑问代词提问划线部分：
Ask questions about the underlined part with an interrogative pronoun:

(1) 他去北京学<u>汉语</u>吗？

(2) 你决定去<u>青岛</u>度假吗？

(3) 从北京到上海，火车要走<u>二十多个</u>小时。

(4) 周末你打算跟<u>格林</u>一起去承德吗？。

(5) 我们坐轮船去上海，你坐<u>飞机</u>去吗？

(6) 北京<u>夏天</u>最热。

(7) 那个电影<u>很有意思</u>。

(8) 今天晚上看京剧，在<u>人民</u>剧场吗？

(9) 你买了<u>三</u>张票吗？座位<u>好不好</u>？

(10) 你的座位在<u>这</u>排吗？<u>十五</u>号吗？

(11) 他<u>病了</u>，没去看京剧。

十九、看 病
kàn   bìng

Seeing a Doctor

181. 你怎么了？哪儿不舒服？

NǏ zěnme le? Nǎr bù shūfu?

What's your trouble?

182. 头疼，还有点儿咳嗽。

Tóu téng, hái yǒudiǎnr késou.

I've got a headache and a cough.

183. 发烧不发烧？

Fā shāo bu fā shāo?

Are you running a fever?

184. 量一量体温吧！

Liáng-yiliáng tǐwēn ba!

Let me take your temperature.

185. 三十七度八，有点儿发烧，张开嘴："A—"。

Sānshí qī dù bā, yǒudiǎnr fā shāo, zhāngkai zuǐ: "A—".

37.8°c. You're having a temperature, but it's not terribly high. Now open your mouth, say "ah—"

186. 请你把上衣解开，我听听。

Qǐng ni bǎ shàngyī jiěkai, wǒ tīngting.

Will you unfasten your jacket? I'll listen to your heart.

187. 这是化验单，请拿到化验室去验血。
Zhè shi huàyàndān, qǐng nádào huànyànshǐ qù yàn xlě.

Please go to the laboratory with this report form, and have your blood tested there.

188. 验完血，把化验单拿回来。
Yànwán xiě, bǎ huàyàndān náhuilai.

Bring the report back with you after the test.

189. 大夫，我得的是什么病?
Dàifu, wǒ dé de shi shénme bìng?

Whati's wrong with me, doctor?

190. 感冒了，吃点儿药就好了。
Gǎnmào le, chī diǎnr yào jiù hǎo le.

You've caught a cold. Take some medicine and you'll be all right.

替换练习 Substitution Drills

1. 量一量 | 体温 | 吧。
　　　　 | 血压 |

2. 请你把 | 上衣解开 | ，我 | 听听 | 。
　　　　 | 嘴张开 | | 看看 |

3. 这是化验单，请拿到化验室去验 | 血 | 。
　　　　　　　　　　　　　　　　 | 尿 |

会 话 Dialogues

甲：你怎么了？
NǏ zěnme le?

乙：大夫，我头疼。
Dàifu, wǒ tóu téng.

甲：咳嗽吗？
Késou ma?

乙：有点儿咳嗽。
Yǒudiǎnr késou.

甲：发烧不发烧？
Fā shāo bu fā shāo?

乙：不知道。
Bù zhīdao.

甲：量一量体温吧！
Liáng-yiliáng tǐwēn ba!

乙：多少度？
Duōshao dù?

甲：三十八度，有点儿发烧。请张开嘴："A—"。
Sānshí bā dù, yǒudiǎnr fā shāo. Qǐng zhāngkai zuǐ:
"A——".

甲：请你把上衣解开，我听听。
Qǐng ni bǎ shàngyī jiěkai, wǒ tīngting.

乙：要化验吗？
Yào huàyàn ma?

188

甲：要。这是化验单，请拿到化验室去验血。验完
血把化验单拿回来。
Yào. Zhè shi huàyàndān, qǐng nádào huàyànshì qù yàn
xiě. Yànwán xiě bǎ huàyàndān náhuilai.

乙：我得的是什么病？
Wǒ dé de shi shénme bìng?

甲：你感冒了，吃点儿药，休息休息就好了。
Nǐ gǎnmào le, chī diǎnr yào, xiūxi-xiāxi jiù hǎo le.

* * *

甲：大夫，我很不舒服。
Dàifu, wǒ hěn bù sūfu.

乙：你哪儿不舒服？
Nǐ nǎr bù sūfu?

甲：头疼，发烧。
Tóu téng, fā shāo.

乙：量一量体温吧——三十九度。咳嗽吗？
Liáng-yiliáng tǐwēn ba —sānshí jiǔ dù. Késou ma?

甲：不咳嗽。
Bù késou.

乙：请把嘴张开："A—"。
Qǐng bǎ zuǐ zhāngkai: "A—".

甲：A—
A—

乙：这是化验单，你到化验室去验验血和尿。
Zhè shi huàyàndān, nǐ dào huàyànshì qù yànyan xiě hé

niào.

甲：对面就是化验室吗？
Duìmiàn jiù shi huàyànshì ma?

乙：是。你把化验单放在化验室外边，他们会叫你。
Shì. Nǐ bǎ huàyàndān fàng zài huàyànshì wàibian,
tāmen huì jiào nǐ.

甲：好，谢谢。
Hǎo, xièxie.

生　词　New Words

1. 舒服	（形）	shūfu	well, comfortable
2. 头	（名）	tóu	head
3. 疼	（形）	téng	ache
4. 有点儿	（副）	yǒudiǎnr	somewhat, a bit
5. 咳嗽	（动）	késou	to cough
6. 发烧		fā shāo	to run a fever
7. 量	（动）	liáng	to take (one's temperature)
8. 体温	（名）	tǐwēn	temperature
9. 度	（量）	dù	degree
10. 张	（动）	zhāng	to open
11. 开	（动）	kāi	to open
12. 嘴	（名）	zuǐ	mouth
13. 把	（介）	bǎ	(a preposition)
14. 上衣	（名）	shàngyī	jacket
15. 解	（动）	jiě	to unfasten
16. 化验单	（名）	huàyàndān	test report form
17. 化验室	（名）	huàyànshì	laboratory
18. 验	（动）	yàn	to test
19. 血	（名）	xiě	blood
20. 回	（动）	huí	to go back, to return

190

21.	大夫	（名）	dàifu	doctor
22.	得	（动）	dé	to suffer from (an illness), to have
23.	感冒	（名）	gǎnmào	cold
24.	药	（名）	yào	medicine
25.	血压	（名）	xuèyā	blood pressure
26.	尿	（名）	niào	urine
27.	外边	（名）	wàibian	outside

语　法　Grammar

"把"字句（一）
Sentences with 把 (A)

　　"把"字句是动词谓语句的一种，用来强调说明动作对某事物有所处置及处置的结果。"把"字句的词序是：

　　　　主语＋把＋宾语＋动词＋其他成分

Sentences with 把 belong to the sentences containing a verbal predicate. They are used to emphasize how things are disposed of, and the result thereof. The word order of the sentence is:

　　　　subject + 把 + object + verb + other sentence elements

　　"把"字的宾语在意义上是谓语动词的受事，"其它成分"是指动态助词"了"、宾语、补语（可能补语除外）或动词本身重叠（单音动词重叠，中间可以加"一"或"了"）。动词必须是及物的，否则不能构成"把"字句（如"来"、"有"、"在"等不能作"把"字句的谓语动词）。例如：

The object of the preposition 把 is the notional object of the verbal predicate. The "other sentence elements" include

191

the aspectual particle 了, the object, the complement (except the potential complement) and the repeated form of the verbal predicate itself. 一 or 了 may be used between a monosyllabic verb and its repeated form. Only transitive verbs can be used in a sentence containing 把. Therefore verbs such as 来, 有 or 在 can never perform as the verbal predicate in it, e.g.

(1) 请你把上衣解开。

(2) 验完血，把化验单拿回来。

(3) 我把这本书看完了。

(4) 请你把这个汉字写写。

(5) 请你把车票给他。

如果说话人不着眼于强调处置意义，也可以不用这类"把"字句，而用一般的动词谓语句。上面的句子可以说成：

It logically follows that any sentence with a verbal predicate is as good as a sentence containing 把 if one's attention is no longer focused on how things are dealt with. In this sense the foregoing sentences can be rewritten as:

(6) 请你解开上衣。

(7) 验完血，拿回化验单来。

(8) 我看完这本书了。

(9) 请你写写这个汉字。

(10) 请你给他车票。

练 习 Exercises

1. 用下列动词的重叠式填空：

Complete the following sentences with the repeated form of the verbs given below:

试　　量　　看　　写　　穿　　吃
　(1) 这个菜味道怎么样？你_____看。
　(2) 发烧吧？你去_____体温。
　(3) 请你_____这个汉字。
　(4) 这本书很好，你可以_____。
　(5) 他_____，说这双布鞋有点小。
　(6) 这双大一点，你_____看。

2. 把下面的句子改成不带"把"的句子：
Change the following into sentences without 把：
　(1) 请你把化验单拿回来。
　(2) 请你把这句话写一写。
　(3) 请你把上衣解开，我听听。
　(4) 请你把这本书给他。

3. 请把下面的句子改成"把"字句：
Rewrite the following sentences with 把：
　(1) 他拿回那本书来了。
　(2) 他吃药了吗？
　(3) 我还没看完那本书。
　(4) 我买完东西就跟他一起走了。

4. 回答下列问题：
Answer the following questions:
　(1) 格林得的是什么病？
　(2) 他说的是英语还是法语？
　(3) 你看的是中国的英文报吗？
　(4) 你给他的是一本新书吗？
　(5) 你拿回来的是刚买的上衣吗？

二十、换 钱
huàn qián
Changing Money

191. 请问，在哪儿兑换外币？
Qǐng wèn, zài nǎr duìhuàn wàibì?

Could you please tell me where I can change my foreign currency?

192. 在中国银行。你住的旅馆也可以兑换。
Zài Zhōngguó Yínháng. Nǐ zhù de lǚguǎn yě kěyǐ duìhuàn.

At Bank of China, or in the hotel where you stay.

193. 我想把美元换成人民币。
Wǒ xiǎng bǎ Měiyuán huànchéng Rénmínbì.

I want to exchange some U.S dollars for Renminbi.

194. 你打算换多少？
Nǐ dǎsuan huàn duōshao?

How much are you going to exchange for?

195. 我换五百美元。
Wǒ huàn wǔbǎi Měiyuán.

Five hundred U.S. dollars.

196. 请您先填一张兑换单。

Qǐng nín xiān tián yì zhāng duìhuàndān.

Fill in the exchange form first, please.

197. 今天美元和人民币的兑换率是多少?

Jīntiān Měiyuán hé Rénmínbì de duìhuànlǜ shì duōshao?

What's the rate of exchange between U.S. dollars and Renminbi today?

198. 今天的兑换率是一比一点九五。

Jīntiān de duìhuànlǜ shì yī bǐ yī diǎn jiǔ-wǔ.

The rate is 1:1.95 today.

199. 请点一点。

Qǐng diǎn-yìdiǎn.

Please check them.

200. 我要十元一张的，或者五元一张的。

Wǒ yào shí yuán yì zhāng de, huòzhě wǔ yuán yì zhāng de.

I want ten-yuan notes or five-yuan ones.

替换练习 Substitution Drills

1. 请问，在哪儿 | 兑换 / 换 | 外币?

2．我想把

| 美元 |
| 日元 |
| 英磅 |
| 法国法郎 |
| 马克 |

换成人民币。

3．我换

| 五百美元 |
| 一千英磅 |
| 二十万日元 |

。

会 话 Dialogues

甲：同志，我想把美元换成人民币。
Tóngzhì, wǒ xiǎng bǎ Měiyuán huànchéng Rénmínbì.

乙：你打算换多少？
Nǐ dǎsuan huàn duōshao?

甲：换八百美元。
Huàn bābǎi Měiyuán.

乙：请你先填一张兑换单。
Qǐng nǐ xiān tián yì zhāng duìhuàndān.

甲：请问，今天美元和人民币的兑换率是多少？
Qǐng wèn, jīntiān Měiyuán hé Rénmínbì de duìhuànlǜ shi duōshao?

乙：今天的兑换率是一比一点八九。
Jīntiān de duìhuànlǜ shi yī bǐ yī diǎn bā-jiǔ.

甲：给你兑换单，请把名字写在这儿。
Gěi ni duìhuàndān, qǐng bǎ míngzi xiě zài zhèr.

乙：你的八百美元换成人民币是一千五百一十二
元，请点一点。
Nǐ de bābǎi Měiyuán huànchéng Rénmínbì shi yìqiān
wǔbǎi yīshí èr yuán, qǐng diǎn-yidiǎn.

甲：我要十元一张的。
Wǒ yào shí yuán yì zhāng de.

乙：好。
hǎo.

甲：谢谢你，再见。
Xièxie nǐ, zàijiàn.

乙：再见。
Zàijiàn.

*　　　*　　　*

甲：劳驾，在哪儿换外币？
Láojià, zài nǎr huàn wàibì?

乙：在中国银行。你住的旅馆也可以兑换。
Zài Zhōngguó Yínháng. Nǐ zhù de lǚguǎn yě kěyǐ
duìhuàn.

甲：我住的旅馆不能兑换。
Wǒ zhù de lǚguǎn bù néng duìhuàn.

乙：那你去中国银行吧！
Nà nǐ qù Zhōngguó Yínháng ba!

甲：中国银行在哪儿？
Zhōngguó Yínháng zài nǎr?

乙：在王府井，离百货大楼不远。
Zài Wángfǔjǐng, lí Bǎihuò Dàlóu bù yuǎn.

甲：好，我明天去。
Hǎo, wǒ míngtiān qù.

乙：你打算换多少?
Nǐ dǎsuan huàn duōshao?

甲：我打算先换四百英磅。
Wǒ dǎsuan xiān huàn sìbǎi Yīngbàng.

生 词 New Words

1. 兑换	(动)	duìhuàn	to exchange
2. 外币	(名)	wàibì	foreign currency
3. 想	(动、能动)	xiǎng	to want, to wish
4. 先	(副)	xiān	first
5. 填	(动)	tián	to fill in
6. 兑换单	(名)	duìhuàndān	exchange form
7. 兑换率	(名)	duìhuànlù	rate of exchange
8. 比	(动)	bǐ	to compare, to
9. 点	(动、名)	diǎn	to count, point
10. 或者	(连)	huòzhě	or

专 名 Proper Nouns

1. 美元	Měiyuán	U.S. dollar
2. 人民币	Rénmínbì	Renminbi (Chinese currency)
3. 王府井	Wángfǔjǐng	name of a place
4. 日元	Rìyuán	(Japanese) yen
5. 英磅	Yīngbàng	pound sterling
6. 法郎	Fǎláng	franc

7. 马克   Mǎkè   mark

语 法 Grammar

"把"字句(二)

Sentences with 把 (B)

"把"字句中"把"的宾语后面为"动词+成+宾语",说明受处置的事物或人通过动作而成为什么。这种"把"字句不能改换成一般动词谓语句。例如:

The 把 sentences whose object is followed by "verb + 成 + object", indicate the result of the diposal of a person or thing. This type of sentences can never be replaced by any other sentence with a verbal predicate, e.g.

(1) 我想把美元换成人民币。

(2) 请你把这个(汉)字换成"把"字。

(3) 他把"太"字写成"大"了。

"把"的宾语后面为"动词+到+宾语",说明受处置的事物或人通过动作到达或处于某地,这种"把"字句也不能改换成一般动词谓语句。例如:

A 把 sentence can not be replaced by any other sentence with a verbal predicate if its object is followed by "verb + 到 + object", indicating the position of a person or thing through the disposal, e.g.

(4) 请你把汽车开到马路对面吧!

(5) 请他把拿来的东西放到302房间里。

"把"字句如果谓语动词后有词组"在…"作补语,说明受处置的事物或人通过动作而存在于某处时,也不能改换成一般动词谓语句。例如:

If its verbal predicate is followed by the phrase "在…" as its complement to indicate the locality of a person or thing, the 把 sentence can never be exchanged with a verbal predicate sentence, e.g.

(6) 请你把名字写在这儿。

(7) 我把房间号填在哪儿？

练 习 Exercises

1. 完成下列句子：

Complete the following sentences:

(1) 我想把英磅＿＿＿＿＿＿＿＿＿＿。

(2) 我打算把这本英文书翻译＿＿＿＿＿＿＿＿＿。

(3) 请你把＿＿＿＿＿＿拿到＿＿＿＿＿＿。

(4) 请问，您把＿＿＿＿＿＿放在＿＿＿＿＿＿？

(5) 你把美元＿＿＿＿＿＿＿＿了吗？

2. 用下面的词语造"把"字句：

Make sentences with 把, using the the words given below:

(1) 日元　换成

(2) 京剧票　放在

(3) 布鞋　拿出去

(4) 书　看完

(5) 电影票　给

(6) 那句话　写完

3. 完成下列对话：

Complete the following dialogues:

(1) A：你住的旅馆可以兑换外币吗？

B：_____。

A：你兑换多少？

B：_____。

(2) A：你昨天买书了没有？

B：_____。

A：我想看看你买的书，可以吗？

B：_____。

A：那我把书拿走了。

B：_____。

(3) A：去年来北京，你住在哪儿？

B：_____。

A：你住的地方可以兑换外币吗？

B：_____。

A：你现在住的地方也可以兑换吗？

B：_____。

(4) A：格林病了吗？他得的什么病？

B：_____。

A：现在他好点儿了吗？

B：_____。

语　法　小　结（二）
yǔ　fǎ　xiǎo　jié

A Short Summary of Grammar (2)

1. 词组　Phrases
   A. 名词词组　Nominal Phrases
      (1) 马路对面的商店
      (2) 人民剧场的票
   B. 形容词词组　Adjectival Phrases
      (1) 比较好的电影
      (2) 很有意思的书
   C. 动词词组　Verbal Phrases
      a. 动宾词组　Verb-Object Phrases
      (1) 教口语的老师
      (2) 不喜欢喝汽水。
      b. 动补词组　Verb-Complement Phrases
      (1) 听不懂的地方
      (2) 填好的兑换单
      c. 状动词组　Adverbial Modifier-Verb Phrases:
      (1) 刚来的学生
      (2) 没学过的汉字
   D. 介词词组　Prepositional Phrases
      (1) 住在西郊
      (2) 离天安门不远

E. 主谓词组　Subject-Predicate Phrases
　　(1) 味道不错的葡萄酒
　　(2) 发音好的同学。
F. "的"字词组　Phrases with 的
　　(1) 买点吃的
　　(2) 有没有喝的
　　(3) 有很多买东西的
2. 补语　Complements
　　A. 结果补语　Resultative Complements
　　　(1) 我没听懂你的话。
　　　(2) 请写好名字，把本子交来。
　　B. 趋向补语　Directional Complements
　　　(1) 他买来三斤苹果。
　　　(2) 同学们进教室去了。
　　　(3) 他拿回来一本新杂志。/他拿回一本新杂志来。
　　　(4) 看京剧的人都走进礼堂去了。
　　C. 可能补语　Potential Complements
　　　(1) 今年我们学得完学不完这本书？
　　　(2) 没有票，进不去。
　　D. 程度补语　Complements of Degree
　　　(1) 张林学英语学得很好。
　　　(2) 他说得慢不慢？
　　E. 时量补语　Time-Measure Complements
　　　(1) 我走了二十分钟，就到东风市场了。
　　　(2) 他学汉语只学了一年多。
　　　(3) 下课十五分钟了，他早回家了。
　　F. 动量补语　Action-Measure Complements
　　　(1) 我只去过那儿一次。

（2）来北京以后，你看过几次中国电影？

G. 时间、处所补语　Time-Locality Complements

（1）保罗住在友谊宾馆。

（3）我把那本书放在那儿了。

练习　Exercises

阅读下列短文并复述：

Read and retell the following passages

（1）打铃了，上课了。同学们都走进教室来了。今天的课是张老师给我们上。张老师是北京人，他教我们口语。他的发音很好，说话说得很慢。他说的话，我们都能听得懂。张老师还会英语和法语，他能看英文书和法文书。他学过四年英语，两年法语。

今天，格林和保罗请假。格林病了，他觉得不舒服。保罗有事，要去大使馆。

老师让我们把书拿出来，他教我们说汉语。玛丽说得很好，史密斯说得也不错。张老师说我们的发音都很好，说得也不慢。

下课以后，老师问我格林去看病了没有，我说他去了。张老师问他得了什么病。我说，格林得的是感冒，不发烧，只是头疼，有点儿咳嗽，大夫说吃一点药就会好的。张老师说下午要去看看格林。

（2）昨天我去朋友家了。我朋友住在西郊学院路52号，离我们学校不太远。我早上九点半出来，上了332路汽车以后，买完票，我问售票员 (shòupiàoyuán, bus conductor)："劳驾，我去学院路，是不是换331路汽车？"他说："是。"我又问，还有几站就到中关村了。他说还有三站。我谢了他，他说："不客气。"

我在中关村换了车，又坐了两站，就到我朋友家了。我朋友和他的夫人、女儿都在家。他们看见我来了，很高兴。请我喝茶、吸烟。吃饭的时候，又请我喝啤酒和葡萄酒。他们作了干烧鱼和香酥鸡，味道好极了。我吃了很多。我朋友还请我吃，我说："够了，我吃不下了。"我朋友说："别客气，就跟在家里一样，好吗？"

吃完饭，半个小时以后，我跟朋友说："不早了，我该走了。谢谢你们。"我朋友说："别客气，欢迎（huānyíng, welcome）你以后常（cháng, often）来。"

（3）周末，我和我的朋友去承德度假了。星期六早上八点十分动身，坐火车走了四个多小时就到了。

走以前，我们到银行去把美元兑换成人民币。我问我朋友："兑换三百美元，够不够？"他说："够了，我想兑换二百美元就行了。"

到了承德，我们住在一个很不错的小饭店里。我们住得很舒服。承德是避暑的好地方，夏天在那儿度假最合适。我们看了几个地方，都很有意思。我们还看了一个电影。来中国以后，我们只看过两次电影。这个电影我和我的朋友以前都没有看过，是一部很好的电影。

我们在那儿住了三天，玩儿（wánr, to enjoy oneself）得高兴极了。星期二晚上我们就回北京了。

二十一、在 邮 局
zài yóu jú
At the Post Office

201. 同志，往东京寄信，贴多少邮票？

Tóngzhì, wàng Dōngjīng jì xìn, tiē duōshao yóupiào?

Comrade, what's the postage for a letter to Tokyo, please?

202. 寄平信还是寄挂号信？

Jì píngxìn háishi jì guàhàoxìn?

Is it an ordinary letter or a registered one?

203. 我寄航空挂号信。

Wǒ jì hángkōng guàhàoxìn.

I want to send it by registered air mail.

204. 这封信超重了，要贴一块四的邮票。

Zhè fēng xìn chāozhòng le, yào tiē yí kuài sì de yóupiào.

This letter is overweight, and the postage will be 1.4 yuan.

205. 我要买纪念邮票，多少钱一套？

Wǒ yào mǎi jìniàn yóupiào, duōshao qián yí tào?

I'd like to get some commemorative stamps. How

much is each set?

206. 邮票让我贴在背面了。
Yóupiào ràng wo tiē zài bèimiànr le.

I put the stamps on the back of the envelope.

207. 请把邮票贴在这儿。
Qǐng bǎ yóupiào tiē zài zhèr.

Please stick the stamps on here.

208. 寄包裹是不是也在这儿?
Jì bāoguǒ shì bu shì yě zài zhèr?

Can I send a parcel from here?

209. 那封信寄出去了吗?
Nà fēng xìn jìchuqu le ma?

Was the letter posted?

210. 他没有接到家里的信。
Tà méiyǒu jiēdào jiālǐ de xìn.

He hasn't received any letter from his family.

替换练习 Substitution Drills

1. 同志,往

东京	寄	信	，贴多少邮票?
巴黎		挂号信	
上海		航空信	
罗马		航空挂号信	

2.

邮票	让（叫）我	贴在背面	了。
化验单		拿走	
电影票		弄丢	

207

3. 他没有接到

| 家里的信 |
| 朋友的信 |
| 母亲的包裹 |
| 王先生寄来的书 |

。

会 话 Dialogues

甲：同志，往巴黎寄信贴多少邮票？
Tóngzhì, wàng Bālí jì xìn, tiē duōshao yóupiào?

乙：你寄平信还是寄挂号信？
Nǐ jì píngxìn háishì jì guàhàoxìn?

甲：我寄平信。
Wǒ jì píngxìn.

乙：贴八毛的邮票。
Tiē bā máo de yóupiào.

甲：是航空信吗？
Shì hángkōngxìn ma?

乙：是。
Shì

......

乙：请把邮票贴在这儿。
Qǐng bǎ yóupiào tiē zài zhèr.

甲：对不起，邮票让我贴在背面了。
Duì bu qǐ, yóupiào ràng wo tiē zài bèimiànr le.

乙：以后请不要再把邮票贴在背面。
Yǐhòu qǐng bú yào zài bǎ yóupiào tiē zài bèimiànr

甲：好。我还要买纪念邮票，多少钱一套？
Hǎo. Wǒ hái yào mǎi jìniàn yóupiào, duōshao qián

yī tào?

乙：这种六毛钱一套。
Zhè zhǒng liù máo qián yī tào.

甲：买三套。
Mǎi sān tào.

*　　　　*　　　　*

甲：约翰，你接到家里寄来的包裹没有？
Yuēhàn, nǐ jiēdào jiāli jìlai de bāoguǒ méiyǒu?

乙：没有。
Méiyǒu.

甲：为什么？
Wèi shénme.

乙：不知道，我接到父亲的信，说寄来了一个包裹。
Bù zhīdao, wǒ jiēdào fùqin de xìn, shuō jìlaile

yī ge bāoguǒ.

甲：会不会被邮局弄丢了？
Huì bu huì ràng yóujú nòngdiū le?

乙：我们去邮局问问吧！
Wǒmen qù yóujú wènwen ba!

⋯⋯

乙：同志，有我的包裹吗？
Tóngzhì, yǒu wǒ de bāoguǒ ma?

丙：你叫什么名字？
Nǐ jiào shénme míngzi?

乙：我叫约翰。
Wǒ jiào Yuēhàn.

丙：你是哪国人?
Nǐ shì nǎguó rén?

乙：我是英国人。
Wǒ shì Yīngguó rén?

丙：这是你的包裹吗?
Zhè shì nǐ de bāoguǒ ma?

乙：是，谢谢。
Shì, xièxie.

生　词　New Words

1. 邮局　　（名）yóujú　　　　　post office
2. 寄　　　（动）jì　　　　　　to post
3. 信　　　（名）xìn　　　　　letter
4. 贴　　　（动）tiē　　　　　to stick on
5. 邮票　　（名）yóupiào　　　stamp
6. 平信　　（名）píngxìn　　　ordinary letter
7. 挂号信　（名）guàhàoxìn　　registered letter
8. 航空　　（名）hángkōng　　air mail
9. 封　　　（量）fēng　　　　（a measure word)
10. 超重　　（动）chāozhòng　　be overweight
11. 纪念　　（动、名）jìniàn　　to commemorate
12. 套　　　（量）tào　　　　　set (a measure word)
13. 让　　　（介、动）ràng　　by, let
14. 背面　　（名）bèimiànr　　back
15. 包裹　　（名）bāoguǒ　　　parcel

210

16. 接	（动）jiē	to receive
17. 叫	（介）jiào	by
18. 弄	（动）nòng	to get
19. 丢	（动）diū	to lose
20. 被	（介）bèi	by

语　法　Grammar

1. "被"字句

Sentences with 被

有些句子，主语是"受事"，谓语中有表示被动的"被、让、叫"等介词，叫做"被"字句。"被、让、叫"的宾语在意义上是谓语的"施事"。这种介词词组一定要放在动词谓语的前边，决不能像英语被动句那样放在句尾。例如：

Senteces with 被 are those of which the subject is the acceptor of the action, and the predicate contains one of the prepositions: 被，让, or 叫. The object of the prepositions indicated above is the notional doer of the action expressed by the predicate of the sentence. Unlike in English, the prepositional phrase always goes before the verbal predicate, e.g.

主语 Subject	谓　语　Predicate				
	介词 Preposition	介词的宾语 Prepositional Object	动词 Verb	补语 Comple- ment	助词 Particle
邮票	让	我	贴	在背面	了。
电影票	被	格林	弄	丢	了。
化验单	叫	他	拿	走	了。

否定词放在介词的前边。例如：

The negative adverb comes before the preposition, e.g.

　　(1) 那套纪念邮票别让他弄去了。

　　(2) 那本书没让他拿走，在我这儿呢。

2. 意义上的被动句

Notional Passive Sentences

谓语中没有表示被动的"被、让、叫"等词，而主语在意义上却是受事，这种句子是意义上的被动句。它在形式上同主语是施事的句子没有区别，只能根据意义来判断。例如：

A notional passive sentence is one whose predicate contains no preposition sucb as 被,让 or 叫, and whose subject is the acceptor of the action in meaning. Formally the sentence with a doer-subject and the sentence with an acceptor-subject are same, therefore can be distinguished only by the meaning, e.g.

　　(1) 那封信寄出去了吗？

　　(2) 上衣解开了。

　　(3) 邮票贴在背面了。

注意：汉语的"被"字句没有英语被动语态用得广泛、频繁。汉语的"被"字句，英语一般译成被动语态；而英语的被动语态，汉语有时用主动句。

Please note that Chinese sentences with 被 are not used as often as the English passive ones. The two may be equal when the former is put into English. However an active sentence sometimes does well for the Chinese translation of the latter.

练 习 Exercises

1. 把下列"被"字句改成主动句（不用"把"字）：
   Change the following into active sentences:
   (1) 那些东西都让他吃完了。
   (2) 那本有意思的书叫他买来了。
   (3) 化验单被他弄丢了。
   (4) 我刚买的书被谁拿走了？

2. 把下列"把"字句改成"被"字句：
   Change the following into sentences with 被:
   (1) 他把电影票弄丢了。
   (2) 我把练习都作完了。
   (3) 格林把你的那本书拿走了。
   (4) 谁把信寄走了？

3. 把下列"被"字句改成"把"字句：
   Change the following into sentences with 把:
   (1) 邮票让我贴在背面了。
   (2) 我刚买的那本书被他弄丢了。
   (3) "太"字叫他写成"大"了。
   (4) 我的英磅被弟弟换成美元了。

4. 把下列句子改成用"是不是"的问句：
   Change the following into interrogative sentences with
   是不是：
   (1) 那封信寄出去了吗？
   (2) 上衣解开了吗？
   (3) 那本书拿回来了没有？
   (4) 你的东西寄回家去了没有？

213

二十二、打 电 话
dǎ diàn huà

On the Telephone

211. 喂，你是哪里？
Wèi, nǐ shi nǎli?

Hello, where is it calling from?

212. 你是北京饭店吗？请转 328 分机。
Nǐ shi Běijīng Fàndiàn ma? Qǐng zhuǎn sān-èr-bā fēnjī.

Is that Beijing Hotel? Extension 328, please.

213. 错了。
Cuò le.

The number is wrong.

214. 你找谁呀？
Nǐ zǎo shuí ya?

Who are you going to speak to?

215. 劳驾，请找一下史密斯先生。
Láojià, qǐng zǎo yíxià Shǐmìsī xiānsheng.

May I speak to Mr. Smith?

216. 好，请等一等。
Hǎo, qǐng děng-yiděng.

Hold on a minute, please.

217. 请你大点儿声，我听不清楚。
Qǐng ni dà diǎnr shēngr, wǒ tīng bu qīngchu.

Please speak louder. I can't hear you.

218. 出租汽车站的电话是多少号？
Chūzū qìchēzhàn de diànhuà shi duōshao hào?

What's the phone number of the taxi company?

219. 我要打个电话叫一辆出租汽车。
Wǒ yào dǎ ge diànhuà jiào yí liàng chūzū qìchē.

I want to make a phone call for a taxi.

220. 我们坐公共汽车进城。
Wǒmen zuò gōnggòng qìchē jìn chéng.

We're going to town by bus.

替换练习　Substitution Drills

1. 你是

| 北京饭店 |
| 友谊商店 |
| 出租汽车站 |
| 北京大学 |
| 语言学院 |

吗？

2. 你找

| 谁呀 |
| 张老师吗 |
| 什么 |
| 信吗 |
| 邮票吗 |

？

3．好，请等
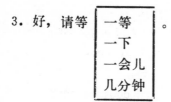
。

4．我们坐
公共汽车
无轨电车
出租汽车
进城。

会　话　Dialogues

甲：喂，你是哪里？
　　Wèi, nǐ shì nǎli?

乙：我是北京语言学院，你是北京饭店吗？
　　Wǒ shì Běijīng Yǔyán Xuéyuàn, nǐ shì Běijīng Fàn-
　　diàn ma?

甲：错了。
　　Cuò le.

乙：对不起。
　　Duì bu qǐ.

　　⋯⋯

乙：喂，是北京饭店吗？
　　Wèi, shì Běijīng Fàndiàn ma?

丙：是啊！
　　Shì a!

216

乙：请转 5024 分机。
Qǐng zhuǎn wǔ-líng-èr-sì fēnjī.

丙：你找谁呀？
Nǐ zhǎo shuí ya?

乙：劳驾，请找一下史密斯先生。
Láojià, qǐng zhǎo yíxià Shǐmìsī xiānsheng.

丙：请等一等。
Qǐng děng-yiděng.

乙：你是史密斯先生吗？
Nǐ shi Shǐmìsī xiānsheng ma?

丁：是，你是谁呀？
Shì, nǐ shi shuí ya?

乙：我是约翰。
Wǒ shì Yuēhàn.

丁：你好，约翰！
Nǐ hǎo, Yuēhàn!

乙：你好！明天我去看你，好吗？
Nǐ hǎo! Míngtiān wǒ qù kàn ni, hǎo ma?

丁：什么？请你大点儿声，我听不清楚。
Shénme? Qǐng ni dà diǎnr shēngr, wǒ tīng bu qīngchu.

乙：明天上午我去看你，好吗？
Míngtiān shàngwǔ wǒ qù kàn ni, hǎo ma?

丁：好。
Hǎo.

乙：我坐出租汽车去，十二点到。
Wǒ zuò chūzū qìchē qù, shí'èr diǎn dào.

丁：好，我等你。
Hǎo, wǒ děng ni.

乙：再见。
Zàijiàn.

丁：再见。
Zàijiàn.

*   *   *

甲：请问，出租汽车站的电话是多少号？
Qǐng wèn, chūzū qìchēzhàn de diànhuà shi duōshao hào?

乙：我不知道，你可以问问114。
Wǒ bù zhīdao, nǐ kěyǐ wènwen yāo-yāo-sì.

甲：喂，是114吗？
Wèi, shì yāo-yāo-sì ma?

丙：是的。
Shì de.

甲：劳驾，出租汽车站的电话是多少号？
Láojià, chūzū qìchēzhàn de diànhuà shi duōshao hào?

丙：55,7661。
wǔ-wǔ-qī-liù-liù-yāo。

甲：谢谢你。
Xièxie ni.

丙：不谢。
Bú xiè

⋯⋯

甲：是出租汽车站吗？
Shì chūzū qìchēzhàn ma?

丁：是。
Shì.

甲：我要一辆出租汽车。
Wǒ yào yí liàng chūzū qìchē.

丁：你是哪里？
Nǐ shi nǎli?

甲：友谊宾馆，246房间，我叫玛丽娅。
Yǒuyì Bīnguǎn, èr-sì-liù fángjiān, wǒ jiào Mǎlìyà.

丁：你去什么地方？
Nǐ qù shénme dìfang?

甲：北京饭店。
Běijīng Fàndiàn.

丁：好的。
Hǎo de.

甲：再见。
Zàijiàn.

丁：再见。
Zàijiàn.

生 词 New Words

1. 喂 （叹）wèi   hello
2. 哪里 （代）nǎli   where
3. 转 （动）zhuǎn   to connect to (an extension)
4. 分机 （名）fēnjī   extension
5. 错 （形）cuò   wrong
6. 找 （动）zhǎo   to look for
7. 一下 yíxià   (a verbal measure word)
8. 等 （动）děng   to wait

9. 声　　　（名）shēngr　　　voice, sound
10. 清楚　　（形）qīngchu　　　clear
11. 出租汽车　　chūzū qìchē　　taxi
12. 电话　　（名）diànhuà　　　telephone
13. 打　　　（动）dǎ　　　to make (a phone call)
14. 叫　　　（动）jiào　　　to call
15. 辆　　　（量）liàng　　　(a measure word)
16. 公共汽车　　gōnggōng qìchē bus
17. 城　　　（名）chéng　　　town
18. 一会儿　　　yíhuìr　　　one minute, a moment

专　名　Proper Nouns

1. 北京大学　　Běijīng Dàxué Beijing University
2. 玛丽娅　　　Mǎlìyà　　　Maria

语　法　Grammar

1. 连动句（二）

Double Verbal Sentences (B)

连动句（一）指的是一个主语的两个动词所表示的行为有先有后，虽然后一行为有时兼表目的。连动句（二）是指后一动词所说的行为只是前一动词所说行为的目的。例如：

In double verbal sentences (A) we discussed how the predicate of a sentence contains two verbs of which the following verb sometimes indicates the purpose of the preceding one. Now in this part we shall deal with the similar sentences in which the following verb of the predicate only indicates the purpose of the preceding one, e.g.

220

(1) 我要打个电话叫一辆出租汽车。

(2) 我打算明天去长城看看。

(3) 我明天到北京饭店找史密斯先生。

注意：表示目的的动词或动词词组一定放在另一动词后面（词序同英语基本相同）。

Please note that the purposive verb or verbal phrase can only be placed behind the other verb (the word order is like the similar English sentences).

2. 连动句（三）

Double Verbal Sentences （C）

连动句（三）是指前一动词所说的行为是后一动词所说行为的方式。例如：

Then there is another type of the double verbal sentences in which the preceding verb of the predicate denotes the way of the action expressed by the following verb, e.g.

(1) 我们坐公共汽车进城。

(2) 格林坐飞机去上海了。

(3) 他学了三年，可以用汉语说了。

注意：这种连动句译成英语一般不用两个动词，表示方式用"by…"或"with…"等介词词组。

N.B. The prepositional phrases such as "by…" or "with …" are very useful for the English translation of the sentences shown above.

3. 动词+"一下"

A Verb Plus 一下

"下"是动量词，"一下"作动词补语，表示一次短促的动作。"了"字放在动词后，名词宾语一般放在"一下"后面。代词宾语则常放在"一下"前面。例如：

下 is a verbal measure word. 一下, meaning a brief action, can be used as a complement. It is often followed by a nominal object, but preceded by a prenominal object. As to 了 it comes directly after the verb as a rule, e.g.

(1) 请等一下，我就来。
(2) 你在这儿坐一下，我去打个电话。
(3) 请找一下史密斯先生。
(4) 让我看一下那本书，好吗？
(5) 你问他一下，电影几点开演？
(6) 他找了一下，说没有。

练 习 Exercises

1. 用连动式完成下列句子：

Complete the following sentences, using double verbal structures:

(1) 今天下午没课，我要_____买东西。
(2) 长城离这儿很远，我们_____去。
(3) 明天我去北京饭店_____。
(4) 我要_____找一下格林先生。

2. 完成下列对话：

Complete the following dialogues:

(1) A：你打电话找谁？

　　B：_____。

　　A：你明天进城吗？

　　B：_____。

　　A：你怎么去？

　　B：_____。

222

（2） A：你打算去长城看看吗？

　　 B：＿＿＿＿＿＿＿＿＿＿＿＿＿。

　　 A：我也打算去。

　　 B：＿＿＿＿＿＿＿＿＿＿＿＿＿。

　　 A：我们怎么去，坐火车还是坐汽车？

　　 B：＿＿＿＿＿＿＿＿＿＿＿＿＿。

（3） A：你找谁呀？

　　 B：＿＿＿＿＿＿＿＿＿＿＿＿＿。

　　 A：他住几号房间？

　　 B：＿＿＿＿＿＿＿＿＿＿＿＿＿。

　　 A：好，请等一下。

（4） A：这双布鞋比较大，您试一下。

　　 B：＿＿＿＿＿＿＿＿＿＿＿＿＿。

　　 A：您再试一下这双。

　　 B：＿＿＿＿＿＿＿＿＿＿＿＿＿。

　　 A：请到那儿交钱。

二十三、看 京 剧
kàn jīng jù
Seeing a Beijing Opera

221. 你在干什么呢？
Nǐ zài gàn shénme ne?

What are you doing there?

222. 我在给格林留条儿。
Wǒ zài gěi Gélín liú tiáor.

I'm leaving Mr. Green a note.

223. 什么事？
Shéme shì?

What for?

224. 通知他看京剧。
Tōngzhī ta kàn jīngjù.

Telling him that we're going to see a Beijing opera.

225. 格林对京剧非常感兴趣。
Gélín duì jīngjù fēicháng gǎn xìngqù.

Mr. Green is very interested in Beijing opera.

226. 明天晚上，学校组织我们看京剧，你去吗？
Míngtiān wǎnshang, xuéxiào zǔzhī wǒmen kàn jīnjù, nǐ
qù ma?

The institute will arrange for us to see a Beijing opera
tomorrow evening. Are you going?

227. 当然去，你拿到票了吗？

Dāngrán qù, nǐ nádào piào le ma?

Certainly I'll go. Have you got the ticket?

228. 张老师让我把这张票给你。

Zhāng lǎoshī, ràng wo bǎ zhè zhāng piào gěi ni.

Mr. Zhang asked me to give you this ticket.

229. 明天晚上几点钟出发？

Míngtiān wǎnshang jǐ diǎnzhōng chūfā?

When are we leaving tomorrow evening?

230. 六点一刻开车，别迟到！

Liù diǎn yí kè kāi chē, bié chídào!

The school bus will leave at 6.15 pm. Don't be late!

替换练习 Substitution Drills

1. 你在 | 干什么呢 | ?
         | 打电话吗 |
         | 看书吗 |
         | 写信吗 |

2. 我在给格林 | 留条儿 | 。
              | 寄包裹 |
              | 打电话 |
              | 写信 |

3. 格林对 | 京剧 | 非常感兴趣。
　　　　| 汉语 |
　　　　| 这部电影 |
　　　　| 旅行 |

4. 明天晚上，| 学校 | 组织我们 | 看京剧 |，你去吗？
　　　　　　| 老师 |　　　　 | 看电影 |

5. 张老师让我把 | 这张票 | 给 | 你 |。
　　　　　　　 | 这本书 |　　| 王丽 |
　　　　　　　 | 这封信 |　　| 玛丽娅 |
　　　　　　　 | 这个本子 |　 | 布朗 |

会 话 Dialogues

甲：你在干什么呢？
　　Nǐ zài gàn shénme ne?

乙：我在给格林留条儿。
　　Wǒ zài gěi Gélín liú tiáor.

甲：什么事？
　　Shéme shì?

乙：通知他看京剧。
　　Tōngzhī ta kàn jīngjù.

甲：什么京剧？
　　Shénme jīngjù?

乙：《闹天宫》，张老师让我把票给他。
《Nào Tiāngōng》, Zhāng lǎoshī ràng wo bǎ piào gěi ta·

甲：你对京剧感兴趣吗？
Nǐ duì jīngjù gǎn xìngqù ma?

乙：非常感兴趣。你呢？
Fēicháng gǎn xìngqù. Nǐ ne?

甲：我也是。
Wǒ yě shì.

乙：你去吗？
Nǐ qù ma?

甲：当然去，
Dāngrán qù.

乙：你拿到票了吗？
Nǐ nádào piào le ma?

甲：拿到了。几点出发？
Nádào le. Jǐ diǎn chūfā?

乙：晚上六点开车，别迟到！
Wǎnshang liù diǎn kāi chē, bié chídào!

甲：知道了。
Zhīdao le.

*   *   *

甲：玛丽在干什么呢？
Mǎlì zài gàn shénme ne?

乙：玛丽在看书呢，有事吗？
Mǎlì zài kàn shū ne, yǒu shì ma?

甲：老师让我通知她看京剧。
Lǎoshī ràng wo tōngzhī ta kàn jīngjù.

乙：在哪儿看？
Zài nǎr kàn?

甲：人民剧场。
Rénmín Jùchǎng.

乙：什么时候？
Shénme shíhou?

甲：明天晚上七点。
Míngtiān wǎnshang qī diǎn.

乙：演什么？
Yǎn shénme?

甲：不知道。请你把这张票给玛丽。
Bù zhīdao. Qǐng nǐ bǎ zhè zhāng piào gěi Mǎlì.

乙：好。
Hǎo.

甲：你对京剧感不感兴趣？
Nǐ duì jīngjù gǎn bu gǎn xìngqù?

乙：很感兴趣。
Hěn gǎn xìngqù.

甲：来中国以后，你看过几次？
Lái Zhōngguó yǐhòu, nǐ kànguo jǐ cì?

乙：我只看过一次。
Wǒ zhǐ kànguo yí cì

甲：明天你去吗？
Míngtiān nǐ qù ma?

乙：当然去！
Dāngrán qù!

甲：你拿到票了吗？
Nǐ nádào piào le ma?

乙：拿到了。
Nádào le.

甲：六点半开车，别迟到！
Liù diǎn bàn kāi chē, bié chídào!

生　词　New Words

1.	干	（动）gàn	to do
2.	给	（介）gěi	to, for
3.	留	（动）liú	to leave
4.	条儿	（名）tiáor	short note
5.	通知	（动、名）tōngzhī	to notify
6.	对	（介）duì	to, for
7.	非常	（副）fēicháng	extremely
8.	感	（动）gǎn	to feel
9.	兴趣	（名）xìngqù	interest
10.	学校	（名）xuéxiào	school, educational institution in general
11.	组织	（动、名）zǔzhī	to organize
12.	当然	（形、副）dāngrán	of course
13.	出发	（动）chūfā	to start off

专　名　Proper Noun

闹天宫　　Nào Tiāngōng　The Monkey Creates Havoc in Heaven

语　法　Grammar

1. **兼语句**

229

Double Functioning Sentences

兼语句是动词谓语句的一种，一般是由一前一后两个动词中间夹一个名词或代词组成。这个名词或代词既是前一个动词的宾语，又是后一个动词的主语，所以叫兼语。兼语句前一个动词常是"让、叫、请"等一类有使令意义的动词。

Double functing sentences are classified as those with a verbal predicate. They have two verbs between which is inserted a noun or pronoun functioning ɔs the object of the first verb, but as the subject of the second one. The first verb is often expressed by a factitive verb such as 让、叫 or 请.

主　语 Subject	谓　　　　　　　　语 Predicate			
	动　词 Verb	兼　　　语 Object-Subject	动　　　词 Verb	宾　语 Object
学校	组织	我们	看	京剧。
格林	叫	我	去	他家。
张老师	让	我	（把这张票)给	你。
他	（没)请	格林	吃	饭。

2. 动词的进行态

The Progressive Aspect of Verbs

要表示一个动作正在进行，可以在动词前加副词"在"、"正在"，也可以在句尾加语气助词"呢"。"在"或"正在"也可以和"呢"同时用。例如：

The progressive aspect of an action may be shown by the adverb 在 or 正在 before the verb, or by the modal particle 呢 at the end of the sentence; 在 or 正在 may go simultaneously with 呢 in one sentence, e.g.

(1) 你在干什么呢？

(2) 我在给格林留条儿。

(3) 张老师正在上课呢！

(4) 他们正在学习。

练 习 Exercises

1. 用疑问代词提问划线部分：

Ask questions about the underlined part with an interrogative pronoun:

(1) 张先生请我进城吃饭。

(2) 我父亲让我到中国去学习汉语。

(3) 格林叫我把信给他。

(4) 玛丽让他给你打电话。

2. 完成下列句子：

Complete the following sentences:

(1) 张先生让我把＿＿＿＿＿＿＿＿。

(2) 格林打电话叫我明天＿＿＿＿＿＿＿＿。

(3) 学校组织＿＿＿＿＿＿＿电影。

(4) 史密斯先生明天让你到他那儿＿＿＿＿＿。

(5) 他打算请张老师＿＿＿＿＿＿＿。

3. 完成下列对话：

Complete the following dialogues:

(1) A：＿＿＿＿＿＿＿＿?

B：我在看书呢。

A：你什么时候去看电影呢？

B：＿＿＿＿＿＿＿，

(2) A：你在写信吗？

B：＿＿＿＿＿＿＿。

A：给谁写信？

B：＿＿＿＿＿＿＿·。

(3) A：你在买什么呢？

B：＿＿＿＿＿＿＿。

A：还打算买别的吗？

B：＿＿＿＿＿＿＿。

A：那买完就走吧。

B：＿＿＿＿＿＿＿。

(4) A：你在给谁打电话？

B：＿＿＿＿＿＿＿。

A：让他来看京剧吗？

B：＿＿＿＿＿＿＿。

二十四、谈 天 气
tán tiān qì

Talking about the Weather

231. 今天天气怎么样?

Jīntiān tiānqì zěnmeyàng?

How's the weather today?

232. 明天下雨吗?

Míngtiān xià yǔ ma?

Is it going to rain tomorrow?

233. 天气预报说，明天晴天，没有雨。

Tiānqì yùbào shuō, míngtiān qíngtiān, méi yǒu yǔ;

The weather forecast says that it's going to be sunny without a drop of rain tomorrow.

234. 你家乡的冬天冷不冷?

Nǐ jiāxiāng de dōngtiān lěng bu lěng?

Is it cold in winter in your home town?

235. 不冷，我家乡的冬天比北京暖和。

Bù lěng, wǒ jiāxiāng de dōngtiān bǐ Běijīng nuǎnhuo.

No. Winter is warmer in my home town than in Beijing.

236. 那里的夏天没有北京热。

Nàli de xiàtiān méiyǒu Běijīng rè.

Summer there is not so hot as in Beijing.

237. 今天跟昨天一样凉快。
Jīntiān gēn zuótiān yíyàng liángkuai.

Today is just as cool as yesterday.

238. 北京的秋天最好，春天常常刮风。
Běijīng de qiūtiān zuì hǎo, chūntiān chángcháng guā fēng.

Autumn is the best season in Beijing,but spring is often
windy.

239. 你对这儿的天气习惯吗?
Nǐ duì zhèr de tiānqì xíguàn ma?

Have you got used to the weather here?

240. 还好，这里的天气跟我家乡差不多。
Hái hǎo, zhèlǐ de tiānqì gēn wǒ jiāxiāng chà bu duō.

I feel it's O.K. Weather here is about the same as we
have in my home town.

替换练习　Substitution Drills

1. 天气预报说，明天 | 晴天 | 。

晴天
阴天
下雨
刮风
下雪
很热
很冷

2.

我家乡
上海
罗马
东京

的冬天比北京暖和。

3.

那里
北京
伦敦

的夏天没有

北京	
南京	这么
上海	那么

热。

4.

今天
这本书
汽车

跟

昨天
那本书
电车

一样

凉快
难
快

。

会 话 Dialogues

甲：今天天气怎么样？
Jīntiān tiānqì zěnmeyàng?

乙：今天天气很好。
Jīntiān tiānqì hěn hǎo.

甲：明天天气好吗？
Míugtiān tiānqì hǎo ma?

乙：天气预报说，明天阴天。
Tiānqì yùbào shuō, míngtiān yīntiān.

甲：明天下不下雨？
Míngtiān xià bu xià yǔ?

235

乙: 明天不下雨。
Míngtiān bú xià yǔ.

甲: 昨天热不热?
Zuótiān rè bu rè?

乙: 不热，昨天跟今天一样凉快。
Bú rè, zuótiān gēn jīntiān yíyàng liángkuai.

甲: 北京的秋天最好，春天常常刮风。
Běijīng de qiūtiān zuì hǎo, chūntiān chángcháng guā fēng.

乙: 是的，我最喜欢北京的秋天，不喜欢北京的春天。
Shì de, wǒ zuì xǐhuan Běijīng de qiūtiān, bù xǐhuan Běijīng de chūntiān.

　　　　　*　　　　　*　　　　　*

甲: 你是哪国人?
Nǐ shi nǎguó rén?

乙: 我是意大利人。
Wǒ shi Yìdàlì rén.

甲: 你家在哪儿?
Nǐ jiā zài nǎr?

乙: 我家在罗马。
Wǒ jiā zài Luómǎ.

甲: 你家乡的冬天冷不冷?
Nǐ jiāxiāng de dōngtiān lěng bu lěng?

乙: 不冷，我家乡的冬天比北京暖和。
Bù lěng, wǒ jiāxiāng de dōngtiān bǐ Běijīng nuǎnhuo.

甲：罗马夏天热吗？
Luómǎ xiàtiān rè ma?

乙：那里夏天没有北京热。
Nàli xiàtiān méiyǒu Běijīng rè.

甲：你对这儿的天气习惯吗？
Nǐ duì zhèr de tiānqì xíguàn ma?

乙：还好，这里的天气跟我家乡差不多。
Hái hǎo, zhèli de tiānqì gēn wǒ jiāxiāng chà bu duō.

生　词　New Words

1.	天气	（名）tiānqì	weather
2.	下	（动）xià	to fall
3.	雨	（名）yǔ	rain
4.	预报	（动、名）yùbào	to forecast
5.	晴天	（名）qíngtiān	sunny
6.	家乡	（名）jiāxiāng	home town (village)
7.	冬天	（名）dōngtiān	winter
8.	比	（介）bǐ	than
9.	暖和	（形）nuǎnhuo	warm
10.	那里	（代）nàli	there
11.	热	（形）rè	hot
12.	凉快	（形）liángkuai	cool
13.	秋天	（名）qiūtiān	autumn
14.	春天	（名）chūntiān	spring
15.	常常	（副）chángcháng	often
16.	刮	（名）guā	to blow (of wind)
17.	风	（动）fēng	wind

18. 习惯	（名、动）	xíguàn	to get used to
19. 差不多		chà bu duō	about same
20. 那么	（代）	nàme	such, so
21. 阴天	（名）	yīntiān	cloudy
22. 雪	（名）	xuě	snow
23. 快	（形）	kuài	quick

专 名　Proper Noun

意大利	Yìdàlì	Italy

语 法　Grammal

1. 用"比"的比较句

Sentences of Comparison with 比

　　有的句子用"比"表示比较，说明两个事物的差别。这种句子一般用形容词作谓语主要成分，即："主语＋比＋宾语＋形容词"。形容词前面可加表示程度增高的副词"更"，后面可带表示程度或表示数量的补语。例如：

In some sentences of comparison 比 is used to indicate the difference of two things. The adjective may serve as the main part of the predicate, i.e. "subject ＋比＋object＋adjective". The adverb of degree 更 often appears before the adjective, and a complement of degree or quantity after it, e.g.

主　　　　语 Subject	谓　　　　　　　语 Predicate				
定语＋名词 Adjectiveal Mo- difier＋Noun	比 比	宾　语 Object	状　语 Adver- bial Modifier	形容词 Adjective	补　语 Comple- ment
我家乡的冬天	比	北京		暖和。	
我们那里	比	这里		冷	多了。
那里的夏天	比	这里	还	热	一点儿。
我哥哥	比	我弟弟		大	五岁。
你的发音	比	他	更	好。	

否定词"不"放在"比"的前面。例如：

The negative adverb should be placed before 比, e.g.

　　(1) 北京的夏天不比上海（的夏天）热。

　　(2) 我写的汉字不比他(写的汉字)好。

　　在不会发生歧义的情况下，可以有省略的说法，如上面的例(1)和例(2)。

It is possible to omit some words as found in the examples (1) and (2) if no ambiguity is caused.

　　注意：在用"比"的句子里，形容词前只能用"更"、"还"等程度副词，不能用"很"、"太"、"非常"、"比较"等副词。

N.B. In a sentence with 比, only the adverbs of degree such as 更 or 还 can be used before the adjective instead of 很，太，非常，比较, etc..

2．用"没有"的比较句

Sentences of Comparison with 没有

　　有的比较句用"没有"表示不及。形容词前常有"这么"或"那么"。例如：

没有 can be used to indicate inequality in comparison. In that case 这么 or 那么 often goes before the adjective, e.g.

主　　　语 Subject	谓　　　　　　　语 Predicate			
定语＋名词 Adjectival Modifier＋Noun	没有	宾　　语 Object	这么 ／ 那么	形容词 Adjective
那里的夏天 那儿 我写的	没有 没有 没有	北京 颐和园 他	 这么 那么	热。 有意思。 好。

3.“跟……一样”

The Structure 跟…一样

有的比较句用“跟…一样”表示相同。例如：

The structure 跟…一样 denotes equality in comparison, e.g.

主　　　语 Subject	谓　　　　　　　语 Predicate			
定语＋名词 Adjectival Modifier＋Noun	跟	宾　　语 Object	一样	形　容　词 Adjeotive
今天 他 他的女儿	跟 跟 跟	昨天 我 我的女儿	一样 一样 一样	凉快。 忙。 大。

4. 无主句

Subjectless Sentences

240

汉语中有些句子是无法说出或无须说出主语的，称无主句。有些无主句是叙述自然现象的，有些是说明生活情况的。例如：

In Chinese it is sometimes impossible or unnecessary to give the subject of a sentence. Some of the subjectless sentences are adopted to describe the natural phenomenon; others are employed to state daily activities, e.g.

主 语 Subject	谓 语 Predicate		语气助词 Modal Particle
	动 词 Verb	宾 语 Object	
	下	雨	了。
	刮	风	了。
	上	课	了。
	打	铃	了。

注意：无主语句和省略主语的句子不同，前者一般是补不出主语的，后者则是可以补出的。

Please note that the subjectless sentence is different from the one whose subject is omitted, because the restoration of the subject is generally impossible for the former.

5. 无主语兼语句

Double Functioning Sentences without a Subject

这种兼语句的第一个动词是"有"，兼语（"有"的宾语）表示的不是确指的人或事物。例如：

Sentences described above have 有 as its first verb, and the duel functioning word (the object of 有) refers to somebody or something in general, e.g.

(1) 格林，有人找你。

(2) 今天有信来吗？

练 习 Exercises

1. 用"比"改写下列句子：

Rewrite the following sentences with 比

(1) 这本书便宜，那本书贵。

(2) 我今年二十，我哥哥二十五。

(3) 昨天热，今天更热。

(4) 北京冬天冷，上海冬天不太冷。

(5) 你写的汉字好，他写的更好。

2. 用"没有"改写下列句子：

Rewrite the following sentences with 没有:

(1) 我今年比去年忙。

(2) 这儿的夏天比我们那儿热。

(3) 今年冬天冷，去年冬天更冷。

(4) 他年纪比我大。

3. 完成下列对话：

Complete the following dialogues:

(1) A：今天天气怎么样？

B：＿＿＿＿＿＿＿＿＿＿＿＿＿。

A：你觉得比昨天热吗？

B：＿＿＿＿＿＿＿＿＿＿＿＿＿。

(2) A：你父亲多大岁数了？

B：＿＿＿＿＿＿＿＿＿＿＿＿＿。

A：＿＿＿＿＿＿＿＿＿＿＿＿＿？

B：我母亲跟我父亲一样大。

242

(3) A：你妹妹多大了？

B：＿＿＿＿＿＿＿＿＿＿。

A：你哥哥比你妹妹大几岁？

B：＿＿＿＿＿＿＿＿＿＿。

(4) A：你工作忙不忙？一天工作几小时？

B：＿＿＿＿＿＿＿＿＿？

A：＿＿＿＿＿＿＿＿＿。

B：那你比我忙多了。

二十五、路　遇
lù　　　　yù

A Chance Meeting

241. 好久没见了，你近来好吗?
Hǎo jiǔ méi jiàn le, nǐ jìnlái hǎo ma?

Haven't seen you for ages ! How are you?

242. 我最近去桂林玩儿了几天。
Wǒ zuìjìn qù Guìlín wánrle jǐ tiān.

I've been to Guilin recently. I stayed there for a few
days.

243. 你是什么时候去的?
Nǐ shì shénme shíhou qù de?

When did you go there?

244. 我是七月十号去的。
Wǒ shì qīyuè shí hào qù de.

I left for Guilin on the tenth July.

245. 你在桂林玩儿得很高兴吧!
Nǐ zài Guìlín wánr de hěn gāoxìng ba !

Did you have a good time in Guilin?

246. 高兴极了，明年还想再去一次。
Gāoxìng jíle, míngnián hái xiǎng zài qù yí cì.

Yes, I enjoyed myself very much. I want to visit

there again next year.

247. 我也很想去。咱们一起去，怎么样?
Wǒ yě hěn xiǎng qù. Zánmen yìqǐ qù, zěnmeyàng?

I want to visit there very much too. Shall we go there together?

248. 那太好了。
Nà tài hǎo le.

That'll be nice.

249. 具体计划我们以后再商量。
Jùtǐ jìhuà wǒmen yǐhòu zài shāngliang.

Let's discuss the details of our plan later.

250. 好，以后电话联系。
Hǎo, yǐhòu diànhuà liánxì.

Fine, we can contact each other by phone later.

替换练习　Substitution Drills

1. 好久没见了，你近来

好吗	?
怎么样	
身体好吗	
工作忙吗	
学习紧张吗	

2. 我是 | 七月十号 | 去的。
　　　　 去年
　　　　 上星期
　　　　 上个月
　　　　 两年以前

3. | 具体计划 | 我们以后再 | 商量 | 。
　 | 具体问题 | 　　　　　 | 讨论 |
　 | 别的事情 | 　　　　　 | 研究 |

会　话　Dialogues

甲：约翰，你好！
　　Yuēhàn, nǐ hǎo!

乙：你好，格林！
　　Nǐ hǎo, Gélín!

甲：好久没见了，你近来好吗？
　　Hǎo jiǔ méi jiàn le, nǐ jìnlái hǎo ma?

乙：很好，谢谢。你呢？
　　Hěn hǎo, xièxie. Nǐ ne?

甲：我最近学习非常紧张。
　　Wǒ zuìjìn xuéxí fēicháng jǐnzhāng.

乙：我学习不太紧张，去桂林玩儿了几天。
　　Wǒ xuéxí bú tài jǐnzhāng, qù Guìlín wánrle jǐ tiān.

甲：你是什么时候去的？
　　Nǐ shi shénme shíhou qù de?

乙：我是七月十五号去的。
　　Wǒ shi qīyuè shíwǔ hào qù de.

246

甲：怎么样？在桂林玩儿得很高兴吧！
Zěnmeyàng? Zài Guìlín wánr de hěn gāoxìng ba?

乙：高兴极了，以后还想再去一次。
Gāoxìng jíle, yǐhòu hái xiǎng zài qù yí cì.

甲：我不想去桂林，我想去杭州玩儿几天。
Wǒ bù xiǎng qù Guìlín, wǒ xiǎng qù Hángzhōu wánr
jǐ tiān.

乙：我也很想去杭州，咱们一起去，怎么样？
Wǒ yě hěn xiǎng qù Hángzhōu, zánmen yìqǐ qù, zěnmeyàng?

甲：那太好了。
Nà tài hǎo le.

乙：具体计划我们以后再商量。
Jùtǐ jìhuà wǒmen yǐhòu zài shāngliang.

甲：好，以后电话联系。
Hǎo, yǐhòu diànhuà liánxì.

*   *   *

甲：好久没见了，你最近到哪儿去了？
Hǎo jiǔ méi jiàn le, nǐ zuìjìn dào nǎr qù le?

乙：我和玛丽到南京玩了几天。
Wǒ hé Mǎlì dào Nánjīng wánrle jǐ tiān.

甲：你们是什么时候去的？
Nǐ men shì shénme shíhou qù de?

乙：我们是上星期一去的。
Wǒmen shì shàng xīngqīyī qù de.

甲：你们是坐火车去的吗？
Nǐmen shì zuò huǒchē qù de ma?

乙：是的，是坐火车去的。
Shì de, shì zuò huǒchē qù de.

甲：南京的天气怎么样？
Nánjīng de tiānqì zěnmeyàng?

乙：热极了，那里的天气比北京热多了。
Rè jíle, nàli de tiānqì bǐ Běijīng rè duō le.

甲：你们去上海了吗？
Nǐmen qù Shànghǎi le ma?

乙：没有。
Méiyǒu

甲：你们是什么时候回来的？
Nǐmen shi shénme shíhou huílai de?

乙：昨天晚上。
Zuótiān wǎnshang.

甲：这个周未，你打算去哪儿度假？
Zhè ge zhōumò, nǐ dǎsuan qù nǎr dù jià?

乙：我打算去内蒙古。
Wǒ dǎsuan qù Nèi-Měnggǔ.

甲：好极了，咱们一起去，好吗？
Hǎo jíle, zánmen yìqǐ qù, hǎo ma?

乙：好，具体问题我们以后再研究。
Hǎo, jùtǐ wèntí wǒmen yǐhòu zài yánjiū.

生 词 New Words

1. 好　　　（副）hǎo　　　quite, very
2. 久　　　（形）jiǔ　　　long
3. 见　　　（动）jiàn　　　to meet
4. 近来　　（名）jìnlái　　recently

248

5.	最近	（名）zuìjìn	lately
6.	玩儿	（动）wánr	to enjoy oneself
7.	咱们	（代）zánmen	we, us
8.	一起	（副、名）yìqǐ	together
9.	具体	（形）jùtǐ	detailed, concrete
10.	计划	（名、动）jìhuà	plan
11.	商量	（动）shāngliang	to discuss, to talk over
12.	去年	（名）qùnián	last year
13.	上星期	shàng xīngqī	last week
14.	上个月	shàng ge yuè	last month
15.	问题	（名）wèntí	question, problem
16.	事情	（名）shìqing	thing
17.	讨论	（动）tǎolùn	to discuss
18.	研究	（动）yánjiū	to consider , to discuss

专 名 Proper Nouns

1.	桂林	Guìlín	name of a place
2.	杭州	Hángzhōu	name of a place
3.	内蒙古	Nèi-Měnggǔ	Inner Mongolia

语 法 Grammar

1. "是…的"句〔注〕

Sentences with the Structure 是…的

汉语用"是…的"的动词谓语句来强调已发生动作的时间、地点、方式等等，"是"字也可以省略。例如：

The structure 是…的 is used in a sentence with a verbal predicate to denote when, where or how an action took place.

是 in the structure may be omitted, e.g.

    (1) 你是什么时候去的?

    (2) 我是七月十号去的。

    (3) 格林是从美国来的。

    (4) 他们是几点出发的?

如果动词有宾语,"的"字常常放在宾语前面。例如:

If the verb takes an object, 的 often comes before the object, e.g.

    (5) 我是在张先生那儿给你打的电话。

    (6) 他坐飞机去的上海。

否定形式是:"不是…的","是"字不能省略。

The negative form of the structure is 不是…的 (here 的 is never omitted).

    (7) 格林不是坐飞机来的,是坐火车来的。

2. 前置宾语(一)

Preposed Objects (A)

为了突出宾语,有时可以使宾语出现在句首,称前置宾语。例如:

A Preposed object is one which prominently appears at the beginning of the sentence, e.g.

宾语 Object	主语 Subject	谓语 Predicate
具体计划	我们	以后再商量。
你要的书	他	已经给你买来了。

练 习 Exercises

1. 用疑问代词提问划线部分:

Ask questions about the underlined part of the following sentences with interrogative pronouns:

(1) 我是七月十号从日本来的。

(2) 我们是坐飞机来中国的。

(3) 格林先生是跟张老师一起去长城玩儿的。

(4) 他是在飞机上给你写信的。

(5) 我是在友谊商店买的上衣。

2. 根据实际情况回答下列问题：

Give your own answers to the following questions:

(1) 你是从哪个国家来的？

(2) 你是什么时候到这儿的？

(3) 你是怎么来的，坐飞机还是坐火车？

(4) 你是一个人来的，还是跟同学一起来的？

(5) 来这儿以后你看过京剧吗？

(6) 你是在哪儿看的？

(7) 你是自己去买的京剧票吗？

(8) 你觉得京剧怎么样？

3. 用下列各组词语造带前置宾语的句子：

Make sentences with a preposed object, using the words given below:

例：学过　汉语　日语 → 汉语我学过，日语我没学过。

(1) 去过　北京　上海

(2) 打算　承德　大同

(3) 能看　英文报　中文报

〔注〕见 166 页的 2. 语气助词"的"。 See *The Stractural particle* 的，page 164

二十六、游览北京

yóu lǎn Běi jīng

Go Sightseeing in Beijing

251. 你是第一次到北京来吧？

Nǐ shi dì-yī cì dào Běijīng lái ba?

Is this your first visit to Beijing?

252. 不，这是第二次，一九八〇年来过一次。

Bù, zhè shi dì-èr cì, yī-jiǔ-bā-líng nián láiguo yí cì

No, this is my second visit. I came here in 1980.

253. 好多名胜古迹你都游览过吧？

Hǎo duō míngshèng gǔjī nǐ dōu yóulǎnguo ba?

Have you visited many places of historical interest and scenic beauty?

254. 上次来，因为家里有事，提前回国了，很多地方没去。

Shàng cì lái, yīnwèi jiāli yǒu shì, tíqián huí guó le, hěn duō dìfang méi qù.

I couldn't go to many places last time, because I got something to attend to at home then, and so left a few days earlier before the due date.

255. 长城去过了吧？

Chángchéng qùguo le ba?

Have you ever been to the Great Wall?

256. 除了长城、故宫以外，你还去过哪些地方?
Chúle Chángchéng, Gùgōng yǐwài, nǐ hái qùguo nǎxiē dìfang?

Where else did you visit apart from the Great Wall and the Palace Museum?

257. 除了长城、故宫以外，我什么地方都没去过。
Chúle Chángchéng, Gùgōng yǐwài, wǒ shénme dìfang dōu méi qùguo.

I haven't been to any places except the Great Wall and the Palace Museum.

258. 人民公社你也可以去参观参观。
Rénmín gōngshè nǐ yě kěyǐ qù cānguan-cānguan.

You may as well visit some people's communes.

259. 参观公社，可以了解中国农民的生活。
Cānguān gōngshè, kěyǐ liǎojiě Zhōngguó nóngmín de shēnghuó.

Visiting people's communes helps one know more about the life of the Chinese farmers.

260. 明天参观人民公社，还要访问社员家庭。
Míngtiān cānguān rénmín gōngshè, hái yào fǎngwèn shèyuán jiātíng.

We're going to visit some families during our tour round the people's commune tomorrow.

替换练习 Substitution Drills

1. 你是

第一次
第二次
第五次

到

北京
中国
上海

来吧!

2. 上次来,因为

家里有事
有病
有事情

,提前回国了,很多地方

没去。

3. 除了

长城
加拿大
说优点

以外,你还

去过哪些地方
准备去哪个国家
打算说缺点吗

?

4. 除了

长城、故宫
颐和园
天坛
加拿大

以外,我

什么地方	都
别的地方	都
哪儿	也
什么国家	也

没去

过。

5.

人民公社
社员家庭
很多名胜古迹

你也可以去

参观参观
访问访问
游览游览

。

254

会 话 Dialogues

甲: 你是第一次到北京来吧？
Nǐ shì dì-yī cì dào Běijīng lái ba?

乙: 不，这是第二次，去年来过一次。
Bù, zhè shì dì-èr cì, qùnián láiguo yí cì.

甲: 好多名胜古迹你都游览过吧？
Hǎo duō míngshèng gǔjī nǐ dōu yóulǎnguo ba?

乙: 上次来，因为家里有事，提前回国了，很多地
方没去。
Shàng cì lái, yīnwèi jiāli yǒu shì, tíqián huí guó le, hěn
duō dìfang méi qù.

甲: 长城去过没有？
Chángchéng qùguo méiyǒu?

乙: 去过了。
Qùguo le.

甲: 除了长城以外，你还去过哪些地方？
Chúle Chángchéng yǐwài, nǐ hái qùguo nǎxiē dìfang?

乙: 除了长城以外，我什么地方都没去过。
Chúle Chángchéng yǐwài, wǒ shénme dìfang dōu méi
qùguo.

甲: 人民公社你也可以去参观参观。
Rénmín gōngshè nǐ yě kěyǐ qù cānguan-cānguan.

乙: 是的，参观公社可以了解中国农民的生活。
Shì de, cānguān gōngshè kěyǐ liǎojiě Zhōngguó nóngmín de shēnghuó.

255

甲：我们星期六上午去参观人民公社，还要访问社
员家庭。
Wǒmen xīngqīliù shàngwǔ qù cānguān rénmín gōngshè,
hái yào fǎngwèn shèyuán jiātíng.

乙：好极了。
Hǎo jíle.

*   *   *

甲：你好，史密斯先生！
Nǐ hǎo, Shǐmìsī xiānsheng!

乙：你好！
Nǐ hǎo!

甲：你是第五次来中国吧？
Nǐ shi dì-wǔ cì lái Zhōngguó ba?

乙：不，这是第六次。
Bù, zhè shi dì-liù cì.

甲：中国的很多地方和名胜古迹你都游览过吧？
Zhōngguó de hěn duō dìfang hé míngshèng gǔjī nǐ dōu
yóulǎnguo ba?

乙：除了云南和西藏以外，别的地方我差不多都去
过了。
Chúle Yúnnán hé Xīzàng yǐwài, biéde dìfang wǒ
chà bu duō dōu qùguo le.

甲：人民公社你也参观过吧？
Rénmín gōngshè nǐ yě cānguānguo ba?

乙：我参观过两个公社。
Wǒ cānguānguo liǎng ge gōngshè.

甲：访问社员家庭了吗？
Fǎngwèn shèyuán jiātíng le ma?

乙：访问了。
Fǎngwén le.

甲：明天有些朋友去参观人民公社，你还想去吗？
Míngtiān yǒuxiē péngyou qù cānguān rénmín gōngshè,
nǐ hái xiǎng qù ma?

乙：不能去了，因为家里有事，我要提前回国，坐
今天晚上的飞机走。
Bù néng qù le, yīnwèi jiāli yǒu shì, wǒ yào tíqián
huí guó, zuò jīntiān wǎnshang de fēijī zǒu.

甲：以后你来北京再去。
Yǐhòu nǐ lái Běijīng zài qù.

乙：好，谢谢。再见！
Hǎo, xièxie. Zàijiàn!

甲：再见！
Zàijiàn!

生 词 New Words

1. 第 　　　（头）dì 　　　(a prefix for ordinal numbers)

2. 名胜古迹 　míngshèng gǔjī 　places of historic interest and scenic beauty

3. 游览 　（动）yóulǎn 　to go sightseeing

4. 因为 　（连）yīnwèi 　because

5. 提前 　（动）tíqián 　before the due date

257

6. 除了…以外　(chúle…yǐwài)　except, besides
7. 人民公社　rénmín gōngshè　people's commune
8. 参观　(动) cānguān　to visit
9. 了解　(动) liǎojiě　to understand
10. 农民　(名) nóngmín　farmer
11. 生活　(名) shēnghuó　life
12. 访问　(动) fǎngwèn　to visit
13. 社员　(名) shèyuán　commune member
14. 家庭　(名) jiātíng　family
15. 国家　(名) guójiā　nation, country
16. 优点　(名) yōudiǎn　good points
17. 缺点　(名) quēdiǎn　weak points
18. 准备　(动) zhǔnbèi　to prepare for

专　名　Proper Nouns

1. 加拿大　Jiānádà　Canada
2. 云南　Yúnnán　Yunnan Province
3. 西藏　Xīzàng　Tibet
4. 天坛　Tiāntán　The Temple of Heaven

语　法　Grammar

1. "除了…以外"

The Structure 除了…以外

"除了"，介词，跟名词、动词、形容词、主谓词组相结合，后面可加"以外"。"除了…以外"可以放在主语前，也可以放在主语后，但不能放在句子末尾。它有两种用法：

除了, a preposition, can go before a noun, verb, an

258

adjective, or a subject-predicate group. The prepositional group, often ended with 以外, may be used before or after the subject, but can never be put at the end of the sentence. It has two usages:

(A) 排除已知，补充其他，后面常用"还"、"也"呼应。例如：

It adds something to what has been known or stated, and is often used with 还 or 也, e.g.

(1) 除了长城、故宫以外，你还去过哪些地方？

(2) 这儿会说汉语的，除了格林，还有玛丽和史密斯。

(3) 我除了想学习汉语以外，还想旅行。

(4) 这儿冬天除了冷以外，还有个缺点，就是风大。

(5) 桂林，除了格林去过以外，我也去过。

(B) 排除特殊，强调一致，后面常用"都"呼应。例如：

It is often used with 都, to exclude what has been otherwise stated, e.g.

(6) 除了格林，美国学生都去长城了。

(7) 除了有病，他每天都上课。

后面用"不"、"没（有）"，强调唯一的事情或动作。例如：

It is used with 不 or 没(有), to indicate the only thing or action, e.g.

(8) 昨天晚上，除了格林，没人来过。

(9) 除了长城、故宫以外，我什么地方都没去过。

(10) 我明天除了去故宫，不去别的地方。

2. 动词重叠(二)

Repeated Verbs (B)

汉语有些双音节动词也可以重叠，意义同单音节动词重叠一样。双音节动词重叠形式是"ABAB"。例如：

Some disyllabic verbs have their repeated forms which,

having the same new meaning as the repeated monosyllabic ones, are formed according to the formula "ABAB", e.g.

    (1) 人民公社你也可以去参观参观。

    (2) 参观人民公社，可以了解了解中国农民的生活。

    (3) 你不去访问访问社员家庭吗？

3. 前置宾语（二）

The Preposed Object (B)

为了突出宾语，也可以使宾语出现在动词之前。例如。

An object may be emphasized by placing it before the verb, e.g.

除了长城以外，	主　语 |Subject	宾　语 Object	谓　语 Predicate
	我	什么地方	都没去过。
	他	汉语	学得很好。
	玛丽	英语	说得好极了。

练　习　Exercises

1. 完成下列句子：

Complete the following sentences:

    (1) 昨天下午除了＿＿＿＿＿，我们没有去别的地方。

    (2) 他除了英语以外，还会＿＿＿＿＿。

    (3) 除了＿＿＿＿＿，我还打算去桂林看看。

    (4) 除了＿＿＿＿＿，别的人都去参观人民公社了。

    (5) 来北京学习的，除了＿＿＿＿＿，还有教汉语的老师。

2. 把下列句子改写成有"除了…以外"的句子：

Change the following sentences with 除了…以外：

例： **我只去过桂林，没有去过别的地方。**

　　除了桂林以外，我什么地方都没有去过

　　(1) 我只游览过长城，没有游览过别的地方。

　　(2) 你去过张老师家，我也去过。

　　(3) 格林访问过人民公社，你也访问过人民公社吗？

　　(4) 你到故宫游览过，还到别的地方游览过吗？

　　(5) 上星期天，我去看朋友，没有去别的地方。

3．回答下列问句：

　　Answer the following questions:

　　（1）你是什么时候到桂林游览的？

　　（2）除了桂林，你还游览过什么地方？

　　（3）你能说英语吗？

　　（4）除了英语，你还能说哪种语言？

　　（5）他英语说得很好，汉语说得怎么样？

　　（6）他汉语说得很好，你呢，也说得很好吗？

　　（7）除了中国，你还到过哪些国家？

　　（8）你汉语能说，中文报也能看吗？

　　（9）中文报比较难，我不能看，你呢？

　　（10）你打算什么时候回国？明年还能再来吗？

二十七、看 电 视
kàn diàn shì
Watching the Television

261. 昨天晚上你干什么去了?
Zuótiān wǎngshang nǐ gàn shénme qu le?

What did you do last night?

262. 我到玛丽那儿聊天儿去了。
Wǒ dào Mǎlì nàr liáo tiānr qu le.

I went to see Mary and had a chat with her there.

263. 你看没看电视?
Nǐ kàn mei kàn diànshì?

Did you watch T.V.?

264. 没看,有什么好节目?
Méi kàn, yǒu shénme hǎo jiémù?

No, I didn't. Was there any good program on T.V.?

265. 昨天电视里有足球比赛。
Zuótiān diànshì li yǒu zúqiú bǐsài.

There was a football match on T.V. yesterday.

266. 哪个队对哪个队?
Nǎ ge duì duì nǎ ge duì?

Between which teams?

267. 中国青年队对国家队，踢得精彩极了。
Zhōngguó Qīngniánduì duì Guójiāduì, tī de jīngcǎi jíle.
Between the Chinese Youth and the National. It was excellent.

268. 哪个队赢了？
Nǎ ge duì yíng le?
Who won the game?

269. 国家队。比分是二比一。
Guójiāduì. Bǐfēn shì èr bǐ yī.
The National did. The score was 2 : 1.

270. 要是以后再有足球比赛，请你告诉我一声。
Yàoshì yǐhòu zài yǒu zúqiú bǐsài, qǐng nǐ gāosu wo yìshēng.
Please tell me if there's any football match in future.

替换练习 Substitution Drills

1. | 昨天晚上 | 你干什么去了？
| 昨天下午 |
| 前天早上 |
| 星期日上午 |

2. 我到 | 玛丽 | 那儿 | 聊天 | 去了。
　　　　 王丽　　　　 看电视
　　　　 王老师　　　 谈话
　　　　 张先生　　　 听录音

3. 有什么 | 好节目 | ？
　　　　　 好电影
　　　　　 好京剧

4. 要是以后再有 | 足球比赛 | ，请告诉我一声。
　　　　　　　　 篮球比赛
　　　　　　　　 好电影
　　　　　　　　 好电视节目

会 话 Dialogues

甲：昨天晚上你干什么去了？
Zuótiān wǎnshang nǐ gàn shénme qu le?

乙：我到玛丽那儿聊天儿去了。
Wǒ dào Mǎlì nàr liáo tiānr qu le.

甲：你看没看电视？
Nǐ kàn mei kàn diànshì?

乙：没有，有什么好节目？
Méiyǒu, yǒu shénme hǎo jiémù?

甲：昨天电视里有足球比赛。
Zuótiān diànshì li yǒu zúqiú bǐsài.

264

乙：哪个队对哪个队？
Nǎ ge duì duì nǎ ge duì?

甲：中国青年队对国家队。
Zhōngguó Qīngniánduì duì Guójiāduì.

乙：踢得怎么样？
Tī de zěnmeyàng?

甲：踢得精彩极了。
Tī de jīngcǎi jíle.

乙：哪个队赢了？
Nǎ ge duì yíng le?

甲：国家队。
Guójiāduì.

乙：比分是多少？
Bǐfēn shi duōshao?

甲：比分是三比一。
Bǐfēn shi sān bǐ yī.

乙：要是以后再有足球比赛，请你告诉我一声。
Yàoshi yǐhòu zài yǒu zúqiú bǐsài, qǐng nǐ gàosu wo
yìshēng.

*   *   *

甲：你喜欢看篮球比赛吗？
Nǐ xǐhuan kàn lánqiú bǐsài ma?

乙：非常喜欢。
Fēicháng xǐhuan.

甲：昨天晚上电视里有篮球比赛，你看了没有？
Zuótiān wǎnshang diànshì li yǒu lánqiú bǐsài, nǐ kànle
méiyǒu?

乙：没有。
Méiyǒu.

甲：你干什么去了？
Nǐ gàn shénme qu le?

乙：我到教室听录音去了。
Wǒ dào jiàoshì tīng lùyīn qu le.

甲：你什么时候回来的？
Nǐ shénme shíhou huílai de?

乙：八点回来的。
Bā diǎn huílai de.

甲：那时候，比赛刚开始。你怎么不来看？
Nà shíhou, bǐsài gāng kāishǐ. Nǐ zěnme bù lái kàn?

乙：我不知道。哪个队对哪个队？
Wǒ bù zhīdao. Nǎ ge duì duì nǎ ge duì?

甲：北京队对上海队。
Běijīngduì duì Shànghǎiduì.

乙：他们打得怎么样？
Tāmen dǎ de zěnmeyàng?

甲：他们打得好极了。
Tāmen dǎ de hǎo jíle.

乙：谁赢了？
Shuí yíng le?

甲：北京队，比分是八十五比七十六。
Běijīngduì, bǐfēn shi bāshí wǔ bǐ qīshí liù.

乙：以后再有篮球比赛，请你告诉我一声。
Yǐhòu zài yǒu lánqiú bǐsài, qǐng nǐ gàosu wo yìshēng.

甲：好。
Hǎo.

生 词 New Words

1. 聊天儿   liáo tiānr   to chat
2. 电视   （名）diànshì   television
3. 节目   （名）jiémù   program
4. 足球   （名）zúqiú   football
5. 比赛   （名）bǐsài   match
6. 队   （名）duì   team
7. 对   （动）duì   versus, against
8. 青年   （名）qīngnián   youth
9. 踢   （动）tī   to kick
10. 精彩   （形）jīngcǎi   excellent
11. 赢   （动）yíng   to win
12. 比分   （名）bǐfēn   score
13. 要是   （连）yàoshi   if
14. 告诉   （动）gàosu   to tell
15. 一声   yìshēng   (a verbal measure word)
16. 前天   （名）qiántiān   the day before yesterday
17. 谈话   tánhuà   to talk
18. 录音   （名）lùyīn   recording
19. 篮球   （名）lánqiú   basket ball
20. 打   （动）dǎ   to play

语 法 Grammar

1. 连动句（四）
Double Verbal Sentences (D)

267

连动句（四）的特点是：后一个动词为"来"或"去"，它前面动词所表示的动作，是主语（施动者）"来"或"去"的目的。"来"或"去"读轻声，后面不能带宾语。例如：

Some double verbal sentences have two verbs of which the second one is 来 or 去, unstressed in pronunciation, without any object; and the first one indicates the purpose of the sentence subject (the doer), e.g.

    (1) 你干什么去了？
    (2) 我聊天儿去了。
    (3) 他干什么来了？
    (4) 他找玛丽来了。
    (5) 玛丽进城买东西去了。

有时在表示目的的动词前面还可以再用一个动词"来"或"去"。例如：

Sometime the verb 来 or 去 may appear a second time before the purposive verb, e.g.

    (6) 他去买东西去了，你等一等吧。

注意："来"或"去"前面的动词不是"上、下、进、出、回、过、起"等这类动词，否则"来"、"去"就应看成是趋向补语。

N.B. The purposive verb is other than 上,下,进,出,回,过,起, or any other of that kind, otherwise it will form with 来 or 去 as the directional complement.

2．用"有"表示存在的句子

Existential Sentences with 有

动词"有"除了表示领有以外，还可以表示存在。表示存在时，主语是处所词。例如：

Apart from the meaning of "possession" the verb 有 also refers to what there exists. The subject before it is a locative word, e.g.

主　　　　　语 Subject	谓　　Predicate　　语	
处所词 Localitive word	有	宾语 Object
电视里	有	足球比赛。
教室里	有	学生。
这儿	没有	中文书。
家里	没有	人。

3. "要是…就…"

The Structure 要是…就…

"要是…就…"用在复句中，表示假设。"要是"可以在分句的主语前，也可以在主语后。例如：

The structure 要是…就… is used in a complex sentence for hypothesis. 要是 may go before or after the subject of the clause, e.g.

(1) 要是你能来北京学习，那就好了。

(2) 要是明天不下雨，我们就去游览长城。

(3) 你下午要是有时间，就到我这儿来吧。

(4) 要是以后再有足球比赛，请你告诉我一声。

(5) 你明天不到我这儿来，我就到你那儿去。

有时只在第一个分句里用"要是"，或只在第二个分句里用"就"，如上面的例(4)和例(5)。

Sometimes only 要是 is used in the first clause, or only 就 used in the second clause as shown in the examples (4) and (5).

练 习 Exercises

1. 完成句子:

   Complete the following sentences:

   (1) 要是明天有课，＿＿＿＿＿＿＿＿。

   (2) 要是＿＿＿＿＿＿＿＿，我就跟你一起去。

   (3) 你要是明年再来北京学习，我就＿＿＿＿＿＿。

   (4) 要是昨天不下雨，我＿＿＿＿＿＿＿＿。

   (5) 要是明天下午没有事，＿＿＿＿＿＿＿。

   (6) 要是＿＿＿＿＿＿＿＿，我就再说一遍。

   (7) 你要是说得慢一点儿，他就＿＿＿＿＿＿。

   (8) 格林要是不来，我们＿＿＿＿＿＿＿。

2. 完成下列对话:

   Complete the following dialogues:

   (1) A: 屋里有人吗?

       B: ＿＿＿＿＿＿＿＿?

       A: 我找格林先生。

       B: ＿＿＿＿＿＿＿＿。

       A: 他到哪儿去了?

       B: ＿＿＿＿＿＿＿＿。

   (2) A: 你在看电视吗?

       B: ＿＿＿＿＿＿＿＿。

       A: 今天电视里有京剧吗?

       B: ＿＿＿＿＿＿＿＿。

       A: 你在看什么节目?

       B: ＿＿＿＿＿＿＿＿。

       A: 明天有京剧吗?

270

B：_____。

(3) A：昨天你去看足球比赛了吗？

B：_____。

A：谁赢了？

B：_____。

A：比分是多少？

B：_____。

A：要是以后再有足球比赛，请告诉我一声。

B：_____。

(4) A：_____？

B：要是不下雨，我就进城了。

A：_____？

B：我在学校跟一个朋友聊天儿了。

(5) A：你们班里有多少学生？

B：_____。

A：有法国学生吗？

B：_____。

A：都是日本学生吗？

B：_____。

A：你们学多长时间了？

B：_____。

A：都会说汉语了吧？

B：_____。

二十八、联 欢 会
lián　huān　huì

At a Party

271. 时间过得真快，学习马上就要总束了。
Shíjiān guò de zhēn kuài, xuéxí mǎshàng jiù yào jiéshù
le.

Time passes quickly. The cause is coming to the end
soon.

272. 今天晚上有晚会，师生一起联欢。
Jīntiān wǎnshang yǒu wǎnhuì, shī-shēng yìqǐ liánhuān.

There'll be a get-together of teachers and students
tonight.

273. 联欢会几点举行？
Liánhuānhuì jǐ diǎn jǔxíng?

When will the party begin?

274. 联欢会上有什么节目？
Liánhuānhuì shang yǒu shénme jiémù?

What's on the party program?

275. 这些节目都是用汉语表演吗？
Zhèxie jiémù dōu shì yòng Hànyǔ biǎoyǎn ma?

Are these items all given in Chinese?

276. 谁代表我们班讲话？
Shuí dàibiǎo wǒmen bān jiǎng huà?

Who'll speak on behalf of our class?

277. 我们要对老师表示感谢。
Wǒmen yào duì lǎoshī biǎoshì gǎnxiè.

We ought to express our thanks to our teachers.

278. 为您的健康干杯！
Wèi nín de jiànkāng gān bēi!

To your health!

279. 为两国人民的友谊干杯！
Wèi liǎng guó rénmín de yǒuyì gān bēi!

To the friendship between the peoples of our two countries!

280. 祝你学习进步，工作顺利！
Zhù ni xuéxí jìnbù, gōngzuò shùnlì!

Wish you progress in your study and success in your work!

替换练习　Substitution Drills

1. 时间过得真快，| 学习 | 马上就要结束了。
　　　　　　　　| 工作 |
　　　　　　　　| 假期 |
　　　　　　　　| 旅行 |

2. 这些节目都是用 | 汉语 / 英语 / 法语 / 日语 | 表演吗？

3. | 谁 / 他 / 格林 / 玛丽 | 代表我们班 | 讲话？ / 讲话。 / 发言。 / 唱歌。 |

4. 我们要对 | 老师 / 您 / 史密斯先生 | 表示感谢。

5. 为 | 您的健康 / 我们的友谊 / 您的进步 | 干杯！

6. 祝你 | 学习进步 / 工作顺利 / 身体健康 / 生活愉快 | ！

会 话　Dialogues

甲：时间过得真快，学习马上就要结束了。
Shíjiān guòde zhēn kuài, xuéxí mǎshàng jiù yào jiéshù le.

乙：今天晚上有晚会，师生一起联欢。
Jīntiān wǎnshang yǒu wǎnhuì, shī-shēng yìqǐ liánhuān.

甲：联欢会几点举行？
Liánhuānhuì jǐ diǎn jǔxíng?

乙：联欢会七点举行。
Liánhuānhuì qī diǎn jǔxíng.

甲：在什么地方？
Zài shénme dìfang?

乙：在礼堂。
Zài lǐtáng.

甲：联欢会有什么节目？
Liánhuānhuì yǒu shénme jiémù?

乙：有老师唱歌儿、同学唱歌儿……很多很多节目。
Yǒu lǎoshī chàng gēr, tóngxué chàng gēr…… hěn duō hěn duō jiémù.

甲：你表演节目吗？
Nǐ biǎoyǎn jiémù ma?

乙：表演，我要用汉语唱一个歌儿。
Biǎoyǎn, wǒ yào yòng Hànyǔ chàng yí ge gēr.

甲：谁代表我们班讲话？
Shuí dàibiǎo wǒmen bān jiǎng huà?

乙：约翰代表我们班讲话。
Yuēhàn dàibiǎo wǒmen bān jiǎng huà.

＊　　　＊　　　＊

甲： 老师好！
Lǎoshī hǎo!

乙： 你们好！
Nǐmen hǎo!

丙： 老师，时间过得真快，学习马上就要结束了。
Lǎoshī, shíjiān guò de zhēn kuài, xuéxí mǎshàng jiù
yào jiéshù le.

乙： 是啊，六个星期很快就要过去了。
Shì a, liù ge xīngqī hěn kuài jiù yào guòqu le.

甲： 我们在中国学了很多东西，还参观了很多 名胜
古迹。
Wǒmen zài Zhōngguó xuéle hěn duō dōngxi, hái
cānguānle hěn duō míngshèng gǔjī.

乙： 你们对这儿的生活习惯了吗？
Nǐmen duì zhèr de shēnghuó xíguàn le ma?

甲： 习惯了。 我在中国就跟在自己家里一样， 生活
得很愉快。
Xíguàn le. Wǒ zài Zhōngguó jiù gēn zài zìjǐ jiāli
yíyàng, shēnghuó de hěn yúkuài.

丙： 我代表我们班同学对老师表示感谢！
Wǒ dàibiǎo wǒmen bān tóngxué duì lǎoshī biǎoshì
gǎnxiè.

乙： 你们太客气了。 你们学习努力， 所以进步很
快。
Nǐmen tài kèqi le. Nǐmen xuéxí nǔlì, suǒyǐ jìnbù hěn
kuài;

丙：谢谢老师!
Xièxie lǎoshī!

甲：老师，请吃一点儿。
Lǎoshī, qǐng chī yìdiǎnr.

乙：好，我自己来。
Hǎo, wǒ zìjǐ lái.

丙：为老师的健康干杯!
Wèi lǎoshī de jiànkāng gān bēi!

甲：祝老师工作顺利，身体健康!
Zhù lǎoshī gōngzuò shùnlì, shēntǐ jiànkāng!

乙：为我们两国人民的友谊干杯!
Wèi wǒmen liǎng guó rénmín de yǒuyì gān bēi!

生 词 New Words

1.	过	（动）guò	to pass
2.	真	（副）zhēn	really
3.	马上	（副）mǎshàng	soon
4.	结束	（动）jiéshù	to finish
5.	晚会	（名）wǎnhuì	evening party
6.	师生	shī-shēng	teachers and students
7.	联欢	（动）liánhuān	to have a get-together
8.	联欢会	（名）liánhuānhuì	get-together
9.	举行	（动）jǔxíng	to hold
10.	用	（动）yòng	to use
11.	表演	（动）biǎoyǎn	to perform
12.	代表	（动、名）dàibiǎo	representative, on behalf of
13.	班	（名）bān	class

14.	讲话	jiǎng huà	to speak
15.	表示	(动、名) biǎoshì	to express
16.	感谢	(动) gǎnxiè	to thank
17.	为	(介) wèi	for
18.	健康	(形、名) jiànkāng	health
19.	干杯	gān bēi	to drink a toast
20.	友谊	(名) yǒuyì	friendship
21.	祝	(动) zhù	to wish
22.	进步	(动、名) jìnbù	progress
23.	顺利	(形) shùnlì	successful, smoothly
24.	假期	(名) jiàqī	holiday
25.	发言	fā yán	to speak
26.	唱	(动) chàng	to sing
27.	歌儿	(名) gēr	song
28.	愉快	(形) yúkuài	pleasant
29.	努力	(形) nǔlì	to try hard, to exert oneself
30.	所以	(连) suǒyǐ	so, therefore

语 法 Grammar

1. 动词的即将发生态——要…了

The Aspect of Immediate Happening Expressed by the Structure 要…了

"要…了" 表示动作或情况即将发生。例如：

The structure 要…了 refers to something that is going to happen soon, e.g.

(1) 火车要开了。

278

（2）天气要冷了。

也可以在"要"前边加上"就"或"快"作状语。"就要"前面可以有时间状语，"快要"不能。例如：

要 may be preceded by the adverbial modifier 就 or 快. An adverbial modifier of time can be placed before 就要, but never before 快要, e.g.

（1）学习马上就要结束了。

（2）请等一下，他就要来了。

（3）火车五点钟就要开了，快点走吧!

（4）张老师快要到日本去旅行了。

有时候也可以省去"要"，说成"就…了""快…了"。口语中"快…了"更常见。例如：

Sometimes 要 may be omitted. The structure therefore becomes "就…了" or "快…了"。In spoken Chinese 快…了 is more often used, e.g.

（5）快开演了，我们进去吧!

2. 介词词组"对…"作状语

The Prepositional Phrase 对… Used as an Adverbial Modifier.

介词"对"有两种用法：

The preposition 对 can be used in two ways:

A. "对"相当于英语的"to"或"for"。例如：

对 means "to" or "for", e.g.

（1）我们要对老师表示感谢。

（2）这些事，不对他说不太好。

（3）别对他母亲说他病了。

B. "对"相当于英语的"as to"或"as for"。"对…"可以放在主语前，也可以放在主语后。否定副词一般在"对…"后面。例如：

对，meaning "as to" or "as for", can be put either before or after the subject. The negative adverb generally appear after "对…", e.g.

（1）格林对京剧非常感兴趣。

（2）刚来的同志对这儿的情况都不很了解。

（3）对这里的天气，我还不太习惯。

（4）对访问社员家庭，他们都有兴趣。

3. 介词词组"为…"作状语

The Prepositional Phrase "为…" Used as an Adverbial Modifier

介词词组"为…"作状语表示原因或目的。"为"后可加"了"。"为（了）…"可放在主语前面。例如：

The prepositional phrase 为… (or 为了…) used before the subject expresses the cause or purpose of an action, e.g.

（1）为你的健康干杯！

（2）我们都为这件事高兴。

（3）为了学习汉语，他来到北京。

（4）为了买那本书，他今天早上八点就进城去了。

练 习 Exercises

1. 完成句子：

Complete the following sentences:

（1）时间过得真快，再过一个星期,我们＿＿＿＿＿了。

（2）车＿＿＿＿＿＿了，请快点上车吧!

（3）你不要给我回信了，我＿＿＿＿＿＿了。

（4）你不要走，他就＿＿＿＿＿＿了。

2．用下列词语造有"对…"作状语的句子：
Make sentences with 对…, as an adverbial modifier, using the words given below:

    (1)   感谢   张老师

    (2)   北京的天气   习惯

    (3)   访问   感兴趣

    (4)   生活   不了解

    (5)   参观游览   没有兴趣

3．回答下列问题：
Answer the following questions:

    (1) 你是为了学汉语到中国来的吗？

    (2) 你对旅行不感兴趣吗？

    (3) 你打算到什么地方去旅行？

    (4) 学习结束以前你们举行联欢会吗？

    (5) 你对联欢会感兴趣吗？

    (6) 你表演节目吗？

    (7) 你打算讲什么？是对老师表示感谢吗？

二十九、买火车票
mǎi huǒ zhē piào
Getting Train Tickets

281. 学习结束以后，你去外地旅行吗？
Xuéxí jiéshù yǐhòu, nǐ qù wàidì lǚxíng ma?

Are you going to visit any places other than Beijing after the cause?

282. 你的旅行路线是什么？
Nǐ de lǚxíng lùxiàn shi shénme?

What's your itinerary?

283. 我准备从北京坐火车到西安，再到成都、重庆，然后由重庆坐船到武汉。
Wǒ zhǔnbèi cóng Běijīng zuò huǒchē dào Xī'ān, zài dào Chéngdū, Chóngqìng, ránhòu yóu Chóngqìng zuò chuán dào Wǔhàn.

I'm going to Xi'an from Beijing by train, and then visit Chengdu and Chongqing. After that I'll go to Wuhan from Chonqing by boat.

284. 回来的时候，你坐飞机还是坐火车？
Huílai de shíhòu, nǐ zuò fēijī háishi zuò huǒchē?

How will you come back: by plane or train?

285. 你去上海坐哪次车?

Nǐ qù Shànghǎi zuò nǎ cì chē?

Which train are you going to take for Shanghai?

286. 我坐 13 次特快。

Wǒ zuò shísān cì tèkuài.

I'll take the express No. 13.

287. 车票是预订还是当天买?

Chēpiào shì yùdìng háishì dàngtiān mǎi?

Are the tickets booked beforehand, or can be bought on the same day when one needs them?

288. 买一张二十号到上海的硬卧票。

Mǎi yì zhāng èrshí hào dào Shànghǎi de yìngwò piào.

A hard berth for Shanghai on the 20th please.

289. 昨天我们班已经走了两个同学。

Zuótiān wǒmen bān yǐjing zǒule liǎng ge tóngxué.

Two of our classmates left yesterday.

290. 你需要在南京站办理签票手续。

Nǐ xūyào zài Nánjīngzhàn bànlǐ qiān piào shǒuxù.

You have to get your ticket signed at Nanjing Station.

替换练习 Substitution Drills

1. 我准备从

北京	坐	火车	到	西安,再到成都、重庆,
东京		飞机		香港
上海		船		青岛

然后由

重庆	坐	船	到	武汉	。
香港		火车		广州	
青岛		飞机		北京	

2.

回来	的时候,你坐飞机还是坐火车?
回国	
来中国	
去南京	

3. 买一张二十号到上海的

硬卧票	。
软卧票	
硬席票	
软席票	

4. 昨天我们班

已经走	了	两个同学	。
来		一位客人	
来		两个参观的	

284

会 话 Dialogues

甲：安东尼，你们学习什么时候结束？
Āndōngní, nǐmen xuéxí shénme shíhou jiéshù?

乙：八月十五号。
Bāyuè shíwǔ hào.

甲：学习结束以后，你去外地旅行吗？
Xuéxí jiéshù yǐhòu, nǐ qù wàidì lǚxíng ma?

乙：去，学校组织我们去外地旅行。
Qù, xuéxiào zǔzhī wǒmen qù wàidì lǚxíng.

甲：你的旅行路线是什么？
Nǐ de lǚxíng lùxiàn shi shénme?

乙：我准备从这里坐火车到西安，再到成都、重庆，
然后由重庆坐船到武汉。
Wǒ zhǔnbèi cóng zhèli zuò huǒchē dào Xī'ān, zài dào
Chéngdū、Chóngqìng, ránhòu yóu Chóngqìng zuò chuán
dào Wǔhàn.

甲：你打算什么时候出发？
Nǐ dǎsuan shénme shíhou chūfā?

乙：八月十六号。
Bāyuè shíliù hào.

甲：回来的时候，你坐飞机还是坐火车？
Huílai de shíhou, nǐ zuò fēijī háishi zuò huǒchē?

乙：坐火车，因为坐飞机太贵了。
Zuò huǒchē, yīnwèi zuò fēijī tài guì le.

甲：这次旅行需要多少天？
Zhè cì lǚxíng xūyào duōshao tiān?

乙：差不多二十天。
Chà bu duō èrshí tiān.

甲：你们班同学都去旅行吗？
Nǐmen bān tóngxué dōu qù lǚxíng ma?

乙：不，有的同学不去旅行，学习结束以后就回国。
昨天我们班已经走了五个同学。
Bù, yǒude tóngxué bú qù lǚxíng, xuéxí jiéshù yǐhòu jiù
huí guó. Zuótiān wǒmen bān yǐjing zǒule wǔ ge
tóngxué.

*　　　　*　　　　*

甲：请问，去上海坐那次车？
Qǐngwèn, qù Shànghǎi zuò nǎ cì chē?

乙：你坐13次特快吧。
Nǐ zuò shísān cì tèkuài ba.

甲：为什么呢？
Wèi shénme ne?

乙：这次车又快又舒服。
Zhè cì chē yòu kuài yòu shūfu.

甲：车票是预订还是当天买？
Chē piào shi yùdìng háishi dàngtiān mǎi?

乙：都可以。
Dōu kěyǐ.

甲：好，买一张十号到上海的票。
Hǎo, mǎi yìzhāng shí hào dào Shànghǎi de piào.

乙：你要硬卧还是要软卧？
Nǐ yào yìngwò háishi yào ruǎnwò?

甲：软卧，一张。
Ruǎnwò, yì zhāng.

乙：九十六块七毛。
jiǔshí liù kuài qī máo.

甲：这次车什么时候开？
Zhè cì chē shénme shíhou kāi?

乙：下午六点十九分。
Xiàwǔ liù diǎn shíjiǔ fēn.

甲：我在南京下车住两天，可以吗？
Wǒ zài Nánjīng xià chē zhù liǎng tiān, kěyǐ ma?

乙：可以，你需要在南京站办理签票手续。
Kěyǐ, nǐ xūyào zài Nánjīngzhàn bànlǐ qiān piào
shǒuxù.

生 词 New Words

1.	外地	（名）wàidì	places other than where one is
2.	路线	（名）lùxiàn	itinerary
3.	然后	（副）ránhòu	afterwards
4.	由	（介）yóu	from
5.	船	（名）chuán	boat
6.	特快	（名）tèkuài	express
7.	预订	（动）yùdìng	to book
8.	当天	（名）dàngtiān	the same day
9.	硬卧	（名）yìngwò	ordinary berth
10.	已经	（副）yǐjing	already
11.	需要	（动）xūyào	to need

12. 办理	（动）bànlǐ	to go about (formalities)
13. 签票	qiàn piào	to sigh a ticket
14. 手续	（名）shǒuxù	formalities
15. 软卧	（名）ruǎnwò	soft berth
16. 硬席	（名）yìngxí	ordinary seat
17. 软席	（名）ruǎnxí	soft seat
18. 客人	（名）kèren	guest
19. 有的	（代）yǒude	some

专 名 Proper Nouns

1. 西安	Xī'ān	name of a place
2. 成都	Chéngdū	name of a place
3. 重庆	Chóngqìng	name of a place
4. 武汉	Wǔhàn	name of a place
5. 香港	Xiānggǎng	Hong kong

语 法 Grammar

1. "…的时候"

The Structure …的时候

"…时候"在句中常作时间状语，它前面可以是动词、动词词组或主谓词组。例如：

The structure …的时候 often functions as an adverbial modifier of time before a verb, verbal phrase or subject-predicate phrase, e.g.

　　(1) 我回来的时候没坐飞机。

　　(2) 回来的时候，你坐飞机还是坐火车？

　　(3) 参观工厂的时候，你到哪儿去了？

288

（4）我打电话的时候，你干什么呢？

（5）上午你给我打电话的时候，我正在上课呢。

2. 存现句

Existential Sentences

表示人或事物在某地点存在、出现或消失的动词谓语句叫存现句。存现句的主语是表示处所的词语，动词常要带动态助词或补语等。宾语是表示存在、出现或消失的人或事物的名词。注意：这种宾语一般不是确指的，不能说"那天走了格林"。例如：

An existential sentence is one that indicates the existence, appearance or disappearance of a person or thing. The subject of the sentence is expressed by a word of locality. The verbal predicate often takes an aspectual particle or a complement. The object is generally an unspecified noun indicating the existence, appearance or disappearance of people or things. N.B. It is incorrect to say 那天走了格林, e.g.

主 语 Subject	谓 语 Predicate	
处所词 Locative word	动词 + 动态助词 / 补语 Verb + Aspectual Particle / Complement	宾 语 Object
我们班 车里 家里	走了 走下来 来了	两个同学。 两个人。 一个客人。

练 习 Exercises

1. 完成下列句子：

Complete the following sentences:

(1) ＿＿＿＿＿＿＿的时候，他正在看书呢。

(2) ＿＿＿＿＿＿＿的时候，他坐飞机还是坐火车？

(3) 我去他家的时候，＿＿＿＿＿＿＿。

(4) 我去寄信的时候，＿＿＿＿＿＿＿？

(5) 格林去找你的时候，＿＿＿＿＿＿？

(6) ＿＿＿＿＿＿＿的时候，格林已经走了。

2．回答下列问题：

Answer the following questions:

(1) 这次来了多少日本学生？

(2) 昨天走了几个学生？

(3) 你家昨天来客人了吗？

(4) 你去的时候，他家里有几位客人？

(5) 张先生家有客人吗？

(6) 今天电视里有什么节目？

(7) 你们班有日本学生吗？

3．把下列句子改成用"还是"的问句：

Change the following into interrogative sentences with
还是：

例：我不坐飞机去上海，坐火车去上海。

你怎么去上海，坐飞机还是坐火车？

(1) 我代表我们班用汉语讲话，不用英语讲话。

(2) 学习结束以后，我不去西安旅行，我去桂林旅行。

(3) 明年我不到上海学习汉语，我到北京学习汉语。

(4) 我打电话请他来吃饭，不是来聊天儿。

三十、送　行
sòng　xíng
Farewell

291. 你的东西都收拾好了吗?

Nǐ de dōngxi dōu shōushihǎo le ma?

Have you finished packing your things up?

292. 收拾得差不多了。

Shōushi de chà bu duō le.

Yes, I've almost finished my packing.

293. 还有什么事情需要我帮忙吗?

Hái yǒu shénme shìqing xūyào wo bāngmáng ma?

Is there anything else that I can do for you?

294. 没有什么了，该办的都办了。

Méi yǒu shénme le, gāi bàn de dōu bànle.

Not at the moment. Everything that should be done has

been done.

295. 护照在桌子上放着呢。

Hùzhào zài zhuōzi shang fàngzhe ne.

The passport is on your table.

296. 希望你以后能再来中国。

Xīwàng nǐ yǐhòu néng zài lái Zhōngguó.

Hope you'll visit China again in future.

297. 欢迎你到我们国家去访问。
Huānyíng nǐ dào wǒmen guójiā qù fǎngwén.

Please visit my country one day and you'll be welcomed.

298. 有机会我一定去，去的时候一定去拜访您。
Yǒu jīhuì wǒ yídìng qù, qù de shíhou yídìng qù bàifǎng nín.

Yes, I will if I have a chance, and I'll go to see you then.

299. 请代我向你家里人问好！
Qǐng dài wo xiàng nǐ jiāli rén wèn hǎo!

Please remember me to your family!

300. 祝你一路平安！
Zhù nǐ yílù píng'ān!

Wish you a pleasant journey!

替换练习　Substitution Drills

1. 你的
| 东西 |
| 行李 |
| 衣服和书籍 |
都收拾好了吗？

2. 没有什么了，该 | 办的 | 都 | 办了 | 。

办的	办了
写的	写了
说的	说了
收拾的	收拾了
准备的	准备了

3. 希望你以后 | 能再来中国 | 。

能再来中国
再来学习
常常来信

4. | 护照 | 在 | 桌子 | 上放着呢。

护照	桌子
衣服	床
书	书架

5. 请代我向 | 你家里人 | 问好。

你家里人
你父亲
布朗教授

会 话 Dialogues

甲：你打算什么时候动身？
　　Nǐ dǎsuan shénme shíhou dòng shēn?

乙：我打算九月三号动身。
　　Wǒ dǎsuan jiǔyuè sān hào dòng shēn.

甲：飞机票买了吗？
Fēijīpiào mǎile ma?

乙：买了。
Mǎi le.

甲：你的东西都收拾好了没有？
Nǐ de dōngxi dōu shōushi hǎo le méiyǒu?

乙：收拾得差不多了。
Shōushi de chà bu duō le.

甲：还有什么事情，需要我帮忙吗？
Hái yǒu shénme shìqing, xūyào wo bāngmáng ma.

乙：谢谢你，没什么了，该办的都办了。
Xièxie ni, méi shénme le, gāi bàn de dōu bànle.

甲：你的护照办了没有？
Nǐ de hùzhào bànle méiyǒu?

乙：已经办了，在桌子上放着呢。
Yǐjing bànle, zài zhuōzi shang fàngzhe ne.

甲：你还有人民币吗？我给你换成美元吧。
Nǐ hái yǒu Rénmínbì ma? Wǒ gěi ni huànchéng Měiyuán ba.

乙：没有了，谢谢。
Méi yǒu le, xièxie.

甲：再有什么事情，打电话告诉我。
Zài yǒu shénme shìqing, dǎ diànhuà gàosu wo.

乙：好的，太麻烦你了。
Hǎo de, tài máfan ni le.

*   *   *

甲：您工作非常忙，还来送我，太感谢了。
Nín gōngzuò fēicháng máng, hái lái sòng wo, tài gǎnxiè le.

乙：希望你以后能再来中国。
Xīwàng nǐ yǐhòu néng zài lái Zhōngguó.

甲：我准备明年假期再来学习汉语。
Wǒ zhǔnbèi míngnián jiàqī zài lái xuéxí Hànyǔ.

乙：欢迎！欢迎！
Huānyíng! Huānyíng!

甲：欢迎您到我们国家去访问。
Huānyíng nín dào wǒmen guójiā qu fǎngwèn.

乙：有机会我一定去。去的时候，一定去拜访你。
Yǒu jīhuì wǒ yídìng qù. Qù de shíhou yídìng qù bàifǎng nǐ.

甲：不敢当。
Bù gǎndāng.

乙：请你常常来信。
Qǐng nǐ chángcháng lái xìn.

甲：一定。
Yídìng.

乙：飞机就要起飞了，请准备上飞机吧！
Fēijī jiù yào qǐfēi le, qǐng zhǔnbèi shàng fēijī ba!

甲：再一次向您表示感谢。
Zài yí cì xiàng nǐ biǎoshì gǎnxiè.

乙：请代我向你家里人问好！
Qǐng dài wo xiàng nǐ jiāli rén wèn hǎo!

甲：谢谢！
Xièxie!

乙：祝你一路平安！
zhù ni yílù píng'ān!

甲：谢谢，再见！
Xièxie, zàijiàn!

乙：再见。
Zàijiàn!

生　词 New Words

1.	收拾	（动）shōushi	to pack up
2.	帮忙	bāng máng	to help
3.	办	（动）bàn	to do
4.	希望	（动、名）xīwàng	to hope
5.	欢迎	（动）huānyíng	to welcome
6.	机会	（名）jīhuì	chance
7.	拜访	（动）bàifǎng	to call upon
8.	代	（动）dài	for
9.	护照	（名）hùzhào	passport
10.	桌子	（名）zhuōzi	table
11.	着	（助）zhe	(a particle)
12.	一路	yílù	all the way
13.	平安	（形）píng'ān	safety
14.	行李	（名）xíngli	luggage
15.	书籍	（名）shūjí	books (in general)
16.	衣服	（名）yīfu	clothes
17.	床	（名）chuáng	bed

18. 书架	（名）shūjià	bookshelves
19. 送	（动）sòng	to see off
20. 起飞	（动）qǐfēi	to take off
21. 不敢当	bù gǎndāng	not deserve praise

语 法 Grammar

1. 动词的持续态

The Continuous Aspect of Verbs

动词后面加动态助词"着"，表示动作状态的持续。否定式是在动词的前面加"没（有）"，即："没（有）+ 动词 + 着"。动词的持续态也常和表示进行态的"正"、"在"连用。例如：

A verb followed by 着 indicates the continuous aspect of an action. The negative form is "没（有）+ verb + 着". The continuous aspect is often used with the progressive adverb 正 or 在, e.g:

    (1) 张老师家坐着几个客人。

    (2) 他穿着一双布鞋。

    (3) 他拿着化验单去找大夫。

    (4) 护照没在桌子上放着。

    (5) 外边正下着雨呢。

正反疑问句是："动词 + 着…没有"。例如：

The affirmative-negative form is "verb + 着…没有", e.g.

    (6) 那里住着人没有？

    (7) 他穿着新上衣没有？

2. 主语和宾语的省略

The Omission of the Subject and the Object

主语在语言环境清楚的情况下，如在对话时，可以省去，宾语也同样可以省去。例如：

The subject and object of a sentence may be omitted in spoken Chinese if the context is clear enough, e.g.

A. 主语省略

The Omission of the Subject

(1) 你的东西都收拾好了吗？

（我的东西）收拾得差不多了。

(2) （我）希望你以后再来中国。

B. 宾语省略

The Omission of the Object

(3) 还有什么事情需要我帮忙吗？

没有什么（事情）了，该办的（事情）都办了。

(4) 请（您）到那儿交款。

C. 主语宾语都有省略

The Omission of Both the Subject and the Object

(5) 昨天他借给我一本书，我看了（这本书），（我）很喜欢（这本书），（我）也借给你（这本书）（你）看看（这本书）吧！

3. 紧缩句

Condensed Sentences

紧缩句是由复句紧缩而成的。所谓紧缩句是指略去一些词语（连词和后一个分句的主语等）。紧缩句很像单句，在语音上中间没有停顿，多用于口语。例如：

A condensed sentence is resulted from a complex one of which some words such as the conjunction and the subject of the second clause, are taken off. The sentence, mostly appearing in dialogues, is similar to a simple one, without any pause in reading it, e.g.

(1) a: 欢迎你到我们国家去。

b: 有机会我一定去。

例(1.b)句是假设条件句的紧缩，意思是："要是有机会，我一定去"。

The example (1.b) is a condensed sentence of hypothesis, meaning "要是有机会，我一定去".

(2) a: 明天要是下雨呢？

b: 下雨就不去。

例(2.b)句意思是："要是下雨，我就不去"。

The example (2.b) means "要是下雨，我就不去".

练 习 Exercises

1. 把"了"、"着"、"过"分别填入下列句子中：

Fill in the following blanks with 了，着 or 过 if appropriate:

(1) 你昨天买____那本书吗？

(2) 你今天上____课没有？

(3) 你以前在上海住____没有？

(4) 我不是第一次来中国，1980年来____。

(5) 到北京以后，你看____京剧吗？

(6) 你刚买的那本书在哪儿放____呢？

(7) 张先生家里坐____两个客人。

(8) 我去的时候，他正在床上坐____看报呢。

2. 用省略主语或宾语的形式完成对话：

Complete the following dialogues with subjectless or objectless sentences:

299

(1) A：你东西都买好了吗？

　　B：＿＿＿＿＿＿＿＿。

(2) A：你还有什么事情要办吗？

　　B：＿＿＿＿＿＿＿＿。

(3) A：欢迎你以后再来北京。

　　B：＿＿＿＿＿＿＿＿。

(4) A：你去过桂林吗？

　　B：＿＿＿＿＿＿＿＿。

　　A：你不想去吗？

　　B：＿＿＿＿＿＿＿＿。

3．用紧缩句完成下列对话：

Complete the following dialogues with condensed sentences:

(1) A：你打算什么时候去游览长城？

　　B：明天去。

　　A：天气预报说明天有雨。

　　B：＿＿＿＿＿＿＿＿。

(2) A：有时间请到我那儿去玩儿。

　　B：＿＿＿＿＿＿＿＿。

(3) A：要是格林先生去，你也去吗？

　　B：＿＿＿＿＿＿＿＿。

(4) A：欢迎你再来参观访问。

　　B：＿＿＿＿＿＿＿＿。

(5) A：星期五去承德旅行，你去不去？

　　B：星期五不上课吗？

　　A：老师说不上课了。

　　B：＿＿＿＿＿＿＿＿。

300

语 法 小 结(三)
yǔ fǎ xiǎo jié
A Short Summary of Grammar(3)

一、词类：Parts of Speech

1. 名词 Nouns
   - (1) 中国 北京
   - (2) 朋友 杂志 主意
   - (3) 左 上 前边
   - (4) 今天 上午 现在

2. 代词 Pronouns
   - A. 人称代词 Personal Pronouns
     我 你 他 我们 你们 他们
   - B. 疑问代词 Interrogative Pronouns
     谁 什么 哪儿 怎么样 几
   - C. 指示代词 Demonstrative Pronouns
     那 这儿 那么 这样

3. 动词 Verbs
   - (1) 去 旅行 觉得
   - (2) 是 有 在

   一部分动词可以重叠：

   Some verbs can be repeatedly used:
   - (3) 问问 听听

(4) 说一说　　讲一讲

(5) 看了看　　想了想

(6) 比较比较　　学习学习

4. 能愿动词　Modal Verbs

　　能　会　要　可以　想

5. 形容词　Adjectives

　　清楚　凉快　努力　早　快　少

一部分形容词可以重叠：

Some adjectives can be repeatedly used:

(1) 好好儿学习

(2) 高高兴兴地回去

6. 数词　Numerals

　A. 基数　Cardinal Numbers

　　五　两　二十　半

　B. 序数　Ordinal Numbers

　　第二　三班　三月二十五日

7. 量词　Measure Words

　A. 名量词　Nominal Measure Words

　　本　层　个　位　句　种

　B. 动量词　Verbal Measure Words

　　次　遍　下儿

8. 介词　Prepositions

　　跟　给　对　比　离　在　把　被　让　为　从

9. 副词　Adverbs

　　很　不　没(有)　都　也　太　已经

10. 连词　Conjunctions

　　和　因为　要是　所以

11. 助词　Particles

A．结构助词　Structural Particles

　　　的　　得　　地

B．语气助词　Modal Particles

　　　吗　　吧　　呢　　了

C．动态助词　Aspectual Particles

　　　了　　着　　过

12．叹词　Interjections

　　　啊

13．象声词　Onomatopoeia

　　　"啊"的一声

二、词组　Phrases

1．名词词组（16课）　Nominal Phrases

　　（1）马路东边是邮局。

　　（2）桌子右边有一个大书架。

2．动词词组（18课）　Verbal Phrases

　　（1）新来的同学都不了解人民公社。

　　（2）我很喜欢喝热茶。

　　（3）买回来的苹果又大又好。

3．形容词词组（17课）　Adjectival Phrases

　　（1）有没有便宜一点儿的布鞋？

　　（2）不清楚的地方可以问我。

　　（3）我觉得凉快极了。

4．主谓词组（11课）　Subject-Predicate Phrases

　　（1）他身体很好。

　　（2）老师说的话我都听懂了。

　　（3）我希望你以后能再来中国。

　　（4）我们都说汉语，好吗？

5．介词词组（7课）　Prepositional Phrases

(1) 我想给我的朋友打个电话。

(2) 张老师把电影票给玛丽了。

(3) 我在北京学习汉语。

(4) 我住在北京西郊。

6. "的"字词组（16课） Phrases with 的

(1) 我是学德语的，他是学英语的，我们两个人学的不一样。

(2) 这本书是新的，那本是旧(jiù, old)的；新的是玛丽的，旧的是我的。

(3) 大夫告诉他，吃这种药的时候，不要吃辣的。

三、句子成分 Sentence Elements

1. 主语 The Subject

(1) 今天很冷，外边有风，要多穿一点儿。

(2) 邮局在哪儿？你知道吗？

(3) 早一点儿比晚一点儿好。

(4) 参观、游览都很有意思。

(5) 你来也可以，他来也可以。

(6) 吃的、穿的、用的都给你准备好了。

2. 谓语 The Predicate （见第四项单句1中的 A·主谓句）

3. 宾语 The Object

(1) 史密斯先生是教授。

(3) 我觉得不舒服。

(4) 请你告诉他，我们希望他明天能来帮忙。

(5) 他怎么过星期天？

(6) 他打算去承德。

(7) 我有点儿咳嗽，想吃淡一点儿的。

前置宾语（25课 26课） The Preposed Object

(8) 今天的报我还没看呢。

304

(9) 他日语说得很好，英语也说得不错。

4．定语　The Adjectival Modifier

(1) 昨天的事我们都知道了。

(2) 我们的宿舍（sùshè, dormitory）在礼堂西边。

(3) 我有一个好主意。

(4) 那是一个很大的房间。

(5) 比他小两岁的弟弟正在大学里学习。

(6) 星期日出来买东西的人多极了。

(7) 我们上课的教室大概在四层。

5．状语　The Adverbial Modifier

(1) 我们已经学完了那本书。

(2) 这个字的发音太难。

(3) 同学们都为他的进步高兴。

(4) 我们要对他表示感谢。

(5) 你从哪儿来？

(6) 他常常是早来晚走。

(7) 我们下午两点半开会。

(8) 请里边坐。

6．补语　The Complement

a．结果补语（13课）The Resultative Complement

(1) 他看完第二个节目就走了。

(2) 旅行要用的东西我都准备好了。

b．程度补语（11课）The Complement of Degree

(1) 他说得不很清楚。

(2) 我看书看得太累了。

c．趋向补语（12课）The Directional Complement

(1) 玛丽城去了。

(2) 我朋友叫来一辆出租汽车。

（3）弟弟跑回家去了。

（4）他从书架上拿下来一本德文书。

   d. 可能补语（14课）The Potential Complement

      （1）够了，我吃不下了。

      （2）那儿那么远，一个小时回得来吗？

   e. 时量补语（15课）The Time-Measure Complement

      （1）他写汉字写了半个小时。

      （2）电影已经开演二十分钟了。

   f. 动量补语（17课）The Action-Measure Complement

      （1）我只去过一次长城。

      （2）我去医院看过他一次。

   g. 数量补语（24课）The Complement of Quantity

      （1）我比他哥哥小两岁。

      （2）这种烟比那种贵一点儿。

   h. 时间、处所补语（8课）The Complement of Time or Locality

      （1）看京剧的时侯，他坐在第八排，我坐在十二排。

      （2）我们的老师住在北京西郊。

      （3）我生（shēng, be born）在一九五九年。

四、句子类型 Different Types of Sentences

（一）单句 Simple Sentences

1. 按句子的结构分为主谓句和非主谓句：

According to the structure, Chinese sentences may be divided into subject-predicate sentences and non subject-predicate sentences:

A. 主谓句

Subject-Predicate Sentences:

(a)名词谓语句(5课)

306

Sentences with a Nominal Predicate

（1）今天星期四。

（2）您今年多大年纪了？——我七十八了。

(b) 动词谓语句（1课　6课）

Sentences with a Verbal Predicate

（1）篮球比赛已经开始了。

（2）我买了一盒火柴。

（3）玛丽给我一张双号的票。

(c) 形容词谓语句（1课）

Sentences with an Adjectival Predicate

（1）这件上衣正合适。

（2）我们家乡的冬天没有北京这么冷。

(d) 主谓谓语句（1课）

Sentences with Subject-Predicate as Its Predicate

（1）你母亲身体怎么样？

（2）我今天头疼，大概感冒了。

B． 非主谓句　Non Subject-Predicate Sentences

(a) 无主句（24课）

Subjectless Sentences

（1）下雪了。

（2）打铃了。

(b) 独词句

One-Word Sentences

（1）看！

（2）火车!

2．按句子的用途或语气分为：

According to the usage or mode, Chinese sentences can be classified as:

A．陈述句

Declarative Sentences

(1) 他女儿在一个公司里工作。

(2) 这儿的夏天很热。

(3) 刮大风了。

B．疑问句（1课　2课　3课　8课　9课）

Interrogative Sentences

(1) 你兑换过人民币吗？在哪儿兑换？

(2) 那个地方离这儿远不远？

(3) 史密斯先生住在北京饭店还是住在友谊宾馆？

(4) 你是不是给他打个电话？

(5) 你的化验单呢？

C．祈使句（10课）

Imperative Sentences

(1) 请坐!

(2) 别客气!

D．感叹句（10课）

Exclamatory Sentences

(1) 啊! 今天的天气太好了!

(2) 时间过得真快啊!

（二）复句　Complex Sentences

1．联合复句

Coordinative Sentences

(1) 他又是我的老师，又是我的朋友。

(2) 他能说法语，我也能说法语。

2．偏正复句（7课）

Subordinative Sentences

(1) 你要是想下星期动身，现在就要去预订飞机票。

308

(2) 王丽因为有病，请了两天假。

五、几种特殊的动词谓语句
Some Special Sentences with a Verbal Predicate

1. "是"字句（2课）

Sentences with 是

(1) 前边就是十字路口。

(2) 他不是布朗先生的秘书。

(3) 这本杂志是不是新的？

2. "有"字句（4课　27课）

Sentences with 有

(1) 我有烟，你有火柴没有？

(2) 今天晚上礼堂里没有电影。

(3) 桌子上有一个纸条儿。

3. "把"字句（19课　20课）

Sentences with 把

(1) 你把包裹寄出去了没有？

(2) 我想把美元换成人民币。

(3) 保罗把找来的钱放在这儿了。

4. "被"字句（21课）

Sentences with 被

(1) 我借来的那本中文书被我妹妹拿走了。

(2) 那瓶汽水让我的小女儿喝了。

意义上的被动句：

Notional Passive Sentences

(3) 我的本子放在保罗的房间里了。

5. "是…的"句（25课）

Sentences with the Structure 是…的

(1) 张老师是坐飞机去武汉的，李平是坐轮船去的。

（2）你是不是在银行看到他的？

6．存在句（29课）

Existential Sentences

　　（1）桌子上放着一个菜单。

　　（2）昨天我们班走了一个同学，他家里有事提前回国了。

　　（3）前边来了一辆出租汽车。

7．连动句（7课22课27课）

Double Verbal Sentences

　　（1）玛丽听见有人叫她，就开门出去了。

　　（2）他想进城到华侨大厦去。

　　（3）在晚会上我们要用汉语表演节目。

　　（4）格林一家人都避暑去了。

8．兼语句（23课　24课）

Donble Functioning Sentences

　　（1）王老师让我通知你一件（jiàn, a measure word）事。

　　（2）下午有个日本同学来找你。

六、动词的态

The Verbal Aspect

1．完成态（12课）

The Perfect Aspect

　　（1）他在中国学习的时候，认识了很多中国朋友。

　　（2）昨天我们参观了人民公社，没有访问社员家庭。

　　（3）这个周末怎么过，你们决定了没有？

2．进行态（23课）

The Progressive Aspect

　　（1）你到他那儿的时候，他正在看电视吗？

　　（2）没有，他正在看书呢。

3．持续态（30课）

The Continuous Aspect

(1) 李平穿着一件新上衣。

(2) 礼堂里正开着联欢会呢。

(3) 我的书上没写着名字。

4．即将发生态（28课）

The Aspect of Immediate Happening

(1) 车要开了，快上去吧!

(2) 我父亲快要退休了。

(3) 我们下个月就要到外地去旅行了。

5．经验态（13课）

The Aspect of Experience

(1) 我去过一次故宫，没去过北海公园。

(2) 你来中国以前吃过饺子没有？

七：比较的方式

The Ways of Comparison

1．表示差别的:

The Ways to Indicate Difference:

(a) "更"、"最" The Adverb 更 or 最

(1) 动物园离我家远，颐和园离我家更远。

(2) 他的发音清楚，你的发音更清楚，玛丽的发音最清楚。

(b) "比"（24课） The Word 比

(1) 我们的工作比他们紧张。

(2) 他来得不比你晚，你们都来得很早。

(c) "没有…那么（这么…）"（24课）

The Structure 没有…那么（这么）…

(1) 这种糖没有那种糖好。

311

（2）我说得没有他那么快。

2．表示异同的：

The Ways to Indicate Similarity and Difference:

"跟…一样"（24课）

The Structure 跟…一样

（1）他住的地方跟我们住的一样远。

（2）妹妹跟我一样喜欢唱歌儿。

（3）这种语言跟那种语言很不一样。

（4）你穿的布鞋跟他穿的一样大不一样大？

练 习 Exercises

阅读下面的短文并复述：

Read and retell the following passages.

（1）今天我从邮局买邮票回来，看见桌子上有一个条儿，是布朗留给我的，通知我今天晚上学校组织我们去看京剧，七点开演，六点出发，提前半小时吃饭。他还说，他对京剧不感兴趣，想在家里看电视，让我把他的票交还（huán, to give back）给老师。

我想，布朗最喜欢看足球，今天晚上的电视节目一定有球赛。我找到电视节目报，看见今天晚上有北京队对上海队的足球赛。上次这两个队在上海（比）赛过一次。我看了，比分是三比二，北京队赢了。这次我不想看了。我想今天晚上的京剧节目一定很精彩，我决定去看京剧。

（2）昨天我给朋友打了一个电话，叫他今天来找我，我们一起去颐和园玩儿玩儿。早上他来了。我们叫了一辆出租汽车，就出发了。

在颐和园玩儿了一个多小时，忽然（hūrán, suddenly）下雨了。我对朋友说:"我们回去吧!"他说:"没关系,早上天气预报说,今天有小雨,下的时间不会太长"。

我到北京一个多月了,对这儿的天气已经习惯了。我朋友告诉我,北京的秋天天气最好,不冷也不热,跟我们家乡差不多。去年他来北京的时候,正好(zhènghǎo: just in time)是秋天,那种天气对他非常合适。他还说,北京的春天常常刮风, 很少下雨,他不太喜欢北京的春天。我说,我还没见过雪,很希望在北京过一个冬天,看看下大雪的情况(qíngkuàng: situation)。

这时候,雨不下了,只刮着一点儿小风,天气非常凉快,我和我的朋友都觉得很舒服。我们又玩儿了一会儿, 就回学校来了。

(3) 我们在中国的学习马上就要结束了,这六个星期我们过得很愉快。除了学习汉语以外,我们还游览了很多大公园。为了了解中国农民的生活情况,我们参观了人民公社,访问了社员家庭。

昨天下午学校组织了一个联欢晚会,师生一起联欢。我代表我们班在会上讲话,对老师表示感谢。我们还表演了一些汉语节目,老师们看了都非常高兴,说我们学习努力,进步很快。我们为老师的健康干杯,还祝他们工作顺利!

下星期我们就要到外地旅行去了,昨天已经预订好了去西安的特快硬卧票,二十二号动身。这次旅行的路线是从北京坐火车到西安,再到成都、重庆,然后由重庆坐船到武汉,从武汉再坐飞机去上海,最后 (zuìhòu: finally) 从上海回国。

昨天我的中国朋友到宿舍来看我们。他问我还有什么事情需要帮忙,我说,没有什么了,该办的都办了,东西也都准备好了。他希望我以后能再来,我对他说,欢迎他到我们国家去旅行。

他祝我一路平安,我祝他身体健康,学习进步。

练 习 答 案
liàn xí dá àn
Key to Exercises

一

1.1 B：很好。/我身体很好。

1.2 B：工作不忙。/工作很忙。

1.3 B：我学习也不很紧张。/我学习很紧张。

1.4 B：他也很好。/张老师也很好。

2.1 A：张老师身体好吗？

2.2 A：工作忙吗？

2.3 A：你好吗？张老师好吗？

2.4 A：你累吗？

3.1 你身体好吗？

3.2 我很忙，你忙吗？

3.3 我工作不很紧张，你工作紧张吗？

3.4 我很好，张老师好吗？

二

1.1 B：他是张老师。

1.2 B：我是。/不是，我是李平。

1.3 B：那位是布朗教授。/他是布朗教授。

314

1.4　B：那位先生是史密斯。

2.1　A：您姓什么？
2.2　A：那位先生是谁？
2.3　A：您是谁？
2.4　A：您叫什么名字？

3.1　谁是布朗教授？/他是谁？
3.2　谁叫王丽？
3.3　您姓什么？
3.4　他身体怎么样？

4.1　我不姓张，我姓王。
4.2　我不很忙，他也不很忙。
4.3　你不累，我也不累。
4.4　我不是格林，我是布朗。
4.5　我身体很好，你身体怎么样？

三

1.1　B：认识，她是我的朋友。
1.2　B：她是格林先生的夫人。
1.3　B：是我的朋友。/不是我的朋友。
1.4　B：他不是格林先生的朋友。/他也是。

2.1　A：谁认识史密斯先生？
2.2　A：谁是格林先生的夫人？/玛丽是谁的夫人？
2.3　A：张先生是谁的老师？/谁是你的老师？

2.4 A: 史密斯先生是谁的朋友?/谁是你的朋友?

3.1 你认识不认识王丽同志?/你认识王丽同志不认识?
3.2 王丽是不是张老师的朋友?/王丽是张老师的朋友不是?
3.3 李平工作紧张不紧张?
3.4 他身体好不好?

四

1. liù diǎn   sān diǎn sìshí
   jiǔ diǎn bàn   qī diǎn líng bā fēn
   shí diǎn sānshí qī   shíyī diǎn wǔshí liú
   shísān diǎn sìshí wǔ   liǎng diǎn sìshí jiǔ

2. chà yí kè liù diǎn   chà shísān fēn sì diǎn
   chà sìfēn sān diǎn   chà wǔ fēn wǔ diǎn
   chà èrshí qī diǎn   chà shí fēn bā diǎn
   chà sān fēn jiǔ diǎn   chà sì fēn shí diǎn

3.1 我们上午八点上课。
3.2 他们下午两点半去颐和园。
3.3 我们今天没(有)课。
3.4 明天我们不上课。

4.1 A: 现在几点?/现在什么时候?
4.2 A: 你们几点下课?/你们什么时候下课?
4.3 A: 你下午几点去?/你什么时候去?
4.3 A: 下午几点开车?/什么时候开车?

5.1 现在几点？

5.2 你几点去颐和园？

5.3 史密斯先生几点下课？

5.4 玛丽小姐今天几点去商店？

6.1 你们今天上午有没有课?/你们今天上午有课没有？

6.2 你们今天下午去不去颐和园?/你们今天下午去颐和园不去？

6.3 史密斯先生今天上不上课?/史密斯先生今天上课不上(课)？

6.4 你明天去不去商店?/你明天去商店不去？

五

1.1 yī–jiǔ–líng–wǔ nián   yī–jiǔ–yī–qī nián
   yī–jiǔ–líng–líng nián   yī–jiǔ–bā–sān nián
   èr–líng–líng–yī nián

1.2 sānyuè èrshí sān rì   sìyuè sānshí rì;
   wǔyuè qī rì   liùyuè yī rì;
   bāyuè shíliù rì

1.3 xīngqīyī shàngwǔ bā diǎn   xīngqīsān xiàwǔ sì diǎn shí fēn

1.4 liùyuè èrshí rì shàngwǔ bā diǎn
   shí'èryuè shíwǔ rì xiàwǔ liù diǎn shíwǔ fēn

2.1 现在十点。

2.2 今天十五号。

2.3 昨天星期三。

2.4 今天不是星期五，是星期四。/是(星期五)。

2.5 现在不是九点十分，是九点十五分。/是九点十分。

2.6 明天不是星期六，是星期五。/明天是星期六。

3.1 今天是不是星期五?/今天是星期五不是?

3.2 明年你来不来中国?/明年你来中国不来?

3.3 史密斯先生明年来不来北京?/史密斯先生明年来北京不来?

3.4 现在是不是三点一刻?/现在是三点一刻不是?

4.1 他几月几号到北京?

4.2 明年你不去中国,后年去不去?

4.3 他星期六下午六点来。

4.4 格林明天不去故宫。

六

1.1 瓶——汽水多少钱一瓶?

1.2 斤——你买几斤苹果?

1.3 盒——你买几盒烟?

1.4 瓶——你买几瓶汽水?

1.5 盒——烟多少钱一盒?

2.1 两位 2.2 两瓶 2.3 十二盒 2.4 两(二)斤
2.5 二十二块 2.6 二十斤(个)

3.1 我给格林先生九十块钱。

3.2 你给他多少钱?

3.3 找你四块三毛。

3.4 我买三斤苹果。

3.5 不要别的东西了,一共多少钱?

七

1.1 买东西 1.2 试试 1.3 学习 1.4 工作 1.5 交钱

2.1 好一点儿　2.2 小一点儿　2.3 贵点儿　2.4 大点儿

3.1 这双布鞋大不大？
3.2 这双合适不合适？
3.3 你明年来不来北京学习？/你明年来北京学习不来？
3.4 你明天去不去商店买东西？/你明天去商店买东西不去？

八

1.1 我家在北京。
1.2 我住在北京西郊学院路8号。
1.3 现在我住在北京饭店。
1.4 我住在三层。
1.5 我住在 306 号房间。

2.1 你家是不是在巴黎？/你家在巴黎，是不是？
2.2 你是不是住在东京？/你住在东京，是不是？
2.3 你明天是不是去颐和园？/你明天去颐和园，是不是？
2.4 你是不是去商店买东西？/你去商店买东西，是不是？
2.5 你住在北京饭店，她是不是也住在那儿？

3.1 张老师在家吗？
3.2 我住在上海，他也住在上海。
3.3 我家在伦敦，他家也在伦敦。
3.4 我去北京，住在北京饭店。
3.5 我到上海，住在一个朋友家。
3.6 我住在朋友家。

九

1.1 A：您多大年纪了？/您多大岁数？

1.2 A：你母亲今年多大年纪了？

1.3 A：你弟弟多大了？/你弟弟十几了？

1.4 A：你妹妹今年多大了？

1.5 A：他几岁了？

1.6 A：你今年二十几了？

2.1 你在公司工作还是在银行工作？

2.2 你家在北京还是在上海？

2.3 格林住在四层还是五层？

2.4 史密斯今年来北京还是明年来北京？/史密斯是今年还是明年
来北京？

3.1 你妹妹是不是在一个公司里工作？ / 你妹妹在一个公司里工
作，是不是？

3.2 现在他是不是在那儿买布鞋？ / 现在他在那儿买布鞋，是不
是？

3.3 你哥哥是不是在这儿学习？ / 你哥哥在这儿学习，是不是？

3.4 格林先生是不是在学院工作？/格林先生在学院工作，是不是？

4.1 今天下午我们没有课，你们呢？

4.2 他父亲退休了，他母亲呢？

4.3 他哥哥身体很好，他妹妹呢？

4.4 格林先在这儿，他的秘书呢？

4.5 张老师和我们都去颐和园，您呢？

4.6 我们买汽水，史密斯先生呢？

1.1 B：我喜欢吃香酥鸡。

1.2 B：我喜欢去颐和园。

1.3 B：穿什么去都行

1.4 B：我住在什么地方都行。

2.1 吃什么，米饭还是饺子？

2.2 买什么，糖还是苹果？

2.3 你明天去哪儿，长城还是故宫？

2.4 你喝什么，啤酒还是汽水？

2.5 你在哪儿学习，北京还是上海？

2.6 你家在什么地方，巴黎还是伦敦？

3.1 来个干烧鱼。

3.2 好，来个干烧鱼。

3.3 味道很好。/味道不大好。

3.4 不，味道很好。/是，味道不大好。

3.5 好，来两瓶。

3.6 喜欢。/不太喜欢吃。

1.1 你会不会说英语？

1.2 他能不能看中文书？

1.3 格林先生汉语说得好不好？

1.4 你汉语说得好不好？

2.1 你能说汉语还是能说日语？

2.2 你会说英语，还是会说汉语？

2.3 格林先生是英国人，还是美国人？

2.4 他英语说得好，还是法语说得好？

3.1 这是他看的中文书。

3.2 你买的布鞋很合适。

3.3 他住的房间大不大？

3.4 你穿的布鞋是多大号的？

3.5 这是玛丽要的汽水。

3.6 这是母亲喜欢喝的茶。

3.7 格林先生喝的酒是什么酒？

3.8 我认识的朋友很多。

十二

1.1 格林昨天来了。

1.2 他去大使馆了。

1.3 他在商店买了布鞋。

1.4 玛丽今天迟到了。

1.5 我懂了。

2.1 格林是不是昨天请假了？/格林昨天是不是请假了？

2.2 我说的你是不是都懂了？

2.3 同学们是不是都进教室去了？

2.4 玛丽没来上课，她是不是病了？

2.5 她昨天是不是去颐和园了？/她是不是昨天去颐和园了？

3.1 昨天他来了没有？

3.2 他去大使馆了没有？

3.3 他买东西了没有？

3.4 他工作了没有？

十三

1.1 过　1.2 了　1.3 过　1.4 了　1.5 过、过　1.6 过

2.1 教你们法语的老师是什么地方（的）人？
　　教我们法语的老师是巴黎人。

2.2 教你们汉语的老师是什么地方（的）人？
　　教我们汉语的老师是北京人。

2.3 教格林口语的老师是哪国人？
　　教格林口语的老师是中国人。

2.4 教王丽英文的老师是哪国人？
　　教王丽英文的老师是美国人。

2.5 教你们日语的老师是哪国人？
　　教我们日语的老师是日本人。

3.1 我在日本学过中文。/我在日本没学过中文。

3.2 我学过一年。

3.3 我以前来过北京。/我以前没来过北京。

3.4 我去过（长城）。/我没去过（长城）。

3.5 我到过（上海）。/我没到过（上海）。

3.6 我在上海住过。/我没在上海住过。

3.7 我在上海住过一年。

3.8 我吃过中国饭。

4.1 这本书你看完了没有？/这本书你看完没看完？

4.2 我说的话，你听懂了没有？/我说的话，你听懂没听懂？

4.3 你以前来过中国没有？/你以前来没来过中国？

4.4 你以前学过中文没有？/你以前学过没学过中文？

4.5 你以前在北京饭店住过没有？/你以前在没在北京饭店住过？
　　/你以前在北京饭店住过没住过？

十四

1.1 你听得懂中国人说话吗？
　　我听不懂。

1.2 中文报你看得懂吗？
　　我看不懂。

1.3 这本书你今天看得完吗？
　　我今天看不完。

1.4 你学得好汉语吗？
　　我学不好。

1.5 你拿得来那本书吗？/那本书你拿得来吗？
　　我拿不来。

2.1 B：昨天我到商店去了。
　　B：我买了。

2.2 A：你昨天上课了吗？
　　A：你去哪儿了？

2.3 B：有些话我还听不懂。
　　B：我只学过一个月。

2.4 B：没没病，我出去了。
　　A：你到那儿去了？

3.1 该　3.2 该　3.3 可以　3.4 可以　3.5 能　3.6 能

十五

1.1 我在朋友家坐了三十分钟。

1.2 我看了一个小时的中文报。

1.3 走了五分钟我就到家了。

1.4 我来中国(有)半个多月了。

1.5 我们上课上了两个多星期了。/我们上了两个多星期的课了。

2.1 A：你来中国(有)多长时间了？

2.2 A：你坐了多长时间的飞机？

2.3 A：你学过多长时间的汉语?/你汉语学过多长时间？

2.4 A：你在上海住过多长时间？

2.5 A：你父亲今年多大年纪了？

2.6 A：你妹妹今年多大了？

2.7 A：北京饭店离这儿远吗？要走多长时间?

十六

1.1 买东西的很多。

1.2 从日本来的都学过汉语吗？

1.3 我认识那个上车的。/那个上车的，我认识。

1.4 那个买票的，我认识，她是我的老师。

1.5 我说的你听得懂听不懂？

2.1 我从北京大学去格林那儿。

2.2 我从中关村去颐和园。

2.3 我下午一点半上车的。

2.4 我今年七月到中国来的。

2.5 我八月二十九号从北京来的。

3.1 我在商店左边的那个车站上的。
3.2 我在331路汽车站右边的那家商店买了双布鞋。
3.3 我们到商店对面的那个饭店去吃饭。
3.4 我们到北京饭店对面的那个汽车站去坐车。

4.1 请给我一张到北京饭店的票。
4.2 我买一张去西安的票。
4.3 我们买两张到北京去的票。
4.4 买一张去颐和园的票。

十七

1.1 这个电影我看过两遍。
1.2 我以前来过北京两次。/我以前来过两次北京。
1.3 来北京以后，我到张老师家去过一次。
1.4 这本书很有意思，我看过三遍。
1.5 这个汉字我写了五遍。

2.1 来中国以前，我学过两年汉语。
2.2 到北京以后，我到北京饭店去过一次。
2.3 以前我在上海住过一年。
2.4 以前我来过中国一次。
2.5 我以后还到中国来学习。/我以后不到中国来学习了。
2.6 昨天下课以后，我到张老师家去了。

3.1 B：北京饭店在前边，离这儿不远，走几分钟就到了

326

3.2　B：长城离这儿远，有一百多里。

　　　B：不，我坐汽车去。

3.3　B：早上八点开。

　　　B：我们该走了。

3.4　B：车几点开？

　　　B：是，该上车了。

4.1　这是一部很有意思的电影。

4.2　那是一本很新的书。

4.3　楼下15排2号，这是个很不错的座位。

4.4　楼下30排28号，那是个很不好的座位。

十八

1.1　B：我打算去北京。

　　　B：我打算在那儿住一个月。

1.2　B：我拿定主意了。

　　　B：我决定去承德。

1.3　B：我打算明年去。

　　　B：我打算学六个星期。

1.4　B：我决定明天去。

　　　B：坐火车去。

　　　B：火车要走20多个小时。

2.1　既然这样，我也去上海。

2.2　你既然有事，就不要去上课了。

2.3　既然你决定明天走，我们就明天走吧。

2.4　你既然决定在这儿学习，就在这儿学习吧！

2.2 既然你去长城，我就跟你一起去长城吧！

3.1 他去北京学什么？
3.2 你决定去哪儿度假？
3.3 从北京到上海，火车要走多少小时？
3.4 周末你打算跟谁一起去承德？
3.5 我们坐轮船去上海，你怎么（坐什么）去？
3.6 北京什么时候最热？
3.7 那个电影怎么样？
3.8 今天晚上看京剧，在哪个剧场？
3.9 你买了几张票？座位怎么样？
3.10你的座位在哪排？多少号？
3.11他为什么没去看京剧？

十九

1.1 吃吃 1.2 量量 1.3 写写 1.4 看看 1.5 穿了穿 1.6 试试

2.1 请你拿回化验单来。/请你拿回来化验单。
2.2 请你写一写这句话。
2.3 请你解开上衣，我听听。
2.4 请你给他这本书。

3.1 他把那本书拿回来了。
3.2 他把药吃了吗？
3.3 我还没（有）把那本书看完。
3.4 我把东西买完就跟他一起走了。

4.1 格林得的是感冒。

4.2 他说的是英语。

4.3 我看的是中国的英文报。

4.4 我给他的是一本新书。

4.5 我拿回来的是刚买的上衣。

二十

1.1 我想把英磅换成人民币。

1.2 我打算把这本英文书翻译成中文。

1.3 请你把这张电影票拿到玛丽那儿。

1.4 请问，您把刚买的那本书放在哪儿了？

1.5 你把美元换成人民币了吗？

2.1 我把日元换成了人民币。

2.2 他把你的京剧票放在我这儿了。

2.3 他把布鞋拿出去了。

2.4 你把那本书看完了吗？

2.5 张老师把电影票给我们了。

2·6 你把那句话写完了没有？

3.1 B：可以兑换。

B：兑换一百美元。

3.2 B：我买了一本。

B：可以。

B：好，你拿走吧!

3.3 B：我住在北京饭店。

B：可以兑换。

B：不能兑换。/也可以兑换。

3.4　B：病了，他得的是感冒。

　　　B：现在好点儿了。

二十一

1.1　他吃完了那些东西。

1.2　他买来了那本有意思的书。

1.3　他弄丢了化验单。

1.4　谁拿走了我刚买的书？

2.1　电影票让他弄丢了。

2.2　练习都叫我作完了。

2.3　你的那本书被格林拿走了。

2.4　信让谁寄走了？

3.1　我把邮票贴在背面了。

3.2　他把我刚买的那本书弄丢了。

3.3　他把"太"字写成"大"了。

3.4　弟弟把我的英磅换成美元了。

4.1　那封信是不是寄出去了？

4.2　上衣是不是解开了？

4.3　那本书是不是拿回来了？

4.4　你的东西是不是寄回家去了？

二十二

1.1　今天下午没课，我要进城去买东西。

1.2　长城离这儿很远，我们坐汽车去。

1.3　明天我去北京饭店看一个朋友。

1.4 我要打电话找一下格林先生。

2.1 B：我找格林先生。
　　B：进城。
　　B：坐公共汽车去。
2.2 B：我打算去。
　　B：那我们一起去吧!
　　B：坐火车去吧。
2.3 B：我找格林。
　　B：302 号房间。
2.4 B：有点儿小。
　　B：好，这双很合适，就买这双。

二十三

1.1 张先生请谁进城吃饭？
1.2 你父亲让你到哪国去学习汉语？
1.3 格林叫你把什么给他？
1.4 玛丽让他给谁打电话？

2.1 张先生让我把这本书给你。

2.2 格林打电话叫我明天到他那儿去。

2.3 学校组织我们去看电影。

2.4 史密斯先生明天让你到他那儿吃饭。

2.5 他打算请张老师去看京剧。

3.1 A：你在干什么呢？
　　B：晚上七点去。

3.2　B：是。

　　　B：给在日本的一个朋友。

3.3　B：我在买苹果。

　　　B：不买别的了。

　　　B：好。

3.4　B：我在给史密斯先生打电话。

　　　B：是的。

二十四

1.1　这本书比那本书便宜。/那本（书）比这本（书）贵。

1.2　我哥哥比我大五岁。/我比哥哥小五岁。

1.3　今天比昨天更热。

1.4　北京冬天比上海（冬天）冷。

1.5　他写的汉字比你写的（汉字）更好。

2.1　我去年没有今年（那么/这么）忙。

2.2　我们那儿夏天没有这儿（夏天）热。

2.3　今年冬天没有去年（冬天）那么冷。

2.4　我年纪没有他大。/我没有他年纪大。

3.1　B：今天天气很热。

　　　B：我觉得比昨天还热。

3.2　B：六十（岁）了。

　　　A：你父亲比你母亲大吧?/你母亲没有你父亲大吧?

3.3　B：我妹妹十八（岁）了。

　　　B：大五岁。

3.4　B：忙，一天要工作九个小时，你呢?

　　　B：我一天要工作十个小时。

二十五

1.1 你是什么时候从日本来的？

1.2 你们是坐什么来中国的？/你们是怎么来中国的？

1.3 格林先生是跟谁一起去长城玩的？

1.4 他是在哪儿给你写信的？/他是在哪儿给你写的信？

1.5 你是在什么地方买的上衣？/你是在什么地方买上衣的？

2.1 我是从法国来的。

2.2 我是七月九号到这儿的。

2.3 我是坐飞机来的。

2.4 我不是一个人来的，是跟同学一起来的。

2.5 我看过京剧。

2.6 在人民剧场看的。

2.7 不是，是老师给我们的。

2.8 我觉得京剧很好。

3.1 北京我去过，上海我没去过。

3.2 承德我打算去，大同（我）不打算去。

3.3 英文报他能看，中文报（他）不能看。

二十六

1.1 昨天下午除了<u>故宫</u>，我们没有去别的地方。

1.2 他除了<u>英语</u>以外，还会<u>说法语</u>。

1.3 除了<u>杭州</u>，我还打算去桂林看看。

1.4 除了<u>格林</u>，别的人都去参观人民公社了。

1.5 来北京学习的，除了<u>学汉语的学生</u>以外，还有<u>教汉语的老师</u>。

2.1 除了长城（以外），我没有游览过别的地方。

2.2 除了你（以外），我也去过张老师家。

2.3 除了格林（以外），你也访问过人民公社吗？

2.4 你除了故宫，还到别的地方游览过吗？

2.5 上星期天，我除了去看朋友，没去别的地方。

3.1 我是今年八月到桂林游览的。

3.2 除了桂林，我还游览过杭州。

3.3 我能说英语。

3.4 除了英语，我还能说点儿汉语。

3.5 他汉语也说得很好。/汉语说得不太好。

3.6 我啊，说得不好。

3.7 除了中国，我还到过日本、英国和法国。

3.8 中文报我不能看。

3.9 我也不能看。

3.10 我打算九月一号回国，明年不能再来了。/我打算九月一号回国，明年还打算来。

二十七

1.1 要是明天有课，我就不去长城了。

1.2 要是明天没有事，我就跟你一起去。

1.3 你要是明年再来北京学习，我就跟你一起来。

1.4 要是昨天不下雨，我就到你家去了。

1.5 要是明天下午没有事，我就跟你一起去参观。

1.6 要是你没听清楚，我就再说一遍。

1.7 你要是说得慢一点儿，他就能听懂了。

1.8 格林要是不来，我们就到他那儿去。

2.1　B：谁呀？有事吗？

　　　B：他不在。

　　　B：他到玛丽那儿去了。

2.2　B：在看电视。

　　　B：没有。

　　　B：看足球比赛。

　　　B：不知道。

2.3　B：去看了。

　　　B：北京队。

　　　B：二比一。

　　　B：好。

2.4　A：你昨天怎么没有进城？

　　　A：你在学校干什么了？

2.5　B：有十个学生。

　　　B：没有。

　　　B：是的。

　　　B：学一个多月了。

　　　B：还不大会说。

二十八

1.1　时间过得真快，再过一个星期，我们<u>就要</u>回国<u>了</u>。

1.2　车<u>就要</u>开<u>了</u>，请快点上车吧!

1.3　你不要给我回信了，我<u>就要</u>走<u>了</u>。

1.4　你不要走，他<u>就要来了</u>。

2.1　我们对张老师表示感谢。

2.2　我们对北京的天气还不习惯。

2.3 我们对访问人民公社很感兴趣。

2.4 我们对社员的生活还不了解。

2.5 他对参观游览没有兴趣。

3.1 我是为了学汉语到中国来的。

3.2 不，我对旅行非常感兴趣。

3.3 我打算到大同去旅行。

3.4 我们举行联欢会。

3.5 我对联欢会很感兴趣。

3.6 我不表演节目。

3.7 我打算讲几句话，对老师表示感谢。/我打算讲点儿对老师表示感谢的话。

二十九

1.1 我去的时候，他正在看书呢。

1.2 回国的时候，他坐飞机还是坐火车？

1.3 我去他家的时候，他正在跟朋友聊天儿呢。

1.4 我去寄信的时候，你正在干什么？

1.5 格林找你的时候，你是在打电话吗？

1.6 我来的时候，格林已经走了。

2.1 这次来了一百多个日本学生。

2.2 昨天走了三个学生。

2.3 我家昨天没来客人。/我家昨天来了客人。

2.4 我去的时候，他家里有两位客人。

2.5 张先生家没有客人。/张先生家有一位客人。

2.6 今天电视里有足球比赛。

2.7 我们班没有日本学生。/我们班有五个日本学生。

3.1 你代表你们班讲话，用汉语讲还是用英语讲？

3.2 学习结束以后，你去哪儿旅行，去西安还是去桂林？

3.3 明年你到哪儿学习，到上海还是到北京？

3.4 你打电话请他来干什么，是吃饭还是聊天儿？

三十

1.1 了　1.2 了　1.3 过　1.4 过　1.5 过　1.6 着　1.7 着　1.8 着

2.1 B：都买好了。

2.2 B：没有了。

2.3 B：有机会一定来。

2.4 B：去过。

2.5 B：想。/不想。

3.1 B：有雨就不去。/有雨也去。

3.2 B：有时间一定去。

3.3 B：格林先生去我就去。/他去我就不去。

3.4 B：有机会一定来。

3.5 B：不上课就去·

词　汇　表

cí　huì　biǎo

Vocabulary

（词后的数字表示课数。The Arabics against each word indicate the lesson numbers.）

A

啊	（叹、助）	à		8

B

八	（数）	bā		4
八月	（名）	bāyuè		5
把	（介）	bǎ		19
吧	（助）	ba		3
拜访	（动）	bàifǎng *visit*	30 —
班	（名）	bān		28
半	（数）	bàn		4
办	（动）	bàn		30
办理	（动）	bànlǐ *to deal with*	29 —
帮忙		bāng máng		30
包裹	（名）	bāoguǒ *parcel*	21 —
报	（名）	bào		11
杯	（名、量）	bēi		10
北	（名）	běi		15
被	（介）	bèi *by*		21

背面	（名）	*at the back* bèimiànr	21 —
本	（量）	běn	6
本子	（名）	běnzi	12
比	（动）	bǐ	20
比	（介）	bǐ *than*	24
比分	（名）	bǐfēn *score*	27 —
比较	（动、副）	bǐjiào *compare*	13 —
比赛	（名）	bǐsài	27
避暑		bì shǔ *to be cool*	18 —
表示	（动、名）	biǎoshì *to express*	28 —
表演	（动）	biǎoyǎn *to perform*	28 —
别	（副）	bié *don't*	10
别的	（代）	biéde	6
病	（动、名）	bìng	12
不错	（形）	búcuò	17
不	（副）	bù	1
不敢当		*do not deserve* bù gǎndāng	30 —
部	（量）	bù *part*	17
布鞋	（名）	bùxié *cloth shoes*	7 —

电话	（名）	diànhuà	22
电视	（名）	diànshì	27
电影	（名）	diànyǐng	17
丢	（动）	diū *lose*	21-
东	（名）	dōng	15
东西	（名）	dōngxi	6
冬天	（名）	dōngtiān	24
懂	（动）	dǒng	11
动身 *start off*		dòng shēn	18-
动物园	（名）*zoo*	dòngwùyuán	15-
都	（副）	dōu	10
度	（量）	dù *degree*	19
度假 *have vacation*		dù jià	18-
短	（形）	duǎn *short*	7
队	（名）	duì	27
对	（介）	duì	23
对	（动）	duì	27
对不起		duì bu qǐ	2
对面	（名）	duìmiàn	16
兑换	（动） *to exchange*	duìhuàn	20-
兑换单	（名） *list of exch.*	duìhuàndān	20-
兑换率	（名） *rate*	duìhuànlù	20-
多	（形、副）	duō	7
多长		duō cháng *how long*	13-
多少	（代）	duōshao	6

E

二	（数）	èr	4

二月	（名）	èryuè	5

F

发烧		fā shāo	19
发言 *make speech*		fā yán	28-
发音 *pronunciation*	（名）	fāyīn	13-
饭	（名）	fàn	14
房间	（名）	fángjiān *room*	8
访问	（动）	fǎngwèn	26
放	（动）	fàng *too to do*	10-
饭店	（名）	fàndiàn *rest.*	8-
非常	（副）	fēicháng	23
飞机	（名）	fēijī	18
分	（量）	fēn	4
分	（量）	fēn	6
分机	（名）	fēnjī *ext.*	22-
分钟	（量）	fēnzhōng *minute*	15-
封	（量）	fēng *meas.*	21
风	（名）	fēng	24
夫人	（名）	fūren	3
父亲	（名）	fùqin *father*	9

G

该	（能动）	gāi *should*	14-
干杯		gān bēi	28
感	（动）	gǎn *feel*	23-
感冒	（名）	gǎnmào *catch cold*	19
感谢	（动）	gǎnxiè	28-

干　　（动）gàn *to do* 23-
刚　　（副）gāng *just* 16
高兴　（形）gāoxìng 3
告辞　（动）gàocí 14
告诉　（动）gàosu 27
歌儿　（名）gēr 28
个　　（量）gè 6
给　　（动）gěi 6
给　　（介）gěi 23
跟…一起　gēn…yìqǐ 18
跟…一样　gēn…yíyàng *the same* 14-
公分　（量）gōngfēn *cm.* 7-
公共汽车　gōnggòng qìchē *bus* 22-
公里　（量）gōnglǐ *km.* 18
公司　（名）gōngsī *company* 9-
工作　（动、名）gōngzuò 1
够　　（形）gòu *enough* 14-
刮　　（动）guā *blow* 24
挂号信　（名）guàhàoxìn *registered letter* 21-
拐　　（动）guǎi *turn* 15-
拐弯　　guǎi wānr 15-
贵　　（形）guì *expensive* 7-
贵姓　（名）guìxìng *what's your surname* 2-
国　　（名）guó 11
国家　（名）guójiā 26
过　　（动）guò 4
过　　（动）guò *pass by* 28
过　　（助）guo *aspect particle* 13

H

还　　（副）hái 6
还是　（连）háishi 9
航空　（名）hángkōng *by air* 21-
好　　（形）hǎo 1
好　　（副）hǎo 25
号　　（名）hào 5
号　　（名）hàor 7-
号　　（名）hào 8
喝　　（动）hē 10
盒　　（名、量）hé *box* 6-
和　　（连）hé 13
合适　（形）héshì *suitable* 7-
很　　（副）hěn 1
后年　（名）hòunián 5
护照　（名）hùzhào *passport* 30-
话　　（名）huà 11
化验单　（名）huàyàndān *test report form* 19-
化验室　（名）huàyànshì *lab* 19-
换　　（动）huàn *to change* 15
欢迎　（动）huānyíng 30
会　　（能动）huì 11
回　　（动）huí 19
火柴　（名）huǒchái *match* 6-
火车　（名）huǒchē 18
或者　（连）huòzhě *or* 20

可口可乐	(名)	kěkǒu-kělè	6-	聊天儿	liáo tiānr *to chat*	27-
可以	(能动)	kěyǐ	14	了解	(动) liǎojiě *to know*	26
刻	(量)	kè	4	铃	(名) líng *bell*	12-
课	(名)	kè	4	留	(动) liú	23
客气	(形)	kèqi *polite*	14	六	(数) liù	4
客人	(名)	kèren	29	六月	(名) liùyuè	5
口语	(名)	kǒuyǔ *oral*	13-	楼	(名) lóu	17
块(元)	(量)	kuài(yuán)	6-	路	(名) lù *road*	15
快	(形)	kuài	24	路线	(名) lùxiàn *route*	29-

录音 (名) lùyīn 27

旅行 (动) lǚxíng 18

L

轮船 (名) lúnchuán *ship* 18-

辣	(形)	là *spicy hot*	10-
辣椒	(名)	làjiāo *spice*	10-
来	(动)	lái	5

M

篮球	(名)	lánqiú	27
劳驾	(动)	láojià *will you*	15-
老师	(名)	lǎoshī	1
了	(助)	le	4
累	(形)	lèi *tired*	1
离	(介)	lí	15
里	(名)	lǐ	9
礼堂	(名)	lǐtáng	17
联欢	(动)	liánhuān *get together*	28-
联欢会	(名)	liánhuānhuì *meeting*	28-
量	(动)	liáng *to measure*	19-
凉快	(形)	liángkuai *cool*	24
两	(数)	liǎng	6
辆	(量)	liàng *m.w. vehicles*	22-

麻烦 (名、动、形) máfan *trouble* 14-

马路 (名) mǎlù *street* 16-

马上 (副) mǎshàng *at once* 28

吗 (助) ma 1

买 (动) mǎi 6

慢 (形) màn 11

忙 (形) máng 1

毛(角) (量) máo(jiǎo) *money* 6

没 (副) méi 4

没有 (副) méiyǒu 12

没关系 méi guānxi 2

妹妹 (名) mèimei 9

米饭 (名) mǐfàn *rice* 10-

秘书	（名）	mìshū secy.	3	弄	（动）	nòng to do something (put)	21
明年	（名）	míngnián	5	努力	（形）	nǔlì	28
明天	（名）	míngtiān	4	女儿	（名）	nǚ'ér	3
名胜古迹	scenic spots míngshèng gǔjī	26	女士	（名）	nǚshì	3
名字	（名）	míngzi	2	暖和	（形）	nuǎnhuo warm	24
母亲	（名）	mǔqin mother	9				

N

P

拿	（动）	ná to take	12	排	（名）	pái volley	17
拿定		nádìng to make a decision	18	朋友	（名）	péngyou	3
哪	（代）	nǎ	11	啤酒	（名）	píjiǔ	10
哪里	（代）	nǎli	22	便宜	（形）	piányi cheap	7
哪儿	（代）	nǎr	7	票	（名）	piào	16
那	（代）	nà	2	瓶	（名、量）	píng bottle	6
那里	（代）	nàli	24	苹果	（名）	píngguǒ	6
那么	（代）	nàme then	24	平安	（形）	píng'ān safe	30
那儿	（代）	nàr	7	平信	（名）	píngxìn letter	21
南	（名）	nán south	15	葡萄酒	（名）	pútaojiǔ	10
难	（形）	nán	13				

Q

呢	（助）	ne	1	七	（数）	qī	4
能	（能动）	néng	11	七月	（名）	qīyuè	5
你	（代）	nǐ	1	起飞	（动）	qǐfēi	30
你们	（代）	nǐmen	3	汽车	（名）	qìchē	15
年	（名）	nián	5	汽水	（名）	qìshuǐr soda water	9
年纪	（名）	niánjì age	9	签票		qiān piào sign ticket	26
尿	（名）	niào urine	19	钱	（名）	qián money	6
您	（代）	nín	2	前	（名）	qián front	15
农民	（名）	nóngmín peasant	26	前边	（名）	qiánbiān	15

前天	(名)	qiántiān *day before*	27
清楚	(形)	qīngchu *clear*	22
青年	(名)	qīngnián *youth*	27
晴天	(名)	qíngtiān *fine day*	24
请	(动)	qǐng	7
请假		qǐng jià *ask for leave*	12
请问		qǐng wèn	3
秋天	(名)	qiūtiān	24
去	(动)	qù	4
去年	(名)	qùnián	25
缺点	(名)	quēdiǎn *short comings*	26

R

然后	(副)	ránhòu *then*	29
让	(介)	ràng *to ask*	21
热	(形)	rè	24
人	(名)	rén	9
人民公社		rénmín gōngshè	26
认识	(动)	rènshi *be ... seat*	3
软卧	(名)	ruǎnwò	29
软席	(名)	ruǎnxí *soft seat*	29

S

三	(数)	sān	4
三月	(名)	sānyuè	5
商店	(名)	shāngdiàn	9
商量	(动)	shāngliang *consult*	25

上	(动)	shàng	4
上个月		shàng ge yuè *last month*	25
上午	(名)	shàngwǔ	4
上星期		shàng xīngqī	25
上衣	(名)	shàngyī	19
少	(形)	shǎo	10
身体	(名)	shēntǐ	1
什么	(代)	shénme	2
社员	(名)	shèyuán	26
声	(名)	shēngr *sound*	22
生活	(名)	shēnghuó *to live*	26
师生		shī-shēng *teacher & student*	28
十	(数)	shí	4
十二月	(名)	shí'èryuè	5
时候	(名)	shíhou	4
时间	(名)	shíjiān *time*	13
十一月	(名)	shíyīyuè	5
十月	(名)	shíyuè	5
十字路口		shízì-lùkǒur *cross road*	15
事	(名)	shì	12
事情	(名)	shìqing	25
试	(动)	shì *to take a temp.*	7
是	(动)	shì	2
是的		shì de *yes*	3
收拾	(动)	shōushi	30
手续	(名)	shǒuxù	29
书	(名)	shū	6

345

书籍	（名）	shūjí *all the books*	30	体温	（名）	tǐwēn *temperature*	19
书架	（名）	shūjià	30	天气	（名）	tiānqì	24
舒服	（形）	shūfu *well*	19	填	（动）	tián *fill in a bar shape*	20
双	（量）	shuāng *two pair*	7	条儿	（名）	tiáor *m.w.*	23
双	（形）	shuāng	17	贴	（动）	tiē *paste*	21
谁	（代）	shuí	2	听	（动）	tīng	12
顺利	（形）	shùnlì *smooth*	28	通知	（动、名）	tōngzhī	23
说	（动）	shuō	11	同学们	（名）	tóngxuémen *classmates*	12
四	（数）	sì	4	同志	（名）	tóngzhì	2
四月	（名）	sìyuè	5	头	（名）	tóu	19
送	（动）	sòng	30	退休	（动）	tuìxiū *retire*	9
岁	（量）	suì *year, age*	9				
岁数	（名）	suìshu *how old*	9		**W**		
所以	（连）	suǒyǐ *so*	28	外币	（名）	wàibì *foreign currency*	20
				外地	（名）	wàidì *foreign place*	29
	T			外边	（名）	wàibian	19
他	（代）	tā	1	完	（动）	wán	13
他们	（代）	tāmen	12	玩儿	（名）	wánr *play*	25
她	（代）	tā	3	晚会	（名）	wǎnhuì *party*	28
太	（副）	tài	7	晚上	（名）	wǎnshang *pm*	17
谈话		tán huà	27	往	（动）	wǎng *trans*	16
糖	（名）	táng	6	往	（介）	wàng	15
讨论	（动）	tǎolùn *to discuss*	25	喂	（叹）	wèi	22
套	（量）	tào *a set of (clothes)*	21	位	（量）	wèi *mea. nt.*	2
特快	（名）	tèkuài *express*	29	为	（介）	wèi *for*	28
疼	（形）	téng *pain*	19	为什么		wèi shéme	18
踢	（动）	tī	27	味道	（名）	wèidao *a taste*	10
提前	（动）	tíqián	26	问题	（名）	wèntí	25

我	(代) wǒ	1	
我们	(代) wǒmen	3	
五	(数) wǔ	4	
五月	(名) wǔyuè	5	
无轨电车	wúguǐ diànchē *no rails tram*	15	

X

西	(名) xī	15
西郊	(名) xījiāo *suburb*	8
吸	(动) xī	14
希望	(动、名) xīwàng *hope*	30
习惯	(动、名) xíguàn *habit*	24
喜欢	(动) xǐhuan	10
下	(动) xià	14
下	(名) xià	15
下	(动) xià	24
下午	(名) xiàwǔ	4
夏天	(名) xiàtiān	18
先	(副) xiān *first*	20
先生	(名) xiānsheng	2
咸	(形) xián *salty*	10
现在	(名) xiànzài	4
想	(动) xiǎng	20
小	(形) xiǎo	7
小姐	(名) xiǎojiě	3
小时	(名) xiǎoshí	18
写	(动) xiě	17

血	(名) xiě *blood*	19
谢谢	(动) xièxie	1
新	(形) xīn	17
信	(名) xìn *letter*	21
星期	(名) xīngqī	5
星期二	(名) xīngqī'èr	5
星期六	(名) xīngqīliù	5
星期日	(名) xīngqīrì	5
星期四	(名) xīngqīsì	5
星期一	(名) xīngqīyī	5
行	(形) xíng *go*	10
行李	(名) xíngli	30
姓	(动、名) xìng *surname*	2
兴趣	(名) xìngqù *interest*	23
需要	(动) xūyào *need*	29
学	(动) xué	13
学生	(名) xuésheng	3
学习	(动) xuéxí	1
学校	(名) xuéxiào	23
学院	(名) xuéyuàn	9
雪	(名) xuě	24
血压	(名) xuèyā *blood pressure*	19

Y

烟	(名) yān *smoke*	6
研究	(动) yánjiū *to research*	25
验	(动) yàn *test*	19
样	(量) yàngr *shape, a kind of*	10

347

348

张	（量）	zhāng *m.w*	16
张	（动）	zhāng *open spread*	19-
找	（动）	zhǎo	6
找	（动）	zhǎo	22
这	（代）	zhè	2
这么	（代）	zhème *this way*	14-
这样	（代）	zhèyàng *such*	18
着	（助）	zhe *aspect part*	30
真	（副）	zhēn *true*	28
正	（副）	zhèng *now*	7-
知道	（动）	zhīdao	5
只	（副）	zhǐ *m.w.*	11
种	（量）	zhǒng *m.w.*	7
周末	（名）	zhōumò *weekend*	18-
主意	（名）	zhǔyi *to note*	18
住	（动）	zhù	8
祝	（动）	zhù *wish*	28
转	（动）	zhuǎn *to turn*	22-
准备	（动）	zhǔnbèi	26
桌子	（名）	zhuōzi	30
自己	（代）	zìjǐ *self*	14
走	（动）	zǒu *to walk*	14
足球	（名）	zúqiú	27
组织	（动）	zǔzhī *organize*	23-
嘴	（名）	zuǐ *mouth*	19-
最	（副）	zuì *most*	18 *pron*
最近	（名）	zuìjìn *recent*	25
昨天	（名）	zuótiān	5

左	（名）	zuǒ	15
左边	（名）	zuǒbiān	16
坐	（动）	zuò *to ride in*	14
座位	（名）	zuòwèi *seat*	17

专名　Proper Nouns

A

| 安东尼 | Āndōngní | 11 |

B

巴黎	Bālí	8
百货大楼	Bǎihuò Dàlóu	15
保罗	Bǎoluó	12
北海公园	Běihǎi Gōngyuán	4
北京	Běijīng	5
北京大学	Běijīng Dàxué	22
北京饭店	Běijīng Fàndiàn	8
北京语言学院	Běijīng Yǔyán Xuéyuàn	16
布朗	Bùlǎng	2

C

长城	Chángchéng	4
承德	Chéngdé	18
成都	Chéngdū	29
重庆	Chóngqìng	29

349

CHENG & TSUI PUBLICATIONS
OF RELATED INTEREST

ESSENTIAL GRAMMAR FOR MODERN CHINESE, by Helen T. Lin, 1984/81 revised second edition, 315 pages. Widely used as a text to supplement primary readers, it provides an exceellent review for those with over one year of Chinese. For first-year students, it should be used topically, not sequentially, to give one a better frame of reference. In pinyin and simplified characters, this book has been given excellent reviews.

0-917056-10-8

MAGIC OF THE BRUSH, by Kai-Yu Hsu and Catherine Woo, 1982, Art Book Co., Taiwan: Art Book Co., and Boston: Cheng & Tsui Co. 7½ × 10¼ ", 90 pages. This book is the result of an introductory course at San Francisco State University on the theory and Tao of Chinese calligraphy and painting, the relationship between poetry and painting, the theory and practice of colors in Chinese painting, etc.

0-917056-33-7

ENGLISH-CHINESE GLOSSARY FOR ELEMENTARY CHINESE, compiled by David J. Daehler 1981/ 77. Reverses the format of Chinese-English glossary at the end of *ELEMENTARY CHINESE,* Part II (Beijing, 1975/2). Useful in search for Chinese words once learned but now forgotten. Also helps in beginning composition writing. 8½ " × 5½ ", 56 pages, simplified characters and pinyin romanization, paperbound.

0-917056-05-1

LU XUN XIAO SHUO JI: VOCABULARY (SELECTED SHORT STORIES OF LU XUN), translated by D.C. Lau, 1979 (Hong Kong: Chinese University Press and Cheng & Tsui Company). 210 pages, original Chinese text in regular characters with vocabulary section in pinyin and English. Designed for third-year use. Paperbound.

0-917056-22-1